CO-OPERATIVE DREAMS

CO-OPERATIVE DREAMS

A History of the Kaweah Colony

Jay O'Connell

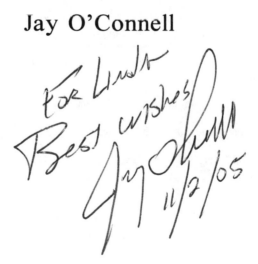

RAVEN RIVER PRESS
VAN NUYS, CALIFORNIA

RAVEN RIVER PRESS
17557 Cohasset St.
Van Nuys, CA 91406

First Edition
02 01 00 99 5 4 3 2 1

Cover design by Jamison Design/J. Spittler

Printed and bound in the United States

Library of Congress Catalog Card Number: 99-64766
ISBN 0-9673370-0-3

*Members of the Kaweah Co-Operative Colony
in front of the Karl Marx Tree.*

CONTENTS

California in the 1880s

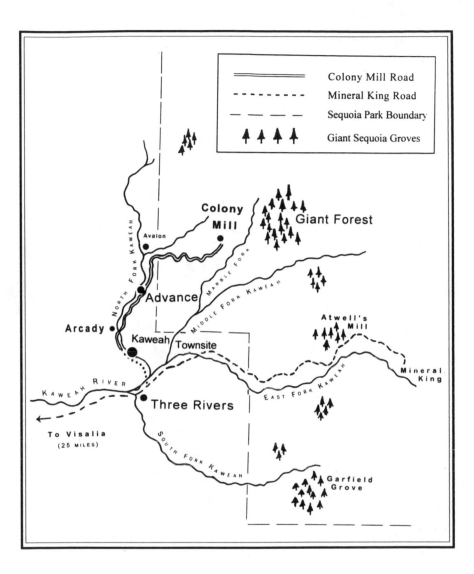

Legend:
- Colony Mill Road
- Mineral King Road
- Sequoia Park Boundary
- Giant Sequoia Groves

Colony Mill

Giant Forest

Avalon

NORTH FORK KAWEAH

MARBLE FORK

Advance

MIDDLE FORK KAWEAH

Arcady

Atwell's Mill

Kaweah Townsite

Mineral King

KAWEAH RIVER

EAST FORK KAWEAH

Three Rivers

To Visalia
(25 MILES)

SOUTH FORK KAWEAH

Garfield Grove

Kaweah Watershed circa 1890

FOREWORD

WHEN I FIRST began researching this book, the largest Marxist-inspired society in history was in the midst of collapse. Monuments to that great experiment were being destroyed—statues were toppled and walls were knocked down. Soviet communism, as established by Lenin and ruthlessly enforced by Stalin, was a distant cry from the communist utopia Marx and Engels had envisioned. Nonetheless, to more than one generation of Americans, the name Marx would forever be linked to the powerful and evil Soviet communist regime—our greatest threat and losers in a long and bitter Cold War.

One monument to an earlier Marxist-inspired utopian endeavor still stands, even though the experimental colony disbanded 100 years prior to the recent dissolution of the great Soviet experiment. There exists an old photograph of this living monument with more than two dozen socialist pioneers standing shoulder-to-shoulder within the width of its massive trunk. The incredibly large redwood tree was christened the Karl Marx Tree by these pioneers, the Kaweah colonists. Being the largest tree in the forest, (in fact, it is the largest tree in the entire world,) it was given a name representing the greatest honor in their eyes.

Today, that giant sequoia is known as the General Sherman Tree and is a major tourist attraction in Sequoia National Park. Those who know the story of the nineteenth-century utopian experiment, however, will always partly look upon this awe-inspiring giant as a monument to a colorful and dramatic chapter of California history: the Kaweah Colony.

Having grown up in Three Rivers, the tiny foothill community at the edge of Sequoia National Park, one could say I was figuratively raised in the shadow of that giant tree. And living so near to

Kaweah, the Colony's story had always been a part of my hometown history. This is not to say that I was interested in local history. As a kid, I was only vaguely aware of this colorful chapter of our local lore, which was one part history, one part rumor, and one part myth. Rumors, when they last over 100 years, graduate to the class of myth, and there are several that surround Kaweah. I had always heard that there had been some sort of Socialist utopian commune experiment up the North Fork road back in the old days. But growing up in the 1960s in a town that attracted its fair share of free thinkers and radicals, I didn't give the story a second thought. I just figured the Kaweah Colony was a bunch of hippies ahead of their time.

Free Love and the Cavalry

One common misconception about the Kaweah Colony is that, because of their Socialist politics, the established local communities generally hated them. Evidence to the contrary can be found in the *Visalia Weekly Delta* and the *Tulare County Times*. Both reported extensively on the Colony, generally in a favorable light. George W. Stewart's *Delta*, however, ultimately turned against the Colony, but even his hypercritical exposé indicted the Colony leaders as scam artists and frauds rather than Socialists. Meanwhile, Ben Maddox's *Tulare County Times* continued to support the Colony, printing editorials that complained of rampant persecution against them.

Proof that local businessmen supported the colonists is found in a circular, signed by the Tulare County Board of Supervisors, which appeared in both papers and stated: "These colonists as a class have proved themselves to be industrious, law abiding and worthy citizens. This treatment of them by the national administration is inexplicable." [1]

One other persistent myth about the Kaweah Colony is that the U.S. Cavalry forcibly chased them off their timber claims, thus preventing them from cutting giant sequoias. The Colony suspended logging operations on their disputed claims for a number of reasons: weather, a washed-out road, and the arrest and conviction of Colony leaders for cutting trees on government land. But the Colony's mill was never even close to Giant Forest—the modern heart of Sequoia National Park—and so they scarcely presented a threat to that spectacular grove of Big Trees. A standoff of sorts did eventually occur between the Colony and Cavalry troops at Atwell's Mill, an area of leased land where the Colony tried to resurrect a defunct logging operation. As we will later see, the real story is far from the popular notion of Cavalry firepower halting Colony axes, but their plan to cut timber in what is today Sequoia National Park naturally contributed to a perception that they intended to destroy the grand forests of giant sequoias.

Perhaps the most salacious and persistent rumor about the Colony was the stigma of a "Free Love" commune. One historian researching the Colony in 1960—nearly seventy years after it disbanded— said of the Tulare County old-timers he spoke with that "everyone here is a historian. They still hate the Kaweans, and call them free lovers."[2] A notice, which ran on the back page of the Colony-published newspaper every week for several months, read: "Kaweah Colony is neither an Anarchist nor a Free Love Colony, and persons of that turn of thought are not desired nor will they be received as members." This is evidence such rumors ran rampant even during the Colony's existence. Many years later, former members of the utopian experiment were still trying to dispel the free love rumor. One local historian recalled a trip to the Colony site in 1948 with Frank Hengst, a former member:

> As we explored the site, Mr. Hengst approached a spot cut in the hillside and viewed it pensively. I asked him why. "I vass yust t'inkin," he said in his German accent, "My oldest boy, George, vass born right here in a tent." He straightened his still massive frame. Fires of long burned-out anger rekindled in his eyes as he said: "Free-luffers, dey called us! Free-luffers!?! My vife and I haff been married fifty-fife years, and I never look at anudder voman!"[4]

Just where these free love rumors started is hard to say. Perhaps it was due to William and Charles Riddell. It has been said they left the Colony and moved up to a secluded nearby lake where they started their own utopian community of sorts. They built two houses—one for the women and one for the men—as they did not believe in conventional marriage and outlawed intercourse. They apparently did not stay entirely true to their Shaker-like beliefs, because babies were born to the women of the group.[5]

Another possible explanation of the free love stigma was due to an earlier American utopian experiment. The Oneida Community, founded in 1848 by John Humphrey Noyes, achieved considerable success and notoriety for several decades. One aspect of Oneida's communalism that surely raised eyebrows was their practice of "complex marriage." Under the system, conventional marriage was abolished and Oneida was transformed into one large "family." Monogamous relationships were forbidden and all adults in the community were considered married to each other and thus could engage in sexual intercourse.[6]

Though the Kaweah Colony did not condone this system, the mere fact that they, too, were an experiment in cooperative (or communal) living invited comparison to Oneida and inevitably contributed to the free love taint. Likewise, Kaweah's Socialist ideology would logically contribute to comparisons with later experiments in Socialist (or Communist) societies.

This is the rumor and myth part of Kaweah's history, and once I became more familiar with the story, I realized the necessity of peeling these layers back to try and discover the real history.

Land, Labor and Conservation

California, Wallace Stegner once wrote, is like the rest of the United States, only more so. Likewise, the Kaweah Colony's story is in many ways like that of California. By examining the concentrated details of the Kaweah Co-Operative Colony's history and the establishment of the state's first national park, a bigger picture of California will ultimately come into frame. What started out as research into local hometown history eventually becomes a lesson on California, and more importantly, a shining example of the human spirit that dreamed up the Colony and settled the West.

Kaweah involved far more than just a local group of early hippies. In fact, three key issues of nineteenth-century California history are illustrated by events at Kaweah. Land and its acquisition; labor and the organization of it; and conservation—a seemingly twentieth-century concept that was very much a headline grabber in the later nineteenth century—are at the heart of this story. They are personified in the early chapters of this book by three major characters in the drama of Kaweah. Via Charles Keller's experiences, we will look at land issues in California. Organized labor will find its voice through Burnette Haskell, who will in turn find his life's calling. And George W. Stewart, who we'll first meet due to his connection with the Land Office, will champion conservation with an effectiveness that even he found surprising.

Land, labor and conservation certainly are not all there is to both the history of California and Kaweah, but during the particular period in question it is impossible to understand what was going on without closely examining the influences these three issues had. (Many will be quick to point out that one can't even discuss the history of California without considering water. Although water certainly plays a part in the story of Kaweah, the dominance of that issue in California belongs to a slightly later period.) Any and all of these aspects of our history have been studied exhaustively, but it is how they intersect and collide, conspire and conflict leading up to and during the time of the Kaweah Colony, and it is how that conspiracy and conflict effected the outcome of Kaweah that we gain a better understanding of the history of California and indeed the American West.

The study of local history obviously helps us to know the place from which we come. My investigation into the Kaweah Colony began with a curiosity about Kaweah and Three Rivers, a place I will always consider home. It has taken me, however, to entirely new places. I have been exposed to stories and histories, aspects and issues I never would have otherwise considered. Just like great literature, art or music, it has opened for me a whole new world.

In that world which we will visit—the Kaweah Colony and California in the 1880s—land, labor and conservation all play a part in the story of a cooperative dream. In this particular story, it is a dream actively pursued by only a few hundred people, but there is no telling how many people have at one time or another dared to share the dream. It is for all of us who share that dream of a better world that this story is told.

The Human Drama

This is not, it should be pointed out, merely a story about issues. Nor is it history of the analytical sort, seeking to prove some theory or put forth a new argument. It is not about the dream itself, but rather a story about the dreamers. Granted, they were people who felt strongly about certain issues, and so to understand the people it is necessary to look closely at the issues that steered their actions. But, as a well-respected local historian once wrote of Kaweah, "the fascinating part is not the principle involved, but the people who made it up. They were a fairly delightful microcosm; to know them with their strengths and failings is to love them." [7]

Joe Doctor, who described himself as a "country journalist," made that statement. He was long considered one of the experts on the Kaweah Colony. Everyone around knew that if you wanted information on the Colony—or just about anything else that had ever happened in Tulare County—you had better go and look up Joe. I finally did just that, shortly before his death in 1995. I had put it off for several years, out of shyness perhaps. Only after years of researching the Colony on my own did I feel qualified to go knocking on Joe's door. I came away not only enriched for having known the outspoken, generous individual, but left with a box full of his original notes and manuscripts on Kaweah, including notes from interviews he conducted in the 1940s with surviving Colony members.

Why Joe decided to entrust me with his archive of Colony materials I can only guess. Well into his eighties and fighting cancer, he obviously knew he was close to the end. Perhaps he sensed from our discussions that I would treat the story as he always felt it should be, as a story of human drama. "If you are half as sincere and enthusiastic as your letter reverberates, " Joe wrote me in answer to my initial request to meet him, "you are an answer to my prayers of many years; that someone would treat the Colony as it should be, a group of idealists who did their thing as human beings, and not as a socialist band of people whose motives should be criticized, rehashed, second-guessed and down graded."

Joe complained that some of the writers who had already written about the Colony were "academics and bureaucrats who didn't really know what the Colony was all about." I, at least, did not fall into either of those dreaded categories. Joe was also disappointed that a young scholar who had contacted him 35 years earlier never wrote his proposed book about the Kaweah Colony. Joe had befriended Oscar Berland, a young labor historian from San Francisco, back in the early 1960s, but theorized that Oscar got carried away "by his own socialistic-communistic convictions which ended in disillusionment," and so abandoned the project.

As I departed from what would be our final visit, Joe urged me to follow through with my efforts on a book about the Colony. He didn't want me to give up and disappear on him like Oscar. He didn't want the writings of academics and bureaucrats to be the final word on Kaweah. I pledged to write this book, and to let the people who dreamed of a utopia at Kaweah tell their story. I write it not as a historian, but rather as a compiler, an editor and a referee. I have worked to present the available information in as logical, clear and even-handed a manner as possible and let the reader, as an active partner in the process, provide the analysis and arguments. I have tried to be true to the spirit of those people involved. More than anything, I have aspired to the role of dramatist presenting a narrative, for perhaps only the dramatist can find that ever-elusive truth, if there is such a thing, in history.

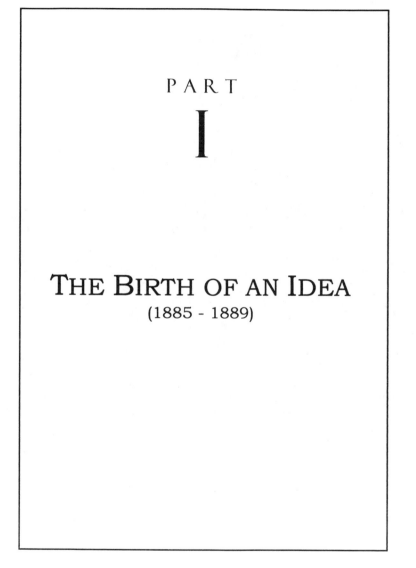

PART

I

THE BIRTH OF AN IDEA
(1885 - 1889)

CHAPTER

1

KELLER AND CALIFORNIA LAND

> *Having occasion to take a train down the valley I was fortunate to find a seat...behind two men who were civil engineers. [One] informed his companion that east of Visalia was the most magnificent forest in the state of giant redwoods [which had] lately been opened for sale. That revelation seemed to me a pointer by God himself...and a beginning of the scheme I had in mind.*
>
> —CHARLES KELLER

THE STORY OF California can be told in terms of land. So stated historian and former title insurance executive W.W. Robinson in his book *Land in California*. "Better still," he continued, "it can be told in terms of men and women claiming the land." [1] One man who lived that story was Charles F. Keller.

In the spring of 1885, Charles Keller, a resolute looking man with a small beard, neatly trimmed to form a point at the chin, was 39 years of age. Born in Germany in 1846, he had come to America with his parents when he was a boy of nine. They had settled in Lock Haven, Pennsylvania, along the Susquehanna River.

In 1864, he ran away from home to enlist in the 7th U.S. Volunteer Cavalry, serving for the remainder of the Civil War. Keller came west to California in 1867, arriving first in San Francisco. The 21-year-old was not much impressed with the town, and before long had signed on with a work party which took him down to the southern part of the state, to the San Bernardino Mountains. There Keller worked building a mill and dam for a

3

mining operation. The pay was excellent—five dollars a day in gold plus board—but the job only lasted six months.

The next stop for Keller was in the valley below, in the town of San Bernardino, where a short stint in the brewery business ended after a flood inundated his adobe brick beer cellar. Keller found himself on the move again, and would be many times before settling in the booming San Joaquin Valley town of Traver, which is where he was headed on a spring day in 1885.[2]

Boom Town of Traver

If the story of California is to be told in terms of land, then that story is never really complete until water is added. While the politics of water had yet to dominate California as it did after the turn-of-the-century with the eras of the Reclamation Board, William Mulholland and the Central Valley Project, water was beginning to permeate every aspect of California's development by the 1880s.

It was water, rather than gold or silver, which fueled the boom in Traver, and Charles Keller had been enthusiastically attracted to the opportunity the blossoming town offered. Situated only 10 miles north of Visalia, the county seat of Tulare, Traver was a product of one of the first large irrigation projects in the Central Valley. The 76 Land & Water Company was formed in 1882, conceived by civil engineer P.Y. Baker. With the aid of several investors, the project set out to develop thousands of acres of land by means of irrigation.

While California's great Central Valley was mostly arid in terms of rainfall, there was a very bountiful water source nearby. The valley is bordered on both the east and west by mountains, and those to the east comprise one of the largest, most spectacular mountain ranges in the world. When the earliest Spanish mission-aries first viewed the range from afar, they described it as *"una gran sierra nevada"*—literally, a great snow-covered range—and the name stuck.

Several major river systems carry the runoff of the Sierra Nevada into the Central Valley. Those rivers draining the watersheds of the northern and central Sierra ultimately flow into the Sacramento and

San Joaquin rivers, which form a complex delta system and eventually meander into the San Francisco Bay. The southern, and steeper, end of the Sierra is drained on the west by three major streams—the Kings, Kaweah and Kern rivers—all of which terminate in the southern San Joaquin Valley. The waters of the Kings and Kaweah once drained into the vast Tulare Lake. (The lake is now usually dry, but prior to the advent of extensive agriculture in the valley, it was the largest body of water west of the Mississippi and boasted perhaps the greatest concentration of game and fish anywhere in America.)[3]

When irrigation projects moved this bountiful water to otherwise arid land, large districts that had afforded nothing more than sheep ranges would be converted into lush gardens, vineyards, orchards and alfalfa pastures, the irrigation promoters promised.

Irrigation certainly was not a new idea to the San Joaquin Valley in the 1880s, although there were still those opponents who claimed irrigation on such a large scale would be disastrous. Skeptics and naysayers feared that the action of the water under the influence of the sun would destroy the substance of the soil, or believed that when the water was put upon the land it would produce chills and fever in such amount that irrigated districts would be uninhabitable.

But by the mid-1880s, local farmers were familiar enough with small-scale irrigation, and investors so motivated by the economic potential, to pay little if any heed to such dire predictions. With water assured for the district, promotion was started on a grand scale early in 1884.

The final step for the 76 Land & Water Company called for the establishment of a town, which was named for one of its directors, Charles Traver. Within one month, Traver could boast of three mercantile stores, two lumberyards, two livery stables, a post office, two hotels, barbershops and a new railway station in the process of being built. Schools and churches soon followed, and the town, situated on the main Southern Pacific line, quickly became the principal shipping point for grain in the area.[4]

While nearby Visalia was a fairly sizable and well-established town, having been around for several decades, Traver had become the rising star in the Central Valley. Charles Keller undoubtedly felt like finally, for once in his life, he was at the right place at the right time. At last, he would obtain a piece of the golden opportunity the California dream had always promised, but which so few had realized.

Bonanza Wheat Farms

As Charles Keller rode the train through the Central Valley that spring day in 1885, the landscape outside his window was dominated by endless acres of wheat—it was the era of the Bonanza wheat farms. Grain farming was one of the first agricultural enterprises in the Central Valley. It could be successfully dry-farmed most seasons, and the coming of the railroad in 1872 provided a boon, opening up vast markets. Additionally, California wheat was able to withstand long shipment by boat, thus opening up the European market.

Not really farming at all, but more like a variety of mining—exploitative farmers would decimate the soil, planting the fields year after year without variation of crops, giving the land neither rest nor manure. Once a section was exhausted they would simply move on to virgin soil elsewhere on their vast landholdings. The same feverish frenzy that characterized mining in Gold Rush California also characterized wheat farming.

In 1885, wheat farming had still to reach its statistical peak in Central California. But the proliferation of irrigation projects, developments in horticulture and viticulture and the completion of additional rail lines were bringing about a change to more of an orchard economy.

Still, in 1886, Tulare County would produce nearly six million bushels of wheat, roughly one-third of the state's entire production. And, in 1888, Traver would ship more wheat than any town in the world ever had. It wasn't until 1891 that the *Traver Advocate* would proclaim that "the reign of King Wheat is nearly over; the orchard, vineyard, apiary and poultry farm is usurping his domain."[5]

Land Monopolization

Monopolization of the land by a relative few had made bonanza farming possible. As Charles Keller traveled through the heart of the great Central Valley, he could look out and see many of these vast holdings. In 1871, 516 men in California owned 8,685,439 acres. In Fresno County, there were 48 landowners with holdings of 79,000 acres or more each. Partners Henry Miller and Charles Lux had managed to acquire 450,000 acres by the early 1870s, and that figure would eventually double.[6]

How had so much land come to be acquired by so few in California? In 1871, an insightful pamphlet, *Our Land and Land Policy*, by San Francisco journalist Henry George, traced the problem back to the Mexican land grants. With them, George lamented, began California's history of "greed, perjury, of corruption, of spoliation and high-handed robbery, for which it will be difficult to find a parallel." Strong words, but Carey McWilliams would later call even that a conservative statement.

In his classic work, *Factories in the Fields*, McWilliams wrote of speculators emerging from "dusty archives with amazing documents," and explained how men who came to be owners of these grants had acquired them from Mexican settlers "who had sold an empire for little or nothing." The Treaty of Guadalupe Hidalgo had guaranteed property rights to Mexicans in California, but the burden to prove the validity of their claims, along with the cost of the proceedings, rested on these native Californians. With few assets beyond the tenuous title to their land, it is easy to imagine how unscrupulous speculators could acquire their already questionable claims.

Many times these holdings became vastly enlarged through liberal and unregulated resurveying. The point, McWilliams emphasized, was not that settlers were swindled and huge profits made, but that the grants, many known to be fraudulent, were not broken up. The monopolistic character of land ownership in California was established.[7]

Keller, himself, had experience attempting to settle on a disputed land grant. In 1869, after his unsuccessful stint as a San Bernardino brewer, he headed to Mission San Buena Ventura, where he learned there was government land to be had.

> This land [Keller once wrote] was in dispute, the Mission claiming it as a Spanish grant whereas people took up the land contending

7

that it was government property, that the grant was false and counterfeit. The settlers employed a lawyer to contest the claim of the Mission. I remained on that claim two years. We employed this lawyer for $2,000 to fight our case and later found that he had taken our retainer and then got $5,000 from our opponents. Of course, the case was dropped; we lost and were ejected.[8]

Keller continued his northward migration, this time into Sonoma County, where he met Caroline Woodard, a teacher at the district school. The two were married in Healdsburg in 1871, where they remained for two years. They were soon able to buy a cattle ranch near Eureka, where they operated a dairy business for three years. Then Keller decided to take on a local monopolist. Looking back in a brief autobiographical manuscript, Keller recalled the episode:

I separated my herd, farmed out the milk cows and drove everything that would make beef to Eureka, the county seat. I opened a market in opposition to a millionaire land and cattle owner who had driven out, by underselling and later buying out, everyone who had ever attempted to oppose him. I determined I would stay to see how long he would last. It was scarcely six months before he came and made terms.[9]

Just how accurate Keller's account was of his triumph against the millionaire is hard to say. But we do get a prime example of an attitude Keller undoubtedly shared with many Californians of the 1870s. After a decade dominated by severe economic depression, the state had been polarized into tight sectors of poverty and wealth. This polarization was caused, according to Henry George, in great part by land monopolization.[10] Charles Keller was one of many who shared that realization and any business success Keller might realize represented a great victory against the wealth and corrupt barony of California.

Railroad Land and Mussel Slough

Wealthy individuals were not the only entities to control vast areas of land in nineteenth-century California. The railroads, most notably the Central Pacific, which eventually merged with the Southern Pacific, owned millions of acres by the 1870s. This land had been granted to them by the government in alternate sections along various right-of-ways of proposed rail lines, which in addition to cash subsidies provided the capital to build and begin operations of the railroads.[11] As Keller, in 1885, was being brought south by the giant locomotive of progress, belching steam and smoke over twin bands of iron, he had to be aware of the railroad's role in shaping the state. And thanks to one particularly painful episode, still a fresh wound in the minds of most residents, Keller's awareness and opinion of the Southern Pacific Railroad's contributions would have been decidedly one-sided.

Frustrated farmers, merchants and land seekers had long blamed their troubles—high transportation rates, a slumping economy, and a frustratingly slow agricultural development—on the highly visible railroad monopoly. In the Mussel Slough area, near Hanford in the west of what was then still Tulare County (now Kings County,) groups of settlers began moving onto railroad-reserved sections of land in the early 1870s. The reserved land had yet to be patented to the railroads, and much as Keller had done on the Mission claim in Buena Ventura, these settlers were betting railroad claims would be voided by the courts.

The settlers tried in vain to file claims on the land. They sent petitions to congress, with no result. In 1878, some Mussel Slough farmers formed the Settlers' Grand League to publicize their position and create solidarity. Seeking to allay growing alarm, the railroad sent out prospectuses, which assured that when the railroad won title, the farmers occupying the land would be offered the right to purchase that land at $2.50 per acre "without regard to improvements."

The railroad received legal title to their grants and began to send land appraisers to evaluate their holdings as a step toward sale. The land was first offered, as promised, to those in possession, but at exorbitant prices of $17 to $40 and even $80 per acre, a value that reflected the improvements made by the settlers. League members refused to pay. The courts, in 1879, upheld the railroad's right to evict the settlers, who were by this time squatters in the eyes of the law.

The situation deteriorated. In May of 1880, U.S. Marshal Alonzo Poole, along with a Southern Pacific land grader and two recent purchasers of railroad land, set out to take possession. While settlers had congregated in Hanford for a picnic, unaware of Poole's mission, two ranches had the furniture removed. After emptying the second ranch house, Poole and his men were met by a contingent of settlers on horseback who "arrested" Marshal Poole and demanded that the other men surrender their guns. Suddenly a horse reared, knocking Poole into the road. Shooting broke out and five of the settlers and one of Poole's men were killed. Another man from the Marshal's party was later found dead in a field with a gunshot wound in his back.[12]

The tragedy at Mussel Slough was an immediate cause celebre. Settlers, frustrated at their inability to acquire land, cast the railroad as pure villain. Nearly 20 years later, Frank Norris summed up their attitude in his historical novel, *The Octopus*. In the fictional account, loosely based on the Mussel Slough affair, he called the railroad:

> The symbol of a vast power, huge, terrible, flinging the echo of its thunder over all the reaches of the valley, leaving blood and destruction in its path; the leviathan, with tentacles and steel clutching into the soil, the soulless Force, the iron-hearted Power, the Monster, the Colossus, the Octopus.[13]

Exposing Dummy Filers

Large corporations, such as the railroad, were easy targets for the disgruntled poor. Their ability to exploit land laws and swindle the government out of countless acres of land was a major cause of the widening gap between poverty and wealth. Charles Keller became well acquainted with just that sort of swindle.

After his triumph against the millionaire competitor in the meat business in Eureka, Keller apparently enjoyed several years as a successful merchant. It was while running that market that he "became acquainted with the fraudulent entries that were being made in government land in Humboldt and Trinity Counties." He described learning of a scheme by lumber companies of using dummy buyers to file claims on government land:

> This news was brought me by various people coming into the meat market, and the stealing was so gross and such a breach of the

10

Charles Keller, who wrote in his memoirs decades later of overhearing about the most magnificent forest of giant redwoods.

government intent to throw these lands open that I induced various of my informants to make affidavits. I forwarded their statements to the Land Office in Washington. Each affidavit stated that the best of the timber lands were being located on by these dummies and were to be transferred later at the request of the companies who hired the locators. Each of these [dummy filers] received fifty dollars when proving-up time came and they turned the land over to the milling companies.

Several of the parties were arrested and I was cited to appear as witness. However, the money influence of those for whom the land was being taken was such that neither of the head men was arrested, but a few of the poor dupes whom they had subverted to do their work were sent to prison. After that my time in Eureka was nearing its end because everyone was so hostile to my movement. Then having a chance to dispose of my business, I sold out.[14]

Again, Charles Keller found himself on the move, this time ending up back in San Francisco where he saw an advertisement for business opportunities in the brand new town of Traver. He quickly jumped at the chance; and it was on a train trip between San Francisco and his new home in the Central Valley that another golden opportunity came his way.

Overheard Opportunity

Keller had learned a valuable lesson from his whistle blowing in Eureka, beyond the obvious one about angering powerful men in the town where you do business. He had become "conversant with the essentials necessary to secure" government land as set forth by the Timber and Stone Act of 1878, designed to provide for the sale of 160-acre tracts of surveyed land, the value of which lay chiefly in the timber and stone upon it. Such land could be purchased for $2.50 per acre. But, as Keller had also learned in Humboldt, this lent itself to fraud.

The Timber and Stone Act was not the first land legislation to avail itself of widespread fraud in California. The Swamp and Overflow Act of 1850 was designed to provide the state with money for reclamation of land deemed more than a certain percentage swamp or overflow, which the state offered for $1.25 per acre. But as this process depended upon locating and determining swamp land, government surveyors found themselves in an easily corruptible position. Some very valuable land was returned to the state of California as swamp and quickly bought up at the bargain price by well-connected and influential men.

One example of such abuse lay just to the east of Traver, in the Sierra Nevada Mountains of Tulare County. In 1883 and 1884, W.H. Norway and P.M. Norboe surveyed the area in and around Giant Forest, where some of the most impressive groves of giant sequoia trees in the world were located. They returned to the state the meadows, which during spring did contain a fair portion of swamped land, along with the dry forest land, deeming it all swamp and overflow. Norway reportedly wrote up his field notes in camp without doing any actual surveying, and for a consideration of 25 cents per acre would declare any land as swamp or overflow. In this way the land became state property and then passed into private hands, allowing the lush meadows of Giant Forest to become summer pasture for Tulare County stockmen.[15]

One of these surveyors, P.M. Norboe, happened to be on the very same train with Charles Keller in the spring of 1885. Also on the train that day was P.Y. Baker, the civil engineer behind the 76 Land & Water Company. Keller's own accounts of their encounter are somewhat contradictory, but in one version Keller claims to have overheard a conversation between Baker and Norboe, wherein "Baker informed his companion that east of Visalia was the most magnificent Forest of giant redwoods...opened for sale by order of the Interior Department." Keller probably played up the element of serendipitous eavesdropping for dramatic effect. In another account, he admits he simply "introduced myself and asked if I might take part in their conversation," and then learned of the "virgin forest of giant redwoods, practically within sight of Visalia, wholly unknown to the average citizen" which belonged to the government and was "actually open to purchase as timber land."[16]

What would this knowledge mean to Charles Keller, a merchant who now owned a market in the thriving valley town of Traver? His future certainly seemed promising without speculating on timber land in the mountains. Keller's only experience with lumbermen involved being run out of town by them in Eureka. But Keller was very interested in this discovery of available timber land, not just for himself, but for a far greater purpose.

Keller belonged, at that time, to the Co-Operative Land Purchase and Colonization Association of San Francisco. The association was an outgrowth of various labor and social reform organizations, most significantly the International Workingmen's Association, to which Keller also belonged. It is likely Keller had even attended a meeting of this association during this last visit to the Bay Area— meetings at which the membership was reminded of its primary duty, which according to Keller was "for each to consider himself a committee of one to seek out opportunities to purchase" land with resources sufficient to sustain a cooperative colony.

It was almost as if this opportunity had sought out Charles Keller. As the train pulled into the Traver depot, still under construction, Keller couldn't wait to further investigate his findings and inform his associates in San Francisco. He became increasingly excited about the prospects for the future. It was now a future he envisioned set in the lush forests of the mighty Sierra Nevada.

2

HASKELL AND
THE LABOR MOVEMENT

*Burnette G. Haskell, of San Francisco, [was] one of the most
erratic and brilliant geniuses in the history of the labor movement on
the Pacific Coast.*

—IRA CROSS, *History of the Labor
Movement in California*

THE CO-OPERATIVE LAND Purchase and Colonization Association in San Francisco, to which Charles Keller belonged, was
spearheaded by Burnette Haskell. He was an intense man of slight
build with a high, prominent forehead and a strikingly penetrating
gaze. He was prone to nervously consuming cigarettes and dominating a conversation with a flood of words. Although not yet 30
years of age in 1885, he had already made considerable impact on
organized labor and seemed destined for even greater notoriety.

Born in 1857, near Downieville in Sierra County, his parents had
both come to California during the Gold Rush. The family was
rather well to do. Haskell's father, Edward Wilder Haskell, was a
Forty-Niner who had achieved considerable success and moved his
family into a fine two-story house in Marysville shortly after
Haskell was born. A daughter and two more sons followed in the
next 10 years.[1] Haskell's mother, Marie Briggs Haskell, once
described her oldest son as extremely curious, getting into everything. "Where ever his mind was," she once wrote, "there is where

he went." She noted he was "not a sleepy child, never slept but little" and even claimed he "could write before he was two." If this hints at a penchant for exaggeration, it was a trait she certainly handed down to her son.

In 1867, at Marie Haskell's suggestion, the family moved to San Francisco so that they could avail themselves to the cultural and social benefits of city life. Haskell's father sold off several hundred acres of orchard property to make this possible. The family moved to a fashionable residence on Rincon Hill, and the elder Haskell began large-scale real estate and mining investments.

Education and Experience

When Haskell was 17 years old, his ever-curious mind investigated mysticism, and with the help of a book on magic he conjured up a spirit, Astaroth, from the netherworld who told him that he had been chosen for great deeds. But throughout his late teens and early twenties, Burnette Gregor Haskell seemed more destined to become a hopeless underachiever.

Haskell attended San Francisco Public High School, but dropped out to take a job as a proofreader in a publishing house, where he learned the printing trade. He returned to high school and eventually went east to attend Oberlin College, but did not register or attend classes. He then moved to Illinois and began studying civil engineering at Illinois University. He left there after a semester and returned to California where he dropped out of the University of California after two months. In her 1950 thesis study on Haskell, Caroline Medan summed up his college career by stating he had been "unduly handicapped by his not registering, not attending class, and not studying." [2]

Haskell set out to make it on his own, and spent two years in Chicago driving a streetcar and clerking, but evidently squandered what little money he earned and found himself more and more in a world of "poverty and pawn shops." In 1877, he accepted his father's suggestion that he return home.

Finally showing signs of settling down, Haskell found a job as a clerk in the law offices of Latimer and Morrow, and began studying law on his own. He passed the bar exam in 1879 and eventually

Burnette G. Haskell, the brilliant and erratic genius.

established his own law practice. He also became interested in politics and served as assistant secretary for the Republican County Convention and later, in 1881, was appointed deputy tax collector. He resigned the post after only one month. He also served a short stint in the California National Guard, earning a commission of captain, but shortly after resigned in part because of an incident involving missing money and records.

During this rather unfocused period of his life, Haskell's parents went through a considerable change. The effects of a nationwide depression—exacerbated by a severe drought and the arrival of cheap eastern goods on the new transcontinental railroad—brought severe financial hardship to California during the "terrible seventies." It was no time to be in the investment business, and under the stress of financial difficulties, Edward and Marie Haskell's marriage ended. She moved to Southern California, and Edward along with the rest of the family weathered an extremely difficult period together, moving six times between 1879 and 1882. Each move took them to less fashionable quarters. On Thanksgiving Day, 1882, the fractured family moved to working-class Howard Street, and were forced to take in boarders.[3]

Truth is Founded

Haskell's instability and early career faltering certainly wasn't from lack of energy, imagination or enthusiasm, but from a definite lack of focus. Law, politics, and the military had influenced the 25-year-old. He displayed a love for the secret and unusual. His capacity for planning and scheming were strikingly apparent and constantly in operation. He had yet, however, to find the great dedication that would be his life's work. It was through the newspaper business that he would ultimately make that discovery.

Haskell's work with the Republican Party led to a position as editor of the *Political Record*, a weekly newspaper in which Haskell hoped to exhort against corruption in politics, which he editorialized was a "danger greater than rebellion and stronger than sectional hatred." But Haskell quickly became disillusioned when he discovered that the publisher had accepted $50 for printing an article favorable to a local candidate for public office.[4] Haskell did the one thing at which he was an expert: he quit. His newspaper career, however, was resurrected when a wealthy uncle on his mother's side set Haskell up with a paper of his own.

While his uncle perhaps hoped the weekly four-sheet paper, called *Truth*, might help promote his own political career, it wasn't long before Haskell had other ideas about the publication's mission. The turning point came one evening in 1882 when, in search of news, Haskell attended a meeting of the Trades Assembly, a Socialist labor organization. Charles F. Burgman spoke at the meeting. It was a speech that opened Haskell's eyes, and he quickly offered to make his weekly paper an organ of the Assembly. In his enthusiasm, he spoke passionately of the corruption he had seen and in which he had even taken part.

Trades Assembly president Frank Roney described the situation in his autobiography:

> [Burnette Haskell] was a lawyer and was employed in the law office of the chairman of the Republican State Central Committee. He had never heard of trade unions or of the movement until he attended the meeting held to hear Burgman's report. Haskell's speech was a frank and uncolored admission of the way politics were run in California at that time. His duties led him to Sacramento to secure by corrupt means passage of measures beneficial to corporations. He did all these things in blissful ignorance of their propriety, believing them to be simply acts in the political game necessary. It shocked most of us and was a revelation that we little expected.[5]

Bitter opposition to Haskell's offer to make the paper the voice of the Assembly was at first expressed by its delegates. However, Roney eventually prevailed upon the members to accept Haskell's proposal and *Truth* became the official organ of the Trades Assembly. "Haskell thereafter," Roney wrote, "was one of the busiest men in the labor movement, and in a short time became a leading exponent of Socialism and then of Anarchism." [6]

The Cause of Labor

It is hard to believe that Haskell had never heard of trade unions or of the movement before attending the Trades Assembly meeting, (although making far-fetched claims was well within his character.) During the 1870s, San Francisco was a town rife with sandlot rallies by torchlight as tensions arose from the extremes of poverty and wealth so evident. Denis Kearney's incendiary speeches and anti-Chinese agitation defined the time. Radical political parties, such as the Workingmen's Party of California, sprang up. Rallies erupted in violence, and a railroad strike in the East ignited widespread riots in San Francisco. This tradition of radicalism prompted California historian Kevin Starr to aptly coin the term "Left Side of the Continent" when describing the state.

In the opening chapter of *Endangered Dreams: The Great Depression in California*, Starr traced the roots of California's unique labor history back to the Gold Rush, explaining how it had created a great need for workers. Labor early on had the advantage and commanded extremely high wages. The Gold Rush also restored dignity to labor, for no matter what a man had done before, he performed hard physical labor in the gold fields. "For a few short years, everyone had been a worker," Starr noted, "and by and through physical work California had been established." [7]

Trade unions gained strength in San Francisco, which due to geographic boundaries and further isolation from the East during the Civil War developed its own manufacturing need and capacity. A heightened influx of immigrants after the completion of the transcontinental railroad created a burgeoning surplus labor force. This situation forced down wages in the state and stoked anti-Chinese sentiment. A severe depression in the mid-1870s—the third and fiercest to hit San Francisco since 1869—further radicalized the labor movement as the search for solutions became more desperate. [8]

Haskell was undoubtedly searching for solutions himself when, in the early 1880s, he devoted himself with a singular fervor to the cause. Haskell had always displayed impatience and a "lack of stability" which biographer Caroline Medan called "the defect of his personality." But with his conversion to the cause of labor, Haskell finally found his "great dedication."

> As editor, lawyer, union organizer, internationalist and cooperationist, [Medan wrote,] Haskell tried to realize a dream of radical reform through socialism. [9]

Anarchy, Revolution and Cooperation

When *Truth* became the official organ of the socialist League of Deliverance, which had evolved from the Trades Assembly, Burgman began the task of converting *Truth*'s young editor. Labor historian Ira Cross once noted that the intellectually insatiable Haskell "within a short time mastered all the available labor and radical literature and became without a doubt the best read man in the local labor movement." [10] By the early 1880s, there was a considerable wealth of material to read. Much of this writing was in response to the social consequences brought on by the Industrial Revolution and the new problems between capital and labor that ensued.

Haskell would have familiarized himself with the French socialists of the late eighteenth and early nineteenth centuries, including the influential thinker Count Henri de Saint-Simon; Charles Fourier, a lonely, saintly man with a tenuous hold on reality who described a socialist utopia in lavish mathematical detail; the more practical Louis Blanc; and Pierre Joseph Proudhon, who wrote the 1840 pamphlet *What is Property*? (The short answer, according to Proudhon, was that all property was profit stolen from the worker.) Haskell very well may have studied social reformers in Britain such as Robert Owen, whose experiments in cooperative and socialist communities included one at New Harmony, Indiana. Undoubtedly the most influential writer Haskell would have read during this period was Karl Marx. Marx, along with Friedrich Engels, published in 1848 what has been called the Bible of Socialism—the *Communist Manifesto*. Marxism united sociology, economics, and all human history in a vast and imposing edifice. By 1880, Haskell also had available to him Marx's 1859 *Critique of Political Economy* and his great 1867 theoretical work, *Capital*. Marx synthesized in his socialism not only French utopian schemes, but English classical economics and German philosophy. Haskell was an eager student, enthused no doubt by the *Communist Manifesto*, which ended with the summons: "Working men of all countries, UNITE!" [11]

Haskell organized a clandestine association—the Invisible Republic—in the summer of 1882, which was basically an elaborate Socialist study group. Steeped in elaborate Roman ritual and a "sense of secret power" that his supposed inside knowledge of state politics made seem meaningful, the Invisible Republic was mostly concerned with, as one observer put it, "talk, talk, talk, and some little swearing too." [12]

Meanwhile, the pages of Haskell's *Truth* were filled with articles by or in praise of such notable figures as John Swinton, Henry George, Victor Hugo, Kropotkin, Marx and Bakunin. Readers were implored to organize themselves into groups of seven, and each in turn organize into another group of seven, and so on until the whole Pacific Coast was organized. Haskell showed an obsession for organizational schemes based on pyramids and geometric progression. *Truth* also contained science fiction articles, many penned by Haskell himself. With titles like "Invisible Men Among Us" and "How to Grow Tall at Will," one can imagine that even these fanciful stories carried a pointed political subtext.[13]

Leagues and associations came and went, were organized or dissolved or merged with confusing frequency. There existed a mish-mash of groups in San Francisco, from the Assembly of the Knights of Labor—by far the largest—to several much smaller groups such as Revolutionary Socialistic Party and Haskell's Invisible Republic. Soon that organization "weeded out the men who could not go as far as we went in radicalism" and was re-christened the Illuminati. *Truth* became more revolutionary in tone, advocating class struggle and anarchy.

By 1883, Haskell became convinced that a complete overhaul of the economic and political structure of America was necessary and that limited educational organizations like his Invisible Republic and Illuminati had insufficient means with which to bring about radical social revolution. Haskell established the International Workingmen's Association, based on, but with no connection to, Marx's International, which was founded in 1864.

The bookish Marx played an important role in the founding of the First International. Following its establishment, he fought successfully to control the organization, using its annual meetings to spread his realistic, "scientific" doctrines of inevitable socialist revolution. This no doubt contributed greatly to the phenomenal growth of socialist political parties worldwide in the 1870s. Various socialist parties emerged in France. Ferdinand Lassalle, a socialist opponent of Marx, organized the Social Democratic Party of Germany. In 1883, Russian exiles in Switzerland founded the Russian Social Democratic party.[14]

Like Marx, Haskell displayed a zeal for practical organization. The purpose of his IWA was, he maintained, to hasten the arrival of a socialist government to "give each man the full product of his labor and his fair share of earthly benefits." Organization was patterned on many secret revolutionary societies, with cells of members, divisions of rank, and encoded membership cards. The secrecy and Haskell's tendency toward exaggeration makes the size of the membership difficult to ascertain, but Ira Cross felt confident that the IWA had at least 19 groups in San Francisco, 10 in Eureka and vicinity, two in Oakland and one each in San Rafael, Berkeley, Healdsburg, Stockton, Sacramento and Tulare County.[15]

Truth, which naturally became the official organ of Haskell's IWA, became now even more revolutionary and extreme, at times even advocating the use of violence. On November 17, 1883, it declared:

> War to the palace, peace to the cottage, death to luxurious idleness! We have no moment to waste. Arm, I say, to the death! For the Revolution is upon you.

In another issue it announced, "Truth is five cents a copy, and dynamite forty cents a pound," and once even published an article entitled "Street Fighting Military Tactics for the Lower Classes" that printed a recipe for dynamite.[16]

These sensational incitements were probably more to attract attention than to really motivate action. Ira Cross had opportunity to interview Haskell shortly before he died, and "he told of having manufactured bombs, of secreting valises filled with them, and of plans to blow up the County Hall of Records," but history cannot trace a single act of violence resulting from Haskell's incendiary writings and extravagant statements.[17]

Haskell's Pacific Coast Division of the IWA did, however, prove to be an important factor in building up the labor movement in California. Haskell's greatest union-organizing effort was the Coast Seamen's Union, which began with Haskell speaking to a couple hundred sailors from a pile of wet lumber on a pier one rainy night and grew to a union over 1200 members strong.[18] For all his organizing and propagandizing success, Haskell realized that approaching Socialism by means of educational groups, revolutionary secret societies or labor unionism was not the way to achieve his dream of a fair and just society.

One summer day in 1884, at a Knights of Labor picnic, Haskell fell into a discussion with some friends: James J. Martin, an Englishman who was active in helping him organize the Coast

Members of what would become the Kaweah Colony including: Burnette Haskell (in white shirt and hat); James J. Martin to the left of him; Haskell's wife Annie in the front row holding her baby; and immediately behind her Andrew Larsen.

Seamen's Union; and John Hooper Redstone, a patriarchal figure among Haskell's associates with a long history of labor and radical activity. An original member of the IWA, Redstone may well have given Haskell the idea for that organization, for he had been at least tangentially involved in the formation of Marx's old International.[19] Haskell felt that a small group or colony operating under the tenets of Socialism would provide the most effective argument for his cause. He envisioned a living example of harmonious cooperation in contrast to the misery and want of the "competitive system," which was the phrase then commonly used as a pejorative term for capitalism.

As well read as Haskell was, it is no surprise he found the blueprint for such an endeavor in Laurence Gronlund's *Co-Operative Commonwealth*, a small volume that had only recently been published and was said to be the "first comprehensive work in English on Socialism." Using the terms "socialism" and "social cooperation" interchangeably, Haskell was naturally attracted to

Gronlund's suggestion of organization, which included a hierarchical scheme of divisions, departments, bureaus, and sections. Haskell and his friends undoubtedly discussed Gronlund's book at the picnic that day, for it would become for them part handbook and part bible.

The very forests surrounding the picnic area where Haskell, Martin and Redstone discussed their plans and dreams provided further inspiration. If a group could settle on land, which offered industrial possibilities or natural resources—a forest, for example—the financial potential would greatly add to a colony's appeal. The trio decided to move forward, to act on their plans and dreams, and a new organization was thus born.

To finance the early phases of their project and to begin implementation of the plan, Haskell and his associates organized a land purchase company. The first meeting of the Co-Operative Land Purchase and Colonization Association was held in October of 1884. Each member agreed to pay a monthly sum, although many were poor and had to "pawn their jewelry or mortgage their homes" to take part, and this money was "devoted to employing searchers for government and other cheap land." [20] Many of these members were also members of the IWA, which drew from groups throughout California, including Traver, California. Charles Keller was one such member.

Family Life

It is hard to imagine, with all of Haskell's activities during the early 1880s, that he would have time for anything else. But in 1881, shortly before his conversion to the causes of labor and socialism, Burnette Haskell was spending a considerable amount of time with a young woman who was a friend of his sister Helen.

Photos of Anna Fader show a woman who, by modern standards, would not be considered a conventional beauty. This is perhaps partly the fault of the camera, which failed to flatter her thin, long, slightly pinched face and crooked smile. But Haskell didn't miss any opportunity to flatter the 23-year-old woman who had come to live with his family. He was obviously, from the start, attracted to her. Her independent spirit—she had come all alone to San Fran-

cisco seeking her own fortune—and intellectual prowess, along
with her physical appearance, had caught his eye. Between Burnette and Annie, as she was called, there was an immediate,
definite attraction. She wrote in her diary shortly after taking a
room with the Haskells:

> Retired at three this morning after discussing the theory of evolu-
> tion until we were wild. Helen's brother is the best informed
> gentleman I have ever had the pleasure of meeting.[21]

Sometime in 1882, Burnette and Annie entered into a home-
drawn marriage contract. Presiding over this ceremony was
Haskell's favorite conjured spirit: Astaroth (the origin of which
was probably Ashtoreth or Astart—the Phoenician goddess of
fertility and sexual love.) By June of 1883, the marriage was
formalized in a legal ceremony. Annie Haskell described her new
husband as a regular socialist, nihilist, communist, red republican.
"He makes me smile," she added.

> I get so mad at Burnette because he just talks Socialism from
> the minute he comes in until he goes out [Annie once wrote in
> her diary]. Well, not all the time, but most. He was very
> pleasant and loving this evening. I listen but I laugh. He loves
> himself the best.[22]

By 1885, Burnette Haskell had begun to talk a great deal about
cooperation and a proposed Colony.

3

STEWART AND
THE LAND OFFICE

Plans were matured with little delay, and on October 5, 1885, thirty-seven persons appeared at the United States Land Office in Visalia to make application to enter tracts of this land under the Timber and Stone Law (Act of 1878).

—GEORGE W. STEWART

WHEN CHARLES KELLER, on his train trip back through the San Joaquin Valley, learned of available timber land, he immediately set out to investigate the matter further. To find out more, he even enlisted the help of the first white man to ever see the giant sequoias of what was already being called the Giant Forest. But first Keller headed to the Land Office in Visalia to confirm what he had heard and acquire maps and surveys of the available forest land. Having checked his information, Keller set out to see for himself all he had heard about the Giant Forest.

> To that end [Keller wrote in 1921,] I interested two neighbors, who agreed to go with me provided I furnished the outfit. Lenny Rockwell, one of those who agreed to go with me, had at one time lived at Three Rivers, and thus was acquainted with the Tharp family.[1]

Rockwell's wife is credited with having named the tiny village of Three Rivers, so christened in the 1870s because it was situated at the convergence of three forks of the Kaweah River, in the hills on the edge of the mighty Sierra.[2] The Kaweah River actually consists of five forks which drain one of the steepest watersheds in all the Sierra. Those forks are the North, Middle, Marble, East and South. In the 30 or so miles from its headwaters to the floor of the San Joaquin Valley, the Kaweah River drops an impressive 12,000 feet, passing through several biological zones, through a wide variation in topography and vegetation, on its swift downward journey.

At a broad widening of the Kaweah foothill valley just below Three Rivers (on land that is today under Lake Kaweah) the homestead and ranch of Hale Tharp, one of the area's earliest settlers, was situated. Tharp's knowledge of the forest that Keller was setting out to explore was unsurpassed by any local settlers, as he had visited that forest before any other white man.

Tharp and the Giant Forest

Hale Tharp had come to Tulare County in 1856, settling on the Kaweah River at the edge of the foothills some 20 miles east of Visalia. Tharp had befriended the local Native American chief, Chappo, who in turn showed Tharp the magnificent redwood forests and lush meadows of the adjacent mountains.

> I had two objects in making this trip [Tharp recalled]. One was for the purpose of locating a high summer range for my stock, and the other was due to the fact that the stories the Indians had told me of the "Big Trees" forest had caused me to wonder, so I decided to go and see.[3]

Since 1861, Tharp had used the area known as the Giant Forest for summer pastures, and had even secured patents on some of the land which had been surveyed and sold by the state as swamp and overflow land—lush meadows which provided ample summer grazing for his stock. On the edge of one meadow Tharp built a cabin from a single fallen sequoia tree which fire had hollowed.

When famed naturalist John Muir visited the spectacular forest in 1876, his exploration included a chance meeting with Hale Tharp, who extended his hospitality to the wandering student of nature. Muir explained to the stockman that he had come south from Yosemite and was only looking at the Big Trees. At Tharp's spacious single log cabin, Muir enjoyed a fine rest and nourishment while he listened to the "observations on trees, animals, adventures, etc." of the "Good Samaritan" Tharp.

Muir later took credit for giving the forest its name when he wrote that "after a general exploration of the Kaweah basin, this part of the sequoia belt seemed to me the finest." He decided to call it "the Giant Forest" and described it as "a magnificent growth of giants grouped in pure temple groves, ranged in colonnades along the sides of meadow, or scattered among the other trees, [extending] from the granite headlands overlooking the hot foothills and plains of the San Joaquin back to within a few miles of the old glacier fountains at an elevation of 5,000 to 8,400 feet above the sea."[4]

Charles Keller obtained permission to use Tharp's fallen log cabin as a base of operation and was told he could count on Tharp's son, Nort, as a guide once he reached the mountain forest. The forest was everything Keller had heard and more. During the summer of 1885, Keller was able to make his own surveys of the area and familiarize himself with the lay of the land.[5]

With his own plats and surveys of the available and heavily timbered land, he sent a report to James Martin in San Francisco, who was secretary of the Land Purchase and Colonization Association. It was the duty of every member to consider themselves "a committee of one to seek out opportunities to purchase, and to notify the Secretary of such finds." Keller, with a sense of urgency, suggested Martin call a meeting, read his report to the members, and ask as many as possible to come to Visalia to view the land and each enter claims for a quarter section of prime forest land. Martin later recalled that "the association thought Mr. Keller's vision excellent." With the Kaweah canyon as an available colony site and the timber as an abundant resource, along with ample water power at hand from the river, Martin realized that "with an eye for the practical," they were indeed "visionaries."[6]

A Busy Land Office

Keller's report to the association in San Francisco "received immediate acceptance," and he was notified to expect "upon a certain day, 40 of our members" to meet him at his home in Traver.

In October of 1885, the General Land Office in Visalia became a very busy place. Visalia was far from being a sleepy little farm town. The county seat of Tulare—a county that had tripled in population during the 1880s—Visalia was also the oldest town between Stockton and Los Angeles. A certain amount of activity and nineteenth-century hustle and bustle was to be expected, but the activities in the Land Office that October were well beyond the range of normal.

On October 5, 37 men, including the Land Purchase Association founder Burnette Haskell, showed up at the Land Office. Each made an entry to purchase 160 acres of timber land at $2.50 per acre, available under the Timber and Stone Act of 1878. It must have been quite a sight as these men, dusty and ragged from their journey down from San Francisco, descended on the Land Office, crowding into the room and filling it with the noise and excitement of their enthusiasm. The registrar must have felt like a harried sales clerk at a candy store, besieged by dozens of clamoring children. (Another group filed on the 30th of the month, bringing the total number of filers to 53.) Keller, of course, had become "uniquely conversant with the necessary endeavoring" (as he once phrased it) to legally secure government land, and so made sure all the rules were carefully followed.[7]

The first rule stated that filers of government land were required to have examined the land they sought to purchase. Keller claimed, in his memoirs, that he organized a "trip of inspection" with each man "sleeping upon the quarter [section] he intended to file on." This may have been an exaggeration—and although written 35 years after the fact, an exaggeration probably first uttered in the Land Office in 1885—as it is hard to imagine being able to lead over 50 filers, most of whom were city-dwellers, into the Sierra forest without benefit of roads or even well-established trails.

Indeed, Keller's memoirs describe one such trip of inspection, which provides some idea of the difficulties in believing that every single filer slept on his applied-for quarter section of land. After a laboriously slow journey "on a very rough trail under Moro Rock into the forest," the party arrived at the plateau situated between the Marble and Middle Forks of the Kaweah. At the western edge juts Moro Rock, a majestic mass of granite rising hundreds of feet from the forest (and dropping off thousands of feet on the valley side). Keller described them as being "pretty much spent" by the time they reached the forest with its unsurpassed stands of sequoias covering some 2,500 acres and containing 20,000 mature sequoias.

While the forest also contains various firs, cedars and pines, it is the concentration of giant sequoias that make the region utterly unique. Native only to the western slope of the Sierra, the massive sequoia's foliage somewhat resembles the incense cedar. But there the similarity ends. Mature sequoias average 15 feet thick at the base and about 250 feet in height. Exceptional trees exceed 300 feet in height and 30 feet in diameter. In age and stature, the *sequoiadendron giganteum* is the unrivaled monarch of the Sierra forest.

Across the canyon of the Marble Fork, with its succession of cascades over marble cliffs, the sequoias thin out and disappear, but there are still vast tracts of pine and fir trees. White fir is dominant here, but also plentiful are incense cedar, ponderosa and Jeffrey pine, Douglas fir, red fir and the majestic sugar pine. These forested slopes and ridges west of the Marble Fork also comprised the land on which Keller and his associates filed claims, and Keller's trip of inspection therefore headed in this direction.

> It now devolved upon me [Keller explained] to assume sole responsibility to guide the party through a trailless wilderness, to a point where I aimed to connect with the North Fork [of the Kaweah River.] I kept my misgivings to myself, and inspired our party by expatiating upon the grandeur and magnificence of the forest.

Dropping west over the saddle ridge which divided the Marble canyon from that of another of the Kaweah's five forks, the group made it down the adjoining canyon to the North Fork. They had to overcome steep descents, shortages of water, thick underbrush,

31

pack horses falling off ledges, individuals becoming separated and lost, and a host of difficulties. They eventually worked their way down to the convergence of the North Fork and a large creek feeding it from the east (today called Yucca Creek, they would name it East Branch,) and finally through the foothill valley of chaparral, woodland and grassland.

Keller noted that "the city people were very much the worse for wear," but all was well as it ended well. Keller, in later correspondence, reiterated the claim that he "led three different parties to the land, constituting 57 in number," and so fulfilled the law demanding that all applicants have been on the land they desired to purchase, to which they all had to swear.[8]

That requirement met, each filer had only to pay a $10 filing fee, arrange to publish notices of their claims in a local newspaper, and then return after 60 days and pay $400 for their individual quarter-sections, at which time they would receive legal title to the land.

Stewart and Shared Suspicions

George W. Stewart was editor of the *Visalia Weekly Delta* when, as he later recalled, he was "reading the proofsheets of the notices, [and] detected the fraudulent nature of the applications and called the attention of the Register of the Land Office to the matter."[9] Looking at the information on those notices today, the only apparent clue that Stewart could have construed as indicating potential fraud was the fact that several of the applicants listed the same San Francisco address—a boarding house on Broadway. More likely, it was the mere circumstances of the mass filing itself, as well as the appearance of the filers themselves, which aroused suspicion.

First of all, San Joaquin Valley residents assumed that this land and its timber were inaccessible except through the expenditure of large sums of money, only possible by some giant corporation. There was, thus, a natural tendency to suspect that these were dummy filers, much like the fraudulent claims Keller had helped to uncover in Northern California years earlier. Suspicion was furthered by the fact that the group, on the very day of the filing, met at the courthouse in Visalia and formed the Tulare Valley and Giant Forest Railroad Company, which might have led suspicious

Visalians to believe they were part of a scheme by the despised Southern Pacific Railroad to obtain and exploit the forest land.

George Stewart, like many Tulare County men, had long been concerned with land matters. Born in Placerville, California, in 1857, Stewart had come to Tulare County with his family in 1866. They were farmers, but young Stewart eventually learned the printing trade and at 19 years of age found a job working for one of the local newspapers, the *Visalia Delta*. Within a few years he became a city editor, and his promising journalism career soon took him to San Francisco and Hawaii before he returned to Visalia to run the *Delta*.[10] Stewart had begun writing editorials urging preservation of mountain watersheds not long after the passage of the Timber and Stone Act of 1878, and many Central Valley citizens shared his concern for what might happen with so much forest land open for sale. As editor of the *Visalia Delta* and a prominent businessman, Stewart was acutely aware of the issues which concerned his readers; and land—its uses, its value, it legitimate or fraudulent acquisition—was a very big concern.

Stewart also mentioned other reasons he and J.D. Hyde, the Register of the Visalia Land Office, became suspicious:

> Fourteen of the members were not citizens of the United States, but made declarations of their intention to become such, in order to be able to apply to enter the lands. The names of several of the applicants were foreign. Many of them appeared to be men who would not be expected to possess the sum of $400, the amount required to pay for the land after the period of publication.[11]

If someone looks like a dummy entryman, sounds like a dummy entryman and acts like a dummy entryman—they must be a dummy entryman. It was common knowledge that big corporations often employed this tactic. Foreign sailors arriving in San Francisco might be offered a few dollars, a jug of whiskey, and even a night in a whorehouse in exchange for filing a land claim under the Timber and Stone Act on a corporation's behalf. Before shipping back out, these sailors would abdicate title to the corporation—there were no restrictions on transfer of ownership—and in such a manner whole forests had been acquired.[12] The appearance of

Keller and his associates, many of whom were in fact sailors, would have easily suggested just such a scheme. Nonetheless, George Stewart published their notices in his newspaper and J.D. Hyde took their applications and filing fees; but the Land Commissioner in Washington, D.C. was contacted and alerted.[13]

Suspended

After 60 days, with notices of the claims printed in the paper, the members of the Land Purchase and Colonization Association could return to the Land Office and pay for their land, which would then be legally deeded to them.

> In the interim [according to Keller's recollection,] certain influential citizens of Visalia took it upon themselves to report to the Interior Department that the people who had filed on these lands were poor and the money they had offered at the land office was not their own; that they were irresponsible, and that the claims should not be allowed.[14]

J.D. Hyde had indeed contacted William Sparks, the Commissioner of the General Land Office in Washington, D.C., at the urging of Stewart and possibly other local citizens. As it turned out, Commissioner Sparks believed that large land and timber baronies were essentially "un-American" and so was more than receptive to suspicions of land fraud. Sparks strongly felt that fraudulent acquisition of land could result in a dangerous situation of "permanent monopoly." Sparks' somewhat radical warning would undoubtedly have found a sympathetic audience in Charles Keller and Burnette Haskell had they read about his fears of monopolists "creating the un-American system of tenant-farming, or dominating the timber supply of states and territories, or establishing conditions of feudalism in baronial possessions and comparative serfdom of employees."[15] While Keller and Haskell shared this contempt for powerful land monopolists, it is ironic that they themselves were suspected of being the puppets of such villains.

An inspector of the General Land Office, in the course of his duties, looked into the matter and filed a report from Visalia on December 1, 1885. In the report, Inspector G.C. Wharton echoed

*Newspaper editor George W. Stewart (left) standing behind
the counter at the Visalia Land Office, where the
Kaweah colonists filed their timber claims.*

local concerns, pointing out that the land was considered
inaccessible and that no access could ever be had except through
the expenditure of large sums of money by some giant corporation.
Wharton also wrote in his report that he "could not learn that these
parties had ever visited or examined the land upon which they had
filed" and surmised that "these men are what are usually called
'dummies', engaged by some corporation, thus evading and violat-
ing the law." [16]

Later that month, just before the first group of applicants were
due to present final proofs and tender, the Visalia Land Office
received a letter notifying Hyde that Sparks had suspended the
claims until a regular investigation could be conducted. Four large
tracts (called "townships" in the nomenclature of land management) containing the land in question, along with several additional
townships, were withdrawn from entry. Sparks gave as his reasons
"supposed irregularities in the surveys, and alleged fraudulent

entries," and promised "an examination in the field... as soon as possible."[17] In a state with a legacy of questionable land grabbing and bureaucrats who either looked the other way or winked while handing out claims to speculators and sharpers, the suspension of the colonists' claims was a surprising action. Such a preemptive strike against suspected land fraud was a rarity indeed. When Keller and the rest returned to find the applications suspended and the registrar refusing to accept payment for the claims, they had to be in a state of utter disbelief.

Upon this action by the Land Office, a meeting was held wherein the members of the association, who had all filed legal legitimate claims to the forest land, debated what had best be done in the face of such extraordinary circumstances.[18] Confident that any investigation would clear them of any supposed fraudulent intent, the would-be colonists decided to proceed with plans.

CHAPTER

4

ROAD WORK BEGINS

So the work began—a work in reality stupendous, contemplating as it did the building of a mountain road for twenty miles to cost not less than a quarter of a million, upon a cash capital of some twenty-five dollars and by about thirty enthusiastic but determined people.

—BURNETTE G. HASKELL
The Commonwealth

WHEN MEMBERS OF the Land Purchase and Colonization Association, immediately after filing claims on timber land in the Sierra Nevada of Tulare County, met at the courthouse in Visalia and organized the Tulare Valley and Giant Forest Railroad Company, their plans were still in the formative stages. Little did they suspect there would be any problem with their applications as they set about refining those plans and investigating their options.

Considering the immediacy in which the articles of incorporation for their proposed railroad were filed—it was done the evening of the very day on which timber land applications had been made—it was apparent that original plans had always involved building a railroad at least part way to the forest and the valuable timber. By late November of 1885, newspapers were already reporting on the proposed railway, which would "run from Tulare City to the Giant Forest, through a belt of the best land that ever laid out of doors." Reports even went so far as to claim that "work on the road is being pushed rapidly forward and grading will be commenced the coming week."[1] This was a generously optimistic prediction.

The Timber Pool

Before any work could begin, the members of the association had to come up with some sort of plan for how to proceed now that they had located their land. In other words, the "Association" was passing from its "Land Purchase" phase to the considerably more complicated "Colonization" phase. Charles Keller's memoirs recount the first important step:

> After we had [filed our claims,] we called a meeting of the timber filers and organized a pool, by entering into an agreement to jointly build a road into the forest to exploit the timber co-operatively, the interest of each timber claimant to be equal to the standing timber upon his holdings: Each was to become, and to remain, the owner of the full value of his claim, but the various quarters were to be exploited completely, each member to receive remuneration according to the equity of each land holder as a member of the pool. Membership in the pool was fixed at $500; which sum was to be expended in the construction of the road.[2]

The "road" by which this timber would be accessed had yet to be defined, and it is interesting to note how Keller avoids any mention of deeding individual claims to the "association," which is exactly what was in effect done.

Charles Keller was elected General Manager of the Timber Pool and James J. Martin its Secretary. Legal Advisor for the new organization was Burnette Haskell and at their initial meeting it was decided that the first order of business was to determine "the most feasible plan to be adopted to reach the source of the Association's wealth [timber] with the least outlay of expense."[3]

Flume vs. Railroad

Two possible plans were discussed. One involved the construction of a flume from a mill site in the forest to the mouth of the Marble Fork of the Kaweah. The other proposal was to build a railroad all the way into the forest, via the North Fork of the Kaweah. Charles Keller was given *carte blanc*, in his own words, to investigate the feasibility of both plans and report back to his associates.

He visited the facilities at the Madera Flume and Lumber Company further north, interviewing station men and repair crews and obtaining estimates of construction costs from the management. Knowing a little something about flumes, he returned to the Marble Fork to determine the practicality of such a flume in its steep canyon. Keller quickly "discarded all ideas regarding the construction of a flume" where the "natural difficulty would be almost impossible to overcome."[4]

Securing the service of an engineer formerly in the employ of the Southern Pacific, Keller then set about investigating the possibility of a railroad into the Giant Forest. Keller's idea was to secure rights of way and obtain bonds from landowners to a five-mile depth on each side of their railroad "for the payment of $5,000 for every running mile of our road; the money to be paid as soon as our road reached Lime Kiln hill on the Kaweah River" [site of present-day Terminus Dam.] The Association, according to Keller himself, was enthusiastic about his plans for a railroad, and instructed him to proceed and "follow his own bend."[5]

Burnette Haskell later recalled that the next year was "spent in raising money to survey the route of the railroad, procure rights of way, etc., etc. Some $25,000 to $30,000 was spent in this direction. Routes were surveyed to three different stations on the S.P.R.R. [main line], many rights of way were secured, and subsidiary bonds were obtained."[6] Newspaper editor George Stewart later claimed only $10,000 was raised to pay for the survey, which was done but "still is unpaid for."[7]

One unexpected turn of events, before any surveying of the proposed railroad commenced, actually created a cash windfall. When the Land Office, in December of 1885, suspended the claims and withdrew the land from entry, the filers could almost look upon the misfortune as an interest-free loan. That was certainly the spin Haskell put on it. With the claims suspended, the members did not have to immediately pay the $400 for each quarter section upon which they had filed claims.

It is also interesting to read Haskell's version of why the applications were suspended. In putting the situation in a positive light, Haskell went so far as to state that it was a "capitalist pool," which had designs on the land themselves, who had influenced the Land Office to suspend their claims. Therefore, when Haskell and his associates returned to offer necessary proofs and tender money, the Land Officer Receiver "declined to receive, but gave on demand a certificate of his declination."

> From his decision an appeal was taken and the Certificate of Declination, proof of tender, claim of title, and notice of taking possession of the lands bought placed on record in the recorder's office of Tulare County. The claimants were advised by their attorney [Haskell] that this constituted them owners and that it was doubtful whether upon appeal they would even be required themselves to pay the money theretofore tendered; it had been illegally refused and the bondsmen of the Receiver and Register were therefore liable.[8]

Thus Haskell saw, and convinced his associates, that they not only legally owned the land for which they had yet to receive title; but that because of the suspensions, payment would be at the very least deferred and perhaps even waived entirely. The members must have concurred to some extent, for they unanimously decided to forge ahead.

Keller continued his work on the proposed railroad. He ran surveys from both Traver and Tulare, hoping to play the citizens of both towns along the main Southern Pacific line off one another. Keller's memoirs suggest he was successful in getting a group of people from Tulare to secure a bonus of $5,000 per mile, and that the city greeted him at the depot with "a grand bonfire in progress" and "the Tulare city band in evidence to give me welcome; it was in fact an acceptance and ratification of my proposal."[9]

But no matter how successful Keller had been in securing rights-of-way and funds for the railroad, he eventually realized that the timber would have to be accessed by wagon road before the railroad could be built. The reason, Keller explained, was "to secure ties and timbers for [rail]road construction from our holdings."[10] His decision was again backed by the membership.

A Wagon Road to the Forest

Haskell recalled the decision a bit differently. Although he conceded that much was accomplished toward realizing their railroad, he recalled the idea of the wagon road as more out of necessity because "the railroad idea [had] been shelved on account of scarcity of means." Haskell also noted that since "large bodies of agricultural and grazing land were discovered on the North Fork and adjacent canyons and were homesteaded, pre-empted or bought by various members of the Pool...the determination was arrived at to found a co-operative colony on the agricultural lands and build a wagon road to the timber."[11]

One has to wonder what Haskell and Keller both left unsaid. Without legal title to the timber lands, it seems highly unlikely they would have been able to raise the necessary capital to build a railroad, or get the support of prominent Tulare County businessmen, who undoubtedly knew the status of their applications. But with their positive spin on the suspended claims and a confidence that once investigated, the claims would be honored, the members—who had begun thinking of themselves as colonists, for they were beginning to settle the area—proceeded with the construction of a wagon road to the forest.

> The stupendous work, for such it was, was begun October 8, 1886, [Haskell wrote] by Captain Andrew Larsen, Horace T. Taylor, John Zobrist, Thomas Markusen, Martin Schneider and Charles F. Keller, Mrs. Taylor and Mrs. Keller cooking for the camp. An average of twenty men worked continuously until done, and without proper tools, powder, or other appliances. At no time was there a dollar ahead in the treasury of the company and it was literally a struggle from hand to mouth.[12]

Haskell's account may have contributed to a later belief that the road was constructed without dynamite, but this was a typical exaggeration on the part of the relentless propagandizer. James Martin, in a letter to the editors of the *Fresno Bee* decades later, corrects the misconception that no blasting powder was used in building the road. "Several hundred pounds, if not tons, of dynamite and black powder were consumed in construction," Martin explained.[13]

Road construction began at the north end of Samuel Halstead's ranch, about three miles up from the North Fork's confluence with the Middle Fork. The road was begun on the west side of the river, as Halstead's property was on this side and one must assume there was already some pre-existing wagon trail up that far. The first road camp was established on a bluff overlooking the river and Andrew Larsen, a tall, muscular sailor from Sweden, built a small cabin there. This would eventually become Burnette Haskell's homestead and be known variously as Haskell's Bluff or Arcady. At the foot of this bluff the road crossed the river and continued up along the east side of the canyon.

Early progress of the road was outlined in the *1st Annual Report of the Executive Committee of the Kaweah Colony Association* from October 1, 1887:

> In January, 1887, the first bridge across the river was completed. Structure consists of seven 20-foot spans and, including the approaches, is about 150 feet in length. In February, 1887, Camp No. 2 was established and about 1½ miles of the road finished. In March, Camp No. 3 was established at Sheep Creek Flat. In April, Camp No. 4 was established at Advance, which has since become a permanent residence.

After the establishment of a permanent camp at Advance, members of the Colony Association and their families began to move to the foothill settlement in the summer of 1887. It was slightly less than a year since road work had begun. The settlement housed families in canvas homes, and grew slowly but steadily its first year and a half. By the spring of 1889, it was reported that Advance had 32 inhabitants "counting old and young" and that on "moonlit nights the voices of the young folks and children fill the air, as they play their outdoor games or join in singing merry chorus songs."[14]

Men of Backbone, Brain and Brawn

Still, even with the growing, idyllic settlement of young and old, all efforts were necessarily focused on building the road, which was

*The "men of backbone, brain and brawn" pause to pose for a photo
while at work on the Colony's road to the timber.*

excruciatingly hard work for the crew which averaged 20 or so
men. Many of the road crew, like Larsen, had been members of the
Coast Seamen's Union. Frank Roney once suggested out-of-work
sailors were profitably used, even exploited, by Haskell's
"scheme." Roney, a San Francisco labor leader who had once been
instrumental in Haskell's conversion to the cause but ended up a
bitter enemy, once wrote:

> When there was no demand for sailors at San Francisco and there
> was a likelihood of wages being reduced, the members of the union
> were sent to Kaweah, where rude shelters were constructed for their
> accommodation and food supplied for their subsistence. No wages
> were paid for their labor, the men being satisfied that they were
> upholding the union. So long as they lived healthily and had all the
> food they needed they were satisfied.[15]

Roney's accusation of exploitation was obviously a subjective
assessment, and the relationship between Haskell and the out-of-

work sailors involved more than just labor for sustenance. Many of these men must have believed they were laboring for a stake in utopia. While many of these sailors came to share Haskell's vision of a social revolution, for others the primary motivation was the promise of some land on which to build a cabin—their own private utopia, perhaps. One sailor whose relationship to Haskell and the cause went far deeper was the big Swede: Andrew Larsen.

A former colonist, who had carried water to the road workers as a teenager, remembered Larsen as a big man, strong and stout. (He was not as big as another worker named Lybeck. In fact, there was a tool at the road camp known as the "Lybeck crowbar" because it was so big no other man could wield it.)[16] Nonetheless, when Haskell called the road crew the men of "backbone, brain and brawn," Larsen had to have been foremost in his mind.

Back in San Francisco, during Haskell's revolutionary period a couple years prior, Larsen had served as a bodyguard while living with the Haskell family. Haskell related an amusing incident in his journal in 1885. He described the household that year as comprised of his father, his 19-year-old brother Benjie, his wife Annie, a roomer named Rose Caffrey and "Andrew Larsen, a sailor, friend and employee who runs the press when he is not engaged in shooting himself to pieces."

The shooting he referred to involved Larsen nearly shooting off his little finger while handling a gun he had obtained for protecting Haskell, who apparently became woozy at the sight of so much blood. According to Haskell's journal, the mishap prompted some teasing remarks from his father:

> You are nice ducks to make a revolution! One shoots himself and
> the other faints away. When the revolution comes on, I shall refuse
> to go out in the same army with Larsen until the hammer and
> trigger are taken out of his pistol.[17]

A few days later Larsen got back at the senior Haskell with a good-natured jibe. One evening, a visiting friend commented that Larsen should try some *Sure Cure*—the health elixir Haskell's father sold—on the wounded hand. "Oh, Edward says it is no good to put that on till the sore is healed," Larsen retorted to general laughter all around.

A New Foreman

As the road work began, the men were supervised on site by the man who had done so much in formulating the plan for the association. Charles Keller, general manager of the Timber Pool—a voluntary association with no real legal status that was now being referred to as the Kaweah Co-Operative Common-wealth Company—served as engineer and foreman of the road project. Under his superintendence the first four or five miles of road were constructed. In March of 1887, articles of incorporation were filed for the Giant Forest Wagon and Toll Road, with Keller, Martin and John Redstone listed among its directors and, in addition, Haskell among others as subscribers of 50 shares valued at $100 each.[18]

But somewhere along the way a rift began. Haskell later described Keller's portion of the road as "not built to grade and runs up hill and down hill in a very annoying and unnecessary way." If continued according to Keller's plan, Haskell claimed, "it would have landed us at the foot of Rommel's hill down in the gully with 2,000 feet elevation to climb by balloon."[19]

Journalist George Stewart recounted the growing rift as symptomatic of Keller's poor treatment of the men and his "attempts to get sole control." Stewart claimed the crews' provisions were "reduced finally to bread and beans only" and that the workers passed a resolution "demanding the right to select their own foreman."[20] That man was Horace T. Taylor. It was once said that he and his German wife were the kind of hard-working, practical individuals who could "make a living on a desert island."[21] Taylor proved to be a manager of rare ability, as one associate observed:

> He was the greatest hand to extract the limit of work from a gang and make them like it, one reason being perhaps his ability to do a little more himself. A little Napolean of a man, but there was no softness or pudginess about him and he never seemed to tire.[22]

Taylor became the new superintendent of road construction and road work proceeded. George Stewart later observed, with an irony he undoubtedly recognized, that the leaders of the association "were much incensed by the assertion of their rights by the laborers" and noted quite accurately that "troubles continued to arise from this time forward." [23]

As the road progressed toward the forest, other matters were headed toward a crisis.

CHAPTER 5

CRISIS AND SETTLEMENT

Far better that the Colony die, than that it be perverted from its first great purpose of demonstrating the fact that men can govern themselves without being "bossed,"—without imperialism.
—BURNETTE HASKELL, *The Crisis*

Well, I don't see the necessity for so much law anyway. I am willing to chuck every law into the fire and go on as we did at first without any law.
—CHARLES KELLER, *The Crisis*

THE GROWING RIFT in the Kaweah Colony had to do with more than just the progression of the wagon road or the manner in which the work crews were treated. It involved a basic fundamental question vital to the future of the endeavor. If the Kaweah experiment were indeed to serve as a shining example of a socialist society—a revolution through example—it would first have to establish a form of organization compliant with the existing laws of the land. It is interesting to note how even a self-professed anarchist became utterly concerned with such compliance. This was self-preservation taking precedence over idealism, and it also became a battle of wills between two men: Burnette Haskell and Charles Keller. The ensuing controversy over defining the legal form of organization of the Kaweah Co-Operative Colony more than anything defined Burnette Haskell as the Colony's guiding force from that point forward.

Haskell Goes to Denver

In January of 1887, just a few months after road construction began, Haskell went to Denver to take over a struggling newspaper: the *Denver Labor Enquirer*. He was serving as its West Coast correspondent when the publisher asked him to come and oversee the paper in Denver. Haskell's own labor paper, *Truth*, had folded a couple years before, and he was still feeling the financial hardships *Truth* had handed him. Haskell had completely exhausted his personal savings and credit trying to keep the journal afloat, and as biographer Caroline Medan suggested, he was "very willing to escape his creditors" and arrived in Denver "in a borrowed overcoat and a new plug hat."[1]

On his way to Denver, Haskell made a detour to visit Kaweah. The Kaweah Co-Operative Colony was still, legally speaking, an informal organization. Their "avowed intention," in Haskell's words, "was to formulate a scheme of organization which should be based upon the doctrines taught in Gronlund's *Co-Operative Commonwealth*, a scheme of pure cooperation based upon purely democratic principles,"[2] but when Haskell visited in January, no legal plan of organization had yet been drafted.

The Executive Board, consisting of Keller, P.N. Kuss, J.G. Wright, W.J. Cuthbertson and James Martin, set a March 1, 1887 deadline for themselves to draft something for the membership's approval, but the deadline passed with nothing submitted. It then fell on Haskell, as legal advisor of the organization, to prepare a brief outlining his suggestions for a legal plan of organization,[3] but by that time he had his hands full with matters in Colorado.

When Haskell arrived in Denver and saw the *Enquirer*'s small subscription list and the pitiful state of its finances, he sat down and cried.[4] To save money, he lived at the newspaper office and, according to his wife, did all the work himself. He nonetheless managed to find time to examine the law and drafted his suggested plan of organization for the Executive Board back in Kaweah. He claimed his plan was then printed in the *Enquirer* and "sent off to the whole membership for their vote."[5] Whatever the outcome of that vote, if indeed any really occurred, is moot. The Executive Board failed to act upon Haskell's plan and while Haskell struggled in Denver to keep the failing newspaper solvent and promote the Socialist labor cause, discontent was on the rise in Kaweah.

Haskell received no word in Denver on his proposed plan of organization, which called for something along the lines of a limited partnership rather than a corporation offering public sale of stock. He did receive "certain documents accompanied by letters of protest and dissent" and learned that the Executive Board had found his "Special Partnership" plan, as he called it, impractical. They had instead, in his absence, decided on incorporation and Haskell found himself in receipt of a set of by-laws for the proposed corporation along with a ballot for members to vote for board directors. He immediately whipped off a letter of protest, and before he heard back received a telegram from dissatisfied members, requesting he return to California.[6] This, along with a nasty case of mountain fever contracted in the unfamiliar climate, was incentive enough to leave Denver less than 10 months after arriving.

Incorporation and Crisis

In October of 1887, Haskell arrived in San Francisco and attended a meeting of that city's members of the Kaweah Colony. As Charles Keller and James Martin were expected in San Francisco soon, they agreed a general meeting should be held to discuss "the stories and charges of imperialism and bossism against the Executive Committee."[7]

In November, a number of meetings were held which boiled down to a debate on whether the Kaweah Colony should organize as a corporation, where capital would be raised through the issuance of shares to be sold publicly; or a limited partnership, where selected and screened candidates would purchase non-transferable memberships in the association. Debate is a polite and perhaps not strong enough term for what transpired. A committee headed by Burnette Haskell issued a circular to the membership entitled "The Crisis," and although it should be read for what it was—one side's version of the story designed to influence membership—it nonetheless offers a detailed and even entertaining summary of the meetings.

At the first meeting, held in San Francisco, Haskell presented his criticisms of the corporation form and its proposed by-laws. His primary complaint with the corporation, as defined by California law, lay in the ownership of transferable shares of stock. Haskell pointed out that anyone could become a member merely by purchasing a share and they could not expel him. As an example, he used Leland Stanford, one of the owners of the Southern Pacific and a man who was symbolic to them of capitalist greed and political corruption.[8]

Keller, on the other hand, strongly favored a corporation, as he felt that only through an open sale of shares could the Colony raise enough capital for their proposed operations. (There were accusations, later on, that Keller had actually approached none other than Leland Stanford about investing in the operation; and that Stanford had told Keller "Go back to your Colony, and if you can change your organization into a corporation and come to me as its legal Board of Directors, authorized to sell your timber, then I will deal with you." [9] The accusation was far-fetched and unsubstantiated.)

Haskell then moved on to the by-laws, pointing out numerous ambiguities and contradictions which rendered them problematic at best. Finally, after a lengthy haranguing by Haskell, a member of the Executive Board spoke:

> *Mr. Cuthbertson*: The Board didn't come here prepared to answer these questions. We want time to meet and consult together about our answers; we should like to have these questions written out.
>
> *Mr. Keller*: Yes, a man can come in and make a speech, and make points and carry a crowd, and carry a point, and we haven't all got the gift of gab.
>
> *Mr. Haskell*: I regret my failings. But the points made will bristle just as well when put upon paper.
>
> *Mr. Keller*: We are willing to concede the request of this meeting if they pass the Law Committee resolution.[10]

Thus a Law Committee, consisting of Keller, Kuss, Cuthbertson, Redstone and Haskell was elected and the meeting was adjourned for one week. In that next meeting, Haskell complained he had received no assistance from the rest of the Law Committee and needed a few more days to prepare a report which, "in whole plain words," would allow the membership to "see plainly all the difficulties in the way of every form of organization, and decide which they will have." This meeting was then adjourned with no resolution made nor any progress to report, except that now another committee was formed, this one to formulate amendments to the by-laws.

Outside Opinions

By early 1888, the opposing sides had accomplished little, but did agree on engaging the services of two judges to draw up a brief showing whether incorporation or a limited partnership would best be suited to the needs of the Kaweah Colony. The judges opined that "of the four forms of organization recognized in this state, the corporate form is alone available for the purpose in view."[11]

The membership heeded this advice and voted 67 to 63 in favor of the corporation,[12] but as one newspaper described, "a small coterie of leaders in the Kaweah movement seemed ambitious to secure absolute control and took exception to [the judge's] opinions."[13] Haskell organized a meeting in San Francisco which declared the corporation illegal and substituted a limited partnership company.

Another vote was held on May 18 and a committee, of which there was never any shortage, met to count the votes. According to another newspaper, "all or part of the ballots for incorporation were kept back" by the committee and the limited partnership favored by Haskell won approval.[14]

The limited objectiveness of all who recounted this episode in the development of the Kaweah Colony hampers the historian's efforts to determine exactly what happened, but at the same time clearly illustrates the emotions and passions aroused. Of course, actions speak louder than words and when Haskell finally succeeded in establishing the limited partnership, or "Joint Stock Company," Keller and nearly 50 other members withdrew from the Kaweah

Colony. Twenty-seven of them formally entered a protest and denounced the undertaking.[15] Many of these, such as Keller, who had done so much in establishing the colony, were original members of the Timber Pool who had filed land claims that were still in a forced state of limbo, awaiting investigation by the government.

Regardless, the Kaweah Colony now had a legal form of organization, albeit one born in crisis. And although membership had been cut by nearly one-third, the Colony, which was ostensibly ruled by a democracy rife with committees, now had one man undeniably at the helm. As legal adviser and trustee of the newly formed company, Burnette Haskell undoubtedly reveled in the role of founding father. The enterprise, however, was crippled by the Keller exodus. While it seems to have made sense for Haskell to push for the limited partnership, the forfeiture of such strong opposition as Keller provided would be a hard loss to overcome. Think of our democracy with its system of checks and balances.

Deed of Settlement

Largely the work of Haskell, the *Deed of Settlement and By-Laws of Kaweah Colony* was adopted March 9, 1888. It was a combination membership contract, Colony constitution and mission statement. University of California professor William Carey Jones, who

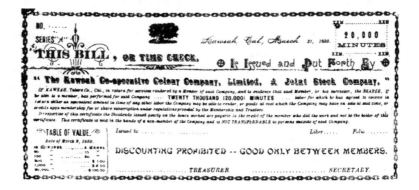

The Kaweah Colony issued time checks in denominations from 10 to 20,000 minutes at a conversion rate of 30 cents per hour.

would eventually become the dean of the School of Jurisprudence at Berkeley, wrote a report on the Colony in 1891 which noted that the *Deed of Settlement* had "a number of ambiguities, resulting from a faulty construction of the sentences," but added that its by-laws were, "in general, lucid and exact."[16]

Simply stated, the Kaweah Colony was organized as a limited partnership, with the number of members fixed at 500. Full membership constituted a contribution of $500, thus proposed capitalization of the company was $250,000. Membership commenced upon payment of the first $10 and acceptance by the Colony trustees. Upon payment of $100 in money, a member was entitled to residence and employment on the Colony grounds. The remainder of the membership could be paid off in labor, goods, or in money.

No person could hold more than one membership, but a married shareholder was entitled to two votes, one of which could be cast by the husband and one by the wife. Applicants were required to fill out a questionnaire which set forth name, place of birth, residence, age, marital status, information on children if any, occupation, capacity for employment, physical condition and religious affiliation. In addition, applicants were asked if they belonged to any trade, labor, or economic organization, and whether they subscribed to any labor or economic journal, and most significantly, if they had read Gronlund's *Co-Operative Commonwealth* and if they believed in "cooperative spirit." The Board of Trustees would provisionally accept or reject all applicants for membership, and those rejected would be refunded any amount of money deposited toward membership.

The "purely democratic" administration was a complicated structure of departments with their appointed superintendents reporting to a duly elected Board of Trustees, who acted as the executive body of the company. Provisions were made for referendums, imperative mandates and initiative, and a general secretary presided over the monthly general meetings.

In addition to granting women an equal vote, other progressive provisions were outlined in the by-laws. Much of this progressive political thought was the result of the Colony leaders' backgrounds in labor and social reform, as well as their adherence to the writings of Laurence Gronlund. These included the declaration that "eight hours shall constitute a day's work in the Colony." All labor paid at an exchange rate of 30 cents an hour, and time checks were issued in denominations of 10 to 20,000 minutes. The by-laws dictated that the Colony would keep a store "for the convenience of members, at which all articles of necessity can be purchased by them with the labor time checks provided by the colony." [17] Indeed, no member or other person was allowed to open a store at the Colony for the sale or exchange of goods, nor could any one colonist employ another.

Historian Robert V. Hine, in his book *California's Utopian Colonies*, described the projected organization as "complex, ponderous, and naïve," and George Stewart once called it a "locomotive's machinery on a bicycle." [18] But by 1888 families had started to arrive and settle at the road camp known as Advance, and by spring of the following year the little village of Advance boasted several dozen full-time residents. The locomotive was chugging along, ignoring or simply unaware that it rode on thin, spindly tires, and infused with an "I think I can" brand of optimism feverishly whipped up by Haskell and other loyal believers in the spirit of cooperation.

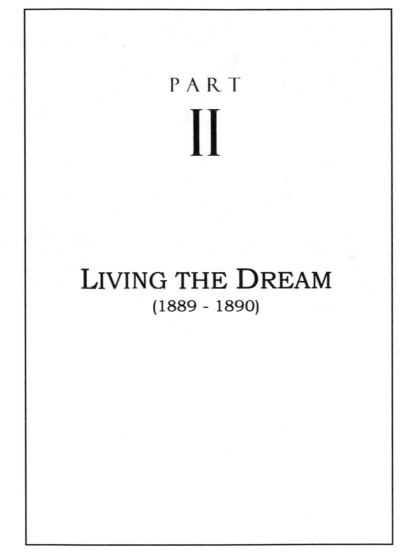

PART

II

LIVING THE DREAM

(1889 - 1890)

6

PIONEERS OF KAWEAH

To me, the fascinating part is not the principle Kaweah involved, but the people who made it up. To know them, with their strengths and failings, is to love them.

—JOSEPH E. DOCTOR, Tulare County Historian

SPANISH EXPLORER GABRIEL Moraga christened it Rio San Gabriel in the early 1800s, but by the middle of the nineteenth century, the river had come to be called Kaweah. Tulare County historians have explained the name as being derived from the Gawia Indians, a band of Yokuts who once lived on its banks. It has also been suggested that the name means "raven," or perhaps more accurately a combination of the Yokuts words for "raven's call" and "water," making the Kaweah the "river of the calling raven."[1]

Burnette Haskell, a brilliant propagandist, once offered his own origin of the name:

> An Indian name—"Ka-we-ah" meaning, "Here we rest;" and one can well imagine the grunt of contentment with which the braves of a century ago uttered [the name] as they reached its clear, cold waters, its sylvan shades, after their dusty desert marches inward from the sea.[2]

In 1887 and 1888, a number of people began to settle along those clear, cold waters and sylvan shades, attracted no doubt by Haskell's description of the place. With the arrival of families at Advance, the Kaweah Colony began a new phase wherein its "Prime Mission," as stated in a pamphlet, to "insure its members against want, or fear of want, by providing comfortable homes, ample sustenance, educational and recreative facilities and to promote and maintain harmonious social relations, on the solid and grand bases of Liberty, Equality and Fraternity,"[3] would finally be put to the very practical test of day-to-day living.

In a tent community, situated in an otherwise lightly settled foothill canyon many miles from the nearest town or village, this experiment was also a test of the pioneer spirit. Would families, many of whom had come from large cities such as San Francisco, be able to adapt to the rugged setting? Did they really expect the Colony to provide all it promised in such glowing terms? Who were these people who would stake everything just to find out if a better life might really await them in the foothills of the Sierra Nevada? They were true pioneers.

Over 500 people were ultimately attracted to, and became members of, the Kaweah Co-Operative Colony.[4] Less than half that number were resident members, with the population at Kaweah hovering around 150 or so at its greatest. They were a varied and diversified lot. "A curious study," Haskell once called the membership, which he claimed represented the United States in microcosm.

> Among the members [Haskell wrote] are old and young, rich and poor, wise and foolish, educated and ignorant, worker and professional man, united only by the common interest in Kaweah.[5]

A brief look at some of the families who lived at Kaweah will help illustrate the diversity of the Colony. Two of these were the families of Colony leaders and organizers: the Martins and the Redstones. The other three families—the Tings, the Hengsts, and the Purdys—are examples of the different kinds of people attracted to the promise and potential at Kaweah.

The Martins and Redstones

James J. Martin, born in Long Milford, England, came to America around 1869 at the age of 25. He became a newspaper reporter in Galveston, Texas, where he met and married Marie Louise, a very beautiful Creole woman from Louisiana. They moved to New Orleans where Martin ran a successful coffee and tea wholesale business. After their daughter, Daisy, was born, the family moved to California, hoping the climate would improve the baby's frail health. They eventually ended up in San Francisco where Martin became interested in labor unions and began his association with Burnette Haskell.[6]

Martin was involved with the Kaweah Colony from its very inception, serving as secretary for nearly every associated organization that evolved along the way: The Land Purchase and Colonization Association, the Timber Pool, the Tulare Valley and Giant Forest Railroad, the Giant Forest Wagon and Toll Road, the short-lived Kaweah Co-Operative Colony Corporation and, finally, the Kaweah Co-Operative Colony Company, Joint Stock, Limited. Throughout much of this early period he kept a home and office in Traver, which Charles Keller had let to him. With the organizational crisis and Keller's exodus from the Colony, Martin established a residence at Advance and before long his family came to join him.

James Martin was described in Will Purdy's poem,"Kaweah: The Saga of the Old Colony," as:

> *A man of genial presence, kindly smile;*
> *A noble head set firm on shoulders square*
> *And crowned with wavy mats of graying hair;*
> *Stern of purpose he, a man to trust,*
> *Whose judgments would be kind as well as just*
> *High faith, and temper firm in word and deed,*
> *He was the type of man e'er born to lead.*

Soon after Martin moved his family to the tent "city" of Advance, Mrs. Martin's tent became a kind of social center in the community. She was a fine cook and had a knack with plants and flowers. Her garden even boasted a fountain, which she had constructed of rock surrounding a pipe to supply water. Daisy, now a healthy, rambunctious and pretty girl of 12 years and Martin's adult son, Albion (Albie), were also active members of the community. Unfortunately, they didn't see much of their father as before long he set up a Colony office in Visalia and spent most of his time living and working there.

John Redstone, considered the patriarch of the entire Kaweah Colony, was, along with Haskell and Martin, one of the primary driving forces behind its organization and management. If Haskell was the great motivator and propagandist and Martin was the business genius of the operation, then Redstone filled the niche of spiritual philosopher and wise old man of the utopian cult. Perhaps nowhere is there a better (albeit overtly glowing) description of Redstone and his remarkable family than that found in the 1932 memoir of Phil Winser, who came to the Colony from England late in its existence.

> The family were such a lovable lot [Winser wrote] manifesting so fine a family affection that to watch it made a good beginning to the esteem which I soon began to feel for the people of my adopted country.
>
> John H. Redstone, or Uncle John as he was commonly called, was the patriarch, though not a very old one at this time; he had traveled in Europe in his youth and the youthful enthusiasms for freedom of thought led him to seek out and talk with Garibaldi and Massini. His profession was that of patent attorney, which he practiced in San Francisco and he was one of the earliest of the Kaweah promoters.
>
> The family moved to Advance and one daughter, Louise, married George Ames there. The other daughters, Dove and Kate, threw themselves actively into the colony work, teaching and doing the many things young, wholesome womanhood found to do amid such novel surroundings.
>
> Al was the youngest and only son. Blessed with great fund of humour, cheerful disposition and strong, active body; he was our best athlete and everyone's friend and favourite, giving us more laughs at our entertainments than all the rest put together.[7]

Members of the Redstone family in front of their tent home at Advance. Seated at right is Dove Redstone Brann with baby Frankie; Al Redstone standing in tent with gun; and the stern looking Sarah Redstone seated next to her grandson Ray Brann.

Little is known of Redstone's wife, Sarah Ann Griffith, except that she was of Welsh descent and apparently not politically minded. Her metier was, in Winser's words, the care of husband, children and grandchildren. When the Redstones came to Advance, one of their daughters was already married to Frank Brann. The young couple, along with their two sons, also became pioneer residents at Advance.

During the early days at the Colony settlement, Redstone still spent much of his time in San Francisco while the family helped establish the community at Advance. The Colony kept offices in San Francisco, where Redstone did much of its recruitment of membership. It is also likely he needed to remain in the city to continue earning a living, for he must have well-realized that the Colony was not yet in a position to furnish the family with all the "ample sustenance" it pledged to provide. An outside source of income was still needed for that.[8]

More Pioneer Families

In 1979, Italia Ting Crooks published a small volume of family history which offers a glimpse into what brought one family, not involved in the establishment of the Colony like the Martins and Redstones, to Kaweah.

In 1887, Peter Ting, a German immigrant who ran a bakery in Pomona, California, married Bessie Miles, the daughter of liberal Unitarian minister Elum Miles. The early days of Bessie and Peter's marriage were happy and full of pleasure. They shared a love and talent for music. Peter got along famously with Bessie's father; he was a "willing student sitting before the learned man, drinking in the ideals of Unitarian faith and liberal politics." It was during this period of his life that Peter became "interested in reforms of all kinds religious and political." But Peter's health was failing. "Long hours of work at the bakery were taking toll," Italia wrote. Peter had found his "so-called nervous disability improved" when he made a visit to Kaweah with his father-in-law. Later, after the death of their first baby and "at the insistence of doctors," Peter turned over the business to a friend. He and Bessie would "try a new life in the mountain colony, Kaweah."[9]

So the couple, along with Elum Miles ("who was waiting for a reason to live there himself") and Bessie's brothers and sisters, George, Waldo, Clara and Kate, moved to the Colony. They had evidently been accepted as members and had paid at least $100 towards their membership, which would make them eligible for residency and employment at the Colony.

"These eager, talented young people were soon integrated into the colony life," their descendant, Italia, boasted. Peter joined the road crew and became a prolific game hunter for the Colony. Along with his musically inclined wife, they were soon taking their places in the social life and the Ting tenthouse became the center of evening social events centered around music. They had the only piano at Advance, and as the Colony newspaper once reported, "If you walk into the Ting tent, you may find Mrs. Ting and Mrs. Frost playing music of the highest class, upon a piano of great excellence." [10]

On October 12, 1889, Peter and Bessie were blessed with a daughter, Italia. Scanning the list of resident children in April 1890, one learns that little Italia was one of five babies at the Colony that spring.

Another child listed was 11-month-old Burnette Kaweah Hengst. Perhaps no other Colony family produced as many descendants that remained in the area as the Hengsts. Several Hengst brothers settled in the area, but two were involved with the Colony. Dedo Hengst was the first to come, followed by his brother Frank Guido Hengst. Frank was duly confirmed for membership on April 2, 1889,[11] and came to Advance, but ultimately settled with his wife at the Colony camp of East Branch, or Avalon, several miles up canyon from Advance. (Avalon was located at the confluence of the North Fork and Yucca Creek, a tributary known to the Colony simply as East Branch.)

Hengst, who was born in Saxony, Germany, in 1863, was one of several German immigrants at the Colony. He worked on the road crew and later at the Colony hay field. His enthusiasm for the Colony was reflected in the name he chose for his son born there. Little Burnette Kaweah Hengst eventually became known, however, as George.[12]

Another family attracted to the promise of reform the Colony offered were the Purdys. George A. Purdy was a veteran of the Union Army and both he and his wife had been members of the fabled "underground railroad" which assisted runaway slaves in escaping to Canada. Mrs. Purdy was once described as "essentially a reformer and in all lines a leader: New Thought, dress reform, women's rights, prohibition— all was as the breath of her life." [13] After the Civil War, they joined the westward movement in a covered wagon and settled in Greenwood, Colorado. It was while living there that they learned of the Kaweah Colony. Its idealistic program appealed to the couple with a strong pioneering spirit and grand sense of justice.[14] In 1889, they came to Kaweah with their teenaged daughter and 11-year-old son. Phil Winser once wrote of the younger generation of Purdys:

Sweet Abbie, the eldest daughter, was the Colony pianist and worked at the printing office. She early attracted my attention by her refinement and Madonna-like face. George Clark, our English harness maker and best violinist, soon annexed her and they were married on the first Christmas Day after my coming [to the Colony.]

Will, the youngest, was a tall, slim lad; he too had the family refinement, with progressive and strongly socialistic leanings and an affection for the environment of Kaweah and its farming; an uphill game for which he was not so well qualified physically.[15]

Will Purdy later described, in poetic verse, the intangible force that brought all these families to the mountains of Kaweah:

> *Ideals, like beauty, are eternal joys;*
> *Their images our vision never cloys;*
> *Fair progeny of the aspiring mind,*
> *Round all her projects are their arms entwined.*

Haskell noted that among those attracted by these ideals were "temperance men and their opposites, churchmen and agnostics, free-thinkers, Darwinists, and spiritualists, bad poets and good, musicians, artists, prophets and priests."[16] The one trait they all shared—a trait often shared by people willing to give up their old life for a chance at something better—was an enthusiasm for new ideas. It was the enthusiasm of the reformer. That was, after all, what made temperance men, churchmen, Darwinists and spiritualists of them all. And it was that enthusiasm which brought them all to Kaweah where they hoped to find, as Haskell believed he had found, a "road to human happiness."[17]

ON THE ROAD TO SUCCESS

...the best mountain road I ever traveled over.

—ANDREW CAULDWELL

WHAT LIFE WAS like for the workers building the Colony's road to the timber can only be imagined. The "men of backbone, brawn and brain," as Haskell once praised them, were not as prone to written communication as some of the Colony leaders. Nonetheless, much can be gleaned from progress reports issued in the spring of 1889 by colonist George Speed:

> We have finished a fraction over three-eighths of a mile, have used some 150 lbs. of [blasting] powder and filled four gulches, one of which is very large. We now dispense of the services of the mule who did all of our water packing, and thereby give him a rest which he deserves. Comrade Brown has been sick for 8 to 10 days. Comrade Dodge has been on the sick list also, but is at work again.[1]

Another report related "having finished a good half mile using some 200 pounds of Giant Powder" and recounted how two large gulches were filled and a wall built "some 300 feet long over a large face of granite, in part of which we drilled holes and put in iron pins in order to hold the rock up, and then filled it in with dirt to the grade."[2] Perhaps this was the section known as "The Elephant,"[3] named for an old Gold Rush term. For the argonauts who flocked to the mountains of California, to "see the Elephant" meant to come across new and foreign sight, and particularly to encounter insurmountable hardships in their exotic adventures.

(For still another, more detailed account of road work see the reprint, on page 67, of an article as it originally appeared in the *Commonwealth*.)

As the Colony road wound its way upwards toward the timber belt and neared completion, many "elephants" of varying shape and size were conquered as cliff after cliff was cut out of solid granite. But for the Kaweah Colony, one other hurdle loomed larger than any elephant, standing squarely between them and the success of their endeavor. This particular beast was the United States government.

Investigation, Finally

While the Kaweah Colony concentrated its efforts on road building and membership recruitment, and had survived an internal crisis that defined its legal and governing structure, the leadership was unable to address one key hurdle in the way of their ultimate success. The applications for the timber land their road approached had been suspended pending investigation. This was an issue that both the Colony leaders and Government Land Office dealt with similarly. It was actively ignored.

In 1887, Government Land Office Commissioner William Sparks, who had suspended the Colony applications and had withdrawn the land from the market, was replaced by S.N. Stockslager.[4] There was, however, little change in policy and Stockslager maintained the suspensions and withdrawals of his predecessor. With the presidential election in November 1888, and Republican Benjamin Harrison's defeat of the incumbent President Grover Cleveland, a change in policy finally stirred some action from the U.S. Department of the Interior. Harrison's appointment to head that department helped undo the excessive and narrow reading of the land laws that had occurred during Cleveland's Democratic

On the Road to Success

The Road Work.

Comrade Speed Writes a Clear and Interesting Description

FAIR VIEW, April 3rd, 1889

Thinking it would be of some interest to our comrades who are at a distance to know something about how we are progressing on the road I write you this brief account of what we have accomplished and how we do it.

We have lately finished one mile of road which is in all probability the most difficult that we have had to contend against as we have had large cliffs of fine granite to go through making the road-bed of solid rock. We have also gone through several ledges of marble and crystallized spar in this work. We have used some 600 lbs. of Giant powder. Besides this we have made some very deep "cuts." I believe the banks will average some 6 or 8 feet; there were also seven large fillings, one about 40 feet long and from 10 to 12 feet deep. This work required considerable time as we had to build walls in some, and "rip-rap in others, that is; putting a layer of brush or rock and then dirt, and so on until you build to grade. We have also been delayed a little by the storms as the banks would cave in after heavy rains which required some cleaning up. But we have had a remarkably fine winter and the slides were few and our progress, considering all things has been fair.

Now as to the way we work: the road being lined out there are stakes, set some 25 feet apart, and each road-workers takes 25 feet; this we call his "claim;" he finishes it up and then goes ahead of the line taking the first untaken claim ahead, and so on. But in the rock-work, of course this cannot be done; there they all work together and fetch up the rear. We have now got only between two and two and a half miles to go to reach the pass or the "saddle" which is on the edge of the timber. The next mile is fair work; we will not have so much rock to contend against and I think we will make good time on it. We are now working some three-quarters of a mile from camp and we have our lunch brought out to us.

Comrade Mackey has got quite a severe bruise on the knee which compelled him to walk on crutches for a few days. it was by a piece of flying rock from a blast. Comrade Williams cut his finger to the bone with a piece of sharp rock but he keeps digging away. As for all the rest, we are all well and hope every other Colonist is the same.

GEORGE SPEED.

Progress report on the construction of the Colony's road to their timber claims as it appeared in the Commonwealth.

67

administration. In 1889, his new Secretary of the Interior, John Noble, made it clear that he disagreed with the policies of his predecessors and promised that he would work to return as much withdrawn land as possible to the market.[5]

In March, 1889, a Special Land Agent was finally directed to visit and investigate the Kaweah Colony for "the purpose of ascertaining the facts regarding the character of the land embraced in the applications and the good faith of the parties making the same."[6]

On October 22, 1889, Land Agent B.F. Allen sent a 29-page, hand-written report to the commissioner of the Land Office in Washington D.C. It began by stating that "in order that you may fully understand the situation both of the land and the parties making the applications to enter, I have found it necessary to make an unusually long report."[7] Long and thorough, the report described the forest land and the Colony settlements. He recounted their history and ideology. He explained the circumstances surrounding the suspension of the application and the local political climate. But more than anything, he paid tribute to the industriousness and honesty of the colonists.

He dispelled any local myths that they were "dummy entrymen" and made a point of stating that "a large majority of them are of American birth and continence and of more than mere ordinary intelligence." He emphasized their plans of permanent settlement and pointed out that "they do not care to build permanent houses of the Shanty kind, preferring to wait until they can use the lumber and put up first class residences." He praised their road, calling it a "work of skill and judgment and sense" and pronounced it "the best mountain road in the state."

Allen did not limit his discussion of the situation to the colonists. After pointing out the improvement the Colony had made, he made mention of damage inflicted upon the land by local stockmen using the high country as summer range for sheep and cattle. "These men are absolutely irresponsible and reckless," Allen wrote, adding that "they delight in forest fires as they clear the country and bring good grass the next season."

> These fires were put out by the colonists [Allen continued] who left their work and rallied to do this labor. Sixteen men at one time had

to fight fire for four days. It spreads slowly underground below the surface of the debris and can only be put out by trenching. This year has been a very dry season and the Colony decided to close their road to all sheep and cattlemen and also to police the forest to prevent damage being done.[8]

And of the damage the Colony-proposed logging would cause, Allen explained their plans in a positive light:

> They do not propose to cut and market the timber in its crude state as mere commercial speculators. They have no idea at all of denuding the forest and leaving it a desert of stumps. They propose to first work up the fallen timber then to thin out the thick growth and foster the remainder, to clear the ground of stumps and cultivate and improve the thus opened places.[9]

Indeed, a more glowing account of the Kaweah Colony exists nowhere else (with the possible exception of Colony-published promotional literature, of which Allen apparently read a great deal.) He certainly didn't look too closely at other sides of the story, such as the stockmen's point of view who were supposedly "destroying the forest." Instead, he seemed to have a naïve faith in all the Colony showed and told him; not unlike the "absolute faith and dependence that all the Colonists have that the government will protect their rights as actual Settlers and improvers," which Allen called "remarkable."

Allen concluded that the colonists should be given patents to the land. The report closed with the following comments:

> Conclusively, it was a misapprehension of the facts that gave the idea that they were either speculators or dummies acting in the interest of some large corporation. I have made this long and possibly worrisome report because it seemed to me that the facts of the case justify it and further for the reason that I believe these people have done and will hereafter really do work of more or less public utility.
>
> It seems to me that the actual settler and improver should be protected as far as possible and if the claims of these men are not recognized now [that] they have built this road, the chance is left

A number of workers on the Colony's road including Andrew Larsen,
in the white shirt perched atop a rock outcropping, chipping
away at the granite face.

open for the corrupt denudation and destruction of the forest by the
way thus opened by the real timber thieves of this coast.[10]

Larsen at Road's End

In the months following Allen's investigation and positive report,
things certainly seemed promising for the Colony. By the spring of
1890, the road had reached the timber belt and work could begin on
the mill, although some road work was needed that spring to repair
what they had already built due to the damaging winter storms.

Spirits were high and optimism flavored the air at Kaweah. Not even the obviously impending death of one of the Colony's own could extinguish the high hopes.

Andrew Larsen returned to Kaweah in June of 1890, the Colony paper reporting that he was "just recovering from a severe illness and will stay until his health is recovered."[11] An original pioneer of Kaweah and one of the first of the road workers, Larsen had gone back to the coast to continue his career as a seaman, captaining for a time the schooner Mary Andersen. But illness ultimately interfered. Larsen looked the part of a rugged man of the sea, tall and muscular with a big droopy mustache, but poor health made him an increasingly delicate invalid. He had to give up his vessel in October of 1889, and spent the next eight months convalescing at the Haskell home in San Francisco. A doctor advised a change of climate, and as his heart longed for Kaweah, he was sent there.[12] A month after his return to Kaweah, it was reported that though he was "suffering from consumption…he is steadily gaining under Dr. S. Guy's treatment."[13] No one would admit the obvious. Andrew Larsen had returned to Kaweah to die.

Decades later, the story would still be told how Larsen refused to die until the road, which he had begun, was complete. An elderly Al Redstone, who was a young man that summer of 1890, remembered Larsen's words as he started out in a wagon one day for the pines on the newly completed road: "All aboard for the graveyard."[14]

In early August, Andrew Larsen, at 28 years of age, died of tuberculosis. Burnette Haskell eulogized him in print:

> He who was one of the founders of Kaweah; he who struck the first blow of the pick in the building of our road; he who swung the first axe in the primeval forest. He is dead; his body lies at the feet of the Pines, and the Marble Fork rushes madly by, sounding the deep notes that his ears may never hear again.[15]

Larsen the man had become Larsen the legend. He lived just long enough to see the completion of the road, which would no doubt lead to the Colony's good fortune. Even the government, in the person of Agent B.F. Allen, was convinced of the Colony's success, and his recommendation that they receive patents on their land claims was the best news they could hope to hear.

Cauldwell, Cranks and the Commonwealth

Agent Allen's report was promptly ignored, and considering the less-than-impartial tone, it is possible to understand why. The following year, a second Special Land Agent was dispatched to investigate the Colony and their applications.

Agent Andrew Cauldwell visited the Colony and did a thorough job of investigating, filing his initial report to the General Land Office in July of 1890. Like Allen, he reported favorably on the Colony and was especially impressed with their road, calling it the "best mountain road I ever traveled over." Cauldwell, however, was somewhat more subdued in his praise of the Colony than his predecessor, as evidenced in the tone of the following passage:

> Without making any comment or prediction as to the ultimate outcome of this cooperative Colony scheme, I cannot help testifying to their industry and perseverance in overcoming almost insurmountable difficulties in building their road.[16]

Cauldwell's report also offers a look at life at the Colony, and by the time he arrived there the settlement of Advance was a flourishing town (although Cauldwell seems to exaggerate the population, evidence that he, too, was caught up in the heady enthusiasm of the Colony at the time):

> At the colony headquarters, called "Advance," I found some 300 men, women and children concentrated in nicely constructed tents, and they appeared to be a wonderfully "happy family" of enthusiasts. They eat from a public table, supplies for which are purchased and issued by officers designated for that purpose. Every colonist who labors in any capacity is credited with his or her time on book, kept for that purpose and no money is circulated in the Colony. Monthly reports are required and published from all officers of the Colony.
>
> The Colony is getting new members daily and weekly from all parts of the Union. So far as my observations went, the colonists on

the grounds are above the average intelligence, but the women as well as the men seemed to me cranky on the subject of cooperation. Quite a number of the new members of the Colony Company have made squatter claims on agricultural lands along the line of their wagon road in the suspended townships referred to in my instructions, have made improvement thereon, and planted grain, set out fruit trees, vines, etc.[17]

Cauldwell also described one very important aspect of Colony life that was first described in Allen's report the year before. Cauldwell mentions the "well-equipped printing office from which a weekly paper is issued," and enclosed four copies in his report. Allen had mentioned in his earlier report that the Colony had just purchased "a cylinder printing press steam engine and a large lot of type and will soon have it in Advance under canvass cover but with wood floor and sides."[18]

By the time of Cauldwell's visit, the *Kaweah Commonwealth* had been publishing weekly for several months at Advance. A continuation of the monthly journal, entitled simply the *Commonwealth* which Burnette Haskell had printed in San Francisco, the *Kaweah Commonwealth* was obviously a propaganda tool for the Colony. It was their sales brochure with which they "sold" memberships. But it was also, in many respects, a typical small town newspaper. And while reports by Agents Allen and Cauldwell offer some description of day to day life at the Colony, the *Kaweah Commonwealth* provides a deluge of detail, from the trivial to the vital, on what life was like for enthusiastic pioneers of above average intelligence who were cranky on the subject of cooperation.

8

FROM THE PAGES
OF THE COMMONWEALTH

Everybody happy.

—*Kaweah Commonwealth*,
July 12, 1890

SCANNING THE PAGES of the *Kaweah Commonwealth*, can one really get an accurate account of what life was like for the colonists? It has been argued that as a reliable historical source, the Colony-published newspaper is terribly lacking—even misleading. The paper was a blatant promotional tool by which the Colony organizers sold memberships to fund their utopian endeavor. In this respect, the *Commonwealth* was pure propaganda. Contemporaries labeled it a "booming sheet."

While it is true that nearly all negative copy concerning life at Kaweah was filtered out, the resulting rose-tinted view presented by the *Commonwealth* does offer an interesting, albeit slanted, glimpse of Colony life. Any one of the 96 issues published at Kaweah contains a wealth of historical detail. And the Arcadian picture painted of the spring and summer of 1890 had at least some basis in truth. This is not to say that all the *Commonwealth* ever reported on were picnics, concerts and ball games.

The newspaper itself was part of an internal dispute that played out in the pages of the weekly journal.

Delivery of Issue Halted

Weekly publication of the *Kaweah Commonwealth* at Advance had been made possible by acquisition of what was billed as the first steam-operated press in all of Tulare County. Dr. M.A. Hunter had turned the press over to the Colony in exchange for membership, time checks and cash when he joined. For the first few months, Hunter served as editor of the Colony-published journal, and the paper generally carried editorials—sermons might be the better term—of a high moral nature by Hunter.

In the March 8, 1890 issue, Hunter wrote one such editorial advocating "true democratic principles" in ruling the Colony and called for "preliminary steps calling for a general election of officers." His primary complaint centered on the "indefinite continuance in office by incumbent [trustees], limited only by a demand for a removal." It was not removal anyone sought, but simply a regular general election making such a choice available. This set off a controversy resulting in some political maneuvering by Martin and Haskell. A battle between the so-called Power Element (Haskell et al.) and the Democratic Element was reminiscent of the schism between the Haskell and Keller factions two years before.[1]

Colony Secretary James Martin, with an office in Visalia, held up distribution and mailing of the issue containing Hunter's bold editorial and Burnette Haskell, based in San Francisco, took control of the situation. Haskell focused the ensuing debate on the manner in which the general membership could nominate and vote on officers; but as most members were non-residents of the Colony, the real issue was to whom and how information would be disseminated to these members. Haskell and Martin realized that whoever controlled the *Commonwealth* controlled the Colony.

Before all was said and done, further controversy erupted over the publishing and releasing of members' names and addresses, which Haskell warned should be kept secret. One account even

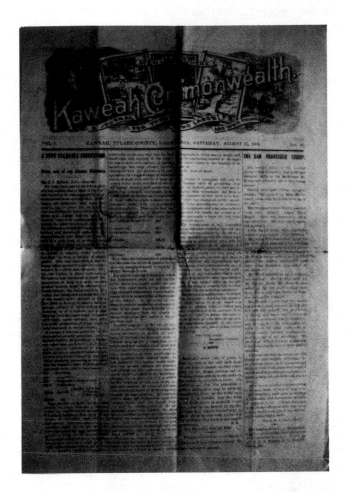

An issue of the Kaweah Commonwealth, published weekly from the Colony on the first steam-operated press in Tulare County.

claimed that "Mr. Haskell stated that someone had given the list of members to the *San Francisco Star*, and that he had one George Moore secure employment in the *Star* office and steal the list."[2]

Nonetheless, by summer the Colony had weathered the storm of internal schism one more time. By publishing weekly from the

Colony itself, the local editorship of the *Commonwealth* represented a growing position of power and influence. Haskell recognized this and, by the sheer force of his bullying personality, took
back complete control of the *Commonwealth*, Hunter having been
"severely abused" at a meeting which he was said to have "left in
tears and resigned" as editor.[3] The Democratic Element continued
to battle Haskell, producing their own propaganda and trying to
appeal to the non-resident membership, but by the time elections were finally held in July, Haskell and Martin were returned
as Trustees.

The *Commonwealth,* which the Democratic Element maintained
was "not a truthful informer of events,"[4] printed the following
account of Hunter's reaction to the election results:

> Dr. M.A. Hunter, rising to his feet, commenced an address to the
> audience which had a most startling effect. He reviewed his long
> years of connection with the labor movement, and how in his old
> age he had come to Kaweah with his all, had laid it upon the Altar
> of Truth, had turned over to the Colony his valuable machinery,
> printing plant and other matter with the hope that he was standing
> upon the bed-rock of freedom; that he had come here for better or
> worse to pass his remaining years in peace and hoped to lie his
> bones to rest amid the sacred bonds of brotherhood and principles
> of co-operation; when he had reached the point of his impressive
> eloquence, the Doctor's eyes were seen to fill and it was at once
> apparent that he was about to break down; Secretary Martin rushed
> forward and clasped him by the hand; this was a signal for the
> whole audience to rise like one man and leaping over benches, etc.,
> hand after hand was extended and grasped in a shake of true
> confidence, love and manliness.[5]

May Day Picnic

The *Commonwealth*, even while the dispute over its control sim-
mered, took every opportunity to depict life at Kaweah as a picnic.
In May of 1890, the paper reported on May Day festivities in the
neighboring village of Three Rivers, which were attended by
several dozen Kaweah colonists. After reading the account, it is

easy to imagine "everyone happy." Music, baseball, and fellowship filled the day, and neighbors became friends. Reporter Laurence Frost painted an idyllic picture when he described how the group of members, including the Colony band "traveled together to the ford of the North Fork, then past Halstead's till we reached the ford of the main river, where we were joined by Mr. Braddock."

> As the river was too high to cross we unhitched, and having provided for the comfort of our animals, commenced to cross the suspension bridge. Having eventually reached the other side, Captain Plaisted formed us into line, paired according to height, and Comrade Vest acting as Drum Major with a bat for a staff, followed by Dillon as Standard Bearer of the immortal stripes, the band, then the ball team, after which the various camp followers...marked time as the band struck up "Welcome Quickstep" and played us into the corral of Mr. Chris Butman's ranch.
>
> The Kaweah people were introduced to the various notabilities of the district. Among the names we heard prominently mentioned were those of Messrs. Blossom, senior and junior, the oldest ranchers in these parts having settled here way back in the sixties.
>
> Mrs. Blossom, a tall and graceful young lady, wore her fair hair in frizzy bangs. Miss H. Bahwell rode to the grounds in a habit of dark ladies cloth with a light Basque trimmed with white lace. Mrs. Trauger, from Mineral King road, wore a dress of dark alpaca.
>
> It was 11:30 before the teams could get into action, the delay being caused by the non-arrival of Mr. Clark, the splendid first base man of the Lime Kiln Club. Our band, however, caused the time to while pleasantly away.

The report then went on to give an account of the game—Lime Kiln beat Kaweah 6 to 0, and the paper made a point of noting the "conspicuous and pleasant absence of all bickering or disputing over the decisions of the umpire."

> After the conclusion of the match [reporter Frost continued], Mr. Warren, on behalf of the residents of Lime Kiln, Three Rivers and adjacent country invited the Kaweah visitors to lunch, elaborate provision for which had been made. During the preparation of the

luncheon, our band played by special request: Capriel, Tube Rose
Waltz, and Overture Queen City. The Pogue's band joined in with
ours, much to the delight of the audience.[6]

A River Runs Through It

Will Purdy, in his poem "Kaweah: The Saga of the Old Colony,"
described how at the Colony "The river ripples blithely over
stones, or roils thru pools with soothing undertones." Not always
so blithely rippling—Purdy also described the river as "that brawl-
ing stream down plunging e'er with zest"—in any event, it played
a major role in the everyday lives of the Kaweah colonists.

First there was the problem of crossing the river. When the
Colony was established there were no substantial bridges across
either the Middle Fork or the North Fork of the Kaweah River.
Small suspension bridges, on which a single person could cross,
were prominent during the Colony days and before, built by the
local ranchers, but horse teams with wagons or buckboards had to
cross the river by fording. This was easily accomplished during
much of the year, but considerably more difficult during winter
storms and the heavy spring runoff.

Construction of a ferry by the Colony solved the problem. Before
its existence, "during the rainy season, goods hauled from beyond
had to be trans-shipped and carried by hand over a very primitive
suspension bridge, so frail that...more than a single person is
forbidden to be on the structure at one time."[7] Crossing on the
ferry, which was a wooden barge attached to cables and which
utilized the current to propel it across the river, was described in
the *Commonwealth* as "exceedingly refreshing. The river runs very
swift and breaks and surges against the punt, making it appear as
though it were traveling at great speed."[8]

The first attempt at building the ferry, however, wasn't successful. An account in the *Commonwealth* in May, 1890, reported:

> On Sunday morning Comrade Carpenter drove our light spring
> wagon to the ferry accompanied by Comrades Christie, Miles and
> Bloomfield. Two Comrades attempted the passage with the wagon,
> some harness and our mail as freight, and a horse swimming

behind. From some cause the boat became a wreck, the wagon went to the bottom of the river, and the harness and mailbags had disappeared.

The rebuilt ferry was far more successful. It was reported that a "four horse leaded team can drive on and cross easily."[9]

In addition to providing a continuing obstacle, the river was also a vital resource and much used recreation site. As summer arrived in earnest, the *Commonwealth* noted that "bathing is a pleasure much indulged in at present, the water just getting warm enough to be enjoyable; during the early part of the season when the snow is melting, the water is too cold to be comfortable, but now it is delightful."[10]

The Colony newspaper also reported that "trout fishing is fashionable now. Nearly every day we see someone en route for the river with the usual outfit used on such occasions." The promotional-minded journal admitted, however, that "the trout is a hard fish to capture and it takes an expert angler to supply the family basket."[11] Perhaps colonist Philip Winser provided a more accurate fishing report when he wrote in his memoirs that as a source of fish, the North Fork "was not much; trout lived in the cold higher reaches—suckers and steelhead constituted the fish stock [near Kaweah] and were not much sought after."[12]

Measles, Broken Bats and a Post Office

One regular section of the *Kaweah Commonwealth*, called "Colony Notes," featured newsy blurbs and social tidbits, some as brief as the "Everybody Happy" declaration quoted at the beginning of this chapter. Subsequent notes in that very same issue included such messages as "Several strangers are among us;" and "Twenty-four horses were accommodated at Advance last week;" and "There is a large number of visiting Comrades sojourning at Advance; the unanimity and harmony prevailing must be very inspiring." Some blurbs provided a little more detail.

> The unavoidable absence of Mrs. Goodwin was noticed by all of us during the 4th of July. She has charge of the culinary matters now at the mill site which is situated in a most attractive spot.[13]

There was even one item which dared to report on something less than happy, inspiring or attractive.

> The measles are prevalent in camp, the following is a list of the afflicted: George Miles, Effie and George Dillon, Dora Tousley, Ida Boggs and Merritt Carpenter. The patients are doing well as the disease has assumed a mild form.[14]

Under the headline "Fourth of July Base Ball" ran an account of "a little ball game worth mentioning." It seems that nearly "all the comrades" were at Advance, down from road or mill work because of the holiday and a General Meeting scheduled the following day. At Comrade O'Farrell's flat about a mile down canyon from Advance the big game was played. Teams were chosen with Howard Plaisted pitching for one team and Al Redstone for the other. The *Commonwealth* described some of the game's highlights:

> Pitcher Plaisted stopped a terrific liner and threw the player out at first. There was no pause in the game nor remark from the pitcher, but a swelling on his wrist the size of a hickory nut showed afterward what the play had cost...Visitor W.T. Hunter and Comrade Botsford had made a pretty double play, when Comrade Waldo Miles took up the bat and struck a high-flyer to centre-field, smashing the bat in the operation. Comrade Hambly saw that ball and went for it. The ball equally went for him and rolled him over handsomely but he came up smiling with the ball in his hands and the side was out. Likewise the game for want of a bat, so the score was announced 15 to 5 in favor of Redstone.[15]

Then, as now, sports reporters could be trusted to provide colorful accounts of the action.

One other item in that same issue of the Colony newspaper did offer a straight news event, announcing the establishment of a U.S. Post Office at Advance. Reporting that "a petition numerously signed asking for a post office" had been sent to Washington some three months prior, the paper noted that "as a result a post office was regularly opened on Monday, July 8th," with H.S. Hubbard, who had been serving as local carrier, in charge. The article then went on to urge all colonists to "send their letters through the office as far as possible, both for safety of delivery and in order that the quarterly report may make as good a showing as possible." The future of their mail facilities, the report maintained, depended on such cooperation. "This is Post Official!"

The Women of Kaweah

It is also possible, via the pages of the *Commonwealth*, to get some idea of how Colony society presented itself to the outside world versus how it really operated. Take, for example, their attitude toward women.

Women were, in theory, on a completely equal footing with men in the Kaweah Colony. They could become members, had an "equal voice and vote in the affairs" of the Colony, and were entitled to an equal wage for their labor.[16] In practice, however, it appears women were subjected to many of the conventional discriminations of the time. On the Board of Trustees for the Colony, no women ever served. Of the 10 or so department superintendents, the name of a woman was a rarity. Among the few examples were Mrs. Christie's service as Domestic Superintendent or Miss Kate Redstone and Miss Mate Hildebrandt as Bureau Chiefs in the Department of Education—Kindergarten teacher and music instructor respectively.[17]

The Kaweah Colony was in reality a man's world. The women were generally seen as wives or daughters who served as homemakers and, in their leisure time, purveyors of culture. It was at the many cultural events—musical entertainments, concerts and literary evenings—that the women made a name for themselves at Kaweah. The pages of the *Commonwealth* would often praise the musical talents of Mrs. Ting, Miss Hildebrandt, Mrs. Frost or Jennie Evans. Social gatherings often featured dramatic recitations by such culturally active women as Kate Redstone and Mrs. Brann. And poetry written by Marie Sandberg, Jennie Sturtevant or Jeannie Peet often graced the pages of the weekly journal.

What these women did accomplish was to bring culture—a sense of finer society—to what was basically a pioneer camp. The tent homes maintained by women such as Mrs. Redstone or Mrs. Ting belied the coarse, temporary nature of the canvas. They were carpeted with homemade rugs, walls lined with tapestry, and decorated with pictures, baskets and "all those things which make up a home." [18] These women made sure the finer arts complemented the natural beauty of where they now lived.

Colony founder Burnette Haskell, in an otherwise bitter article he penned after the demise of the endeavor, wrote:

> I have no words except of praise for the women of Kaweah; the men did most of the gossiping, kicking [complaining], and loafing; the women were uniformly kind, cheerful, hard-working, and patient. They cooked, washed, baked, sewed, canned fruit, and on one notable occasion they fought a forest fire for twenty hours and by their heroic work, attested by burned and bleeding hands and faces, saved that glorious plateau [Giant Forest] for posterity." [19]

The episode of which Haskell made note was reported in the *Commonwealth* as well. Explaining that most of the men working the mill were down below at Advance for a General Meeting, the paper reported that only Mrs. Theophilus, Mrs. Bishop along with her daughter, and Comrade Saint-Dizier were up at the Mill camp. A fire started and "in this emergency all the afternoon and night of Saturday Mr. Saint-Dizier, Mrs. Theophilus and Mrs. Bishop, the latter with her baby most of the time on her arm, fought the flames with water in buckets and wet blankets until finally its course was turned down the gully and the mill was saved." [20]

The nature of the praise these women received, together with the fact that they were not in attendance at the General Meeting and thus apolitical citizens in the Colony, speaks volumes on their true place in Colony society. This was perhaps unfortunate, for Haskell believed, in the end, that the women possessed a greater sense of cooperative responsibility than many men, citing that he had "seen a woman getting in firewood with an ax and bucksaw in plain sight of thirteen men gathered for six solid hours around a stump excitedly discussing a rule of order improperly construed at the last meeting." [21]

TWO RISING MOVEMENTS

Evolution is the rock upon which Nationalism is founded.
—Denver Labor Enquirer

The movement looking toward the reservation of a tract of timber land
near the summit of the Sierra has at last taken definite shape.
—Visalia Weekly Delta

AS THE FINAL decade of the nineteenth century began and a springtime optimism prevailed at Advance, hopes for the future of the Kaweah Colony were dependent upon two completely unrelated movements of thought and action.

These movements were kindled by the influential writings of two notable figures. The first was John Muir, a Scottish-born sheepherder, explorer, journalist and essayist, self-taught naturalist and self-described tramp. He was a man whose name would become almost synonymous with the Sierra Nevada, the mountains he called the "Range of Light." The other was Edward Bellamy, a Massachusetts-born son of a Baptist clergyman, a lawyer-turned-journalist who had achieved a modest literary reputation when the publication of his fifth novel brought him sudden and worldwide acclaim.

Muir and Bellamy were two of the most influential writers of the late nineteenth century, and perhaps nowhere would that influence be as greatly felt or celebrated, realized and lamented, as at the

Kaweah Colony. To examine how these writers and the concurrent movements they launched would effect the Colony that summer of 1890 and afterward, it is necessary to double-back in time and bring each up to speed.

Early Conservation Attempts

John Muir first came to the Sierra Nevada in 1869. While Muir spent much of the early 1870s exploring the Yosemite area—his name will forever be associated with Yosemite—his curiosity regarding the Sierra was boundless. By the end of the decade he had explored much of the spectacular mountain range, including Mt. Whitney, Kings Canyon, and the vast sequoia groves of Grant Grove and the Giant Forest.

> The Big Tree is nature's forest masterpiece [Muir once wrote] and so far as I know, the greatest of living things. It belongs to an ancient stock, as its remains in old rocks show, and has a strange air of other days about it, a thoroughbred look inherited from the long ago—the auld lang syne of trees.[1]

As pointed out in Lary Dilsaver and William Tweed's *Challenge of the Big Trees*, Muir's newspaper accounts brought about a greater appreciation of the features of the Sierra, and his writings about the sequoias added to the understanding of the Big Trees. "The primary significance of Muir's visits," the book proclaims, "would not become apparent for a number of years."[2]

By 1878, others began writing about the sequoias and lamenting their potential destruction. On October 11, 1878, the new and rather young 21-year-old editor of the *Visalia Delta* wrote an editorial attacking the cutting of a giant sequoia for exhibition back east, a destructive practice first exposed and decried by Muir himself. George W. Stewart called for enforcement of state laws to prohibit the cutting of the giant trees.[3] Little came of these pleas.

As the 1870s drew to a close, however, other prominent men had been drawn into what was definitely becoming a popular cause. Prompted by a growing presence of lumbermen in the readily accessible Grant Grove area (then known as the Fresno-Tulare Grove) in January, 1880, Tipton Lindsey, receiver at the U.S. Land

Office in Visalia and J.D. Hyde, the land office registrar, were able to convince the land commissioner to withdraw from sale the sections which contained the stately grove.[4] Stewart's *Delta* was also recommending some sort of permanent preservation of the grove, and later that year George Stewart was finally able to bend the ear of someone who might really be in a position to effect a permanent solution.

During his 1880 campaign for the U.S. Senate, General John F. Miller came to Visalia and met with the editors of the local newspapers. Stewart was able to brief the senatorial candidate on a broad spectrum of local conservation issues, including the Kings and Kern canyons, Mt. Whitney, and the preservation of the "grand old redwoods." Miller not only won appointment to the U.S. Senate, but he apparently well remembered all that Stewart had told him.

On December 31, 1881, Senator Miller introduced a bill in the Senate to set apart a certain tract of land "as a public park and forest reservation for the benefit and enjoyment of the people." The bill was given no serious consideration in the committee on public lands, to which it was referred, simply because of the vast territory it sought to set aside. The proposed park encompassed all of the upper Kern, Kaweah and Kings River watersheds—an area covering all of modern-day Sequoia and Kings Canyon National Parks along with substantial timber belts to the west. It was so extensive that even Stewart stated that "opposition was universal."[5]

The idea of scenic preservation, which was the original impetus for all our earliest national parks, was nothing new. Alfred Runte, in his 1979 book, *National Parks: The American Experience,* explains that a sense of national pride and monumentalism—a search for cultural identity in a relatively infant culture—was one motivation for preservation. He also notes that there evolved in Congress "a firm (if unwritten) policy that only 'worthless' lands might be set aside." Worthless, that is, in terms of lacking accessible, available natural resources or potential as agricultural land—a criteria many scenic mountain lands easily met.[6] Cultural nationalism could not compete with a national obsession with productivity and the exploitation of any available natural resource.

Even a later awareness about a growing need for wilderness, wildlife and biological conservation did not change the primary criterion of preservation, Runte noted. National parks must begin and remain worthless to survive. While the forested land outlined in Miller's bill was far from worthless, compared to agricultural land it was certainly low-worth, and the difficulty in accessing its natural resources further kept its relative value in check. Nonetheless, no tract of land as expansive as the one Miller proposed to reserve could be perceived as anything but potentially very valuable.

Sequoia National Park historian Douglas Strong, in his 1964 doctoral thesis for Syracuse University, pointed out an ironic source of opposition to Miller's proposal—a source that strongly supported the argument for the preservation only of "worthless" lands.

> The earliest park proposals attracted little comment [Strong wrote], however, one unusual source of opposition appeared in a San Francisco anti-monopoly weekly periodical entitled *Truth*. Although not opposing government reservation in principle, *Truth* condemned the Miller bill for playing into the hands of lumber, railroad and other monopolies. It insisted that the park reservation would withdraw from the people vast supplies of timber and extensive mining districts in Tulare and Fresno counties. *Truth* could only approve the park if it were restricted to the highest mountain districts where no lumber or mining interest existed.[7]

Truth's editor, Burnette G. Haskell, could not have known when he wrote that in 1882 just how prescient his opinion would prove. Miller's bill quickly died, but by the end of the 1880s, Haskell would be keeping a very close eye on the proposals made by men such as John Muir, George Stewart and the growing forest preservation movement in Tulare County.

Bellamy's Look Backward

In 1888, with the publication of a work of fiction by Edward Bellamy, Haskell's attention was drawn to a considerably different kind of movement that sprang up almost overnight. Few books in the history of American literature have had a more stimulating influence on the social thought of the time as Bellamy's *Looking Backward*.

In what Bellamy described as a "romance of future happiness posed against present sorrow,"[8] the book tells of a young man, Julian West, who wakes up from a mesmerized sleep and finds himself in the Boston of 2000 A.D. Leaving behind a nineteenth-century world dominated by the waste, greed, cruelty and madness of the competitive system, the inadvertent time traveler finds an unrecognizable America in the future. The country operates under a system of state socialism; private property has been abolished, all share equally in the wealth of the country, and all contribute equally—to the best of their capacities—in their service to the industrial army which produces the wealth. Cooperation has replaced competition; acquisitiveness and aggression have disappeared in the tide of plenty for all, and no man seeks to dominate another. The transition, Julian West learns, from the tortured old society to this new utopia was effected painlessly; and the new conditions provide an answer to an ancient question—human nature is essentially good. Society has arrived, in short, at a rational and humane order devoted to the noblest ends of man.

The book had immediate political impact. That same year, 1888, the first Bellamy Club was founded in Boston to propagate the principles of Nationalism, as the system of social organization Bellamy's depiction of the future outlined was quickly labeled. A wave of clubs, more than 150 in less than two years, swept across the nation and gave meteoric rise to the Nationalist movement.[9] To Burnette Haskell, working fervently to publicize, promote and fund the Kaweah Co-Operative Colony, the Nationalist movement couldn't have happened at a better time.

Although the Kaweah Colony's political and social structure was based on another book, Laurence Gronlund's *Co-Operative Commonwealth*, Bellamy's utopian look at the future proved more accessible to the general reading public. Gronlund had provided a blueprint of socialist cooperation, but Bellamy came up with a full-color model, complete with action figures and moving parts. It wasn't long before Haskell was claiming that the Kaweah Colony was Bellamy's model realized.

Three early clubs were formed on the West Coast—in Oakland, San Francisco, and Los Angeles—before the movement took hold under Haskell's leadership. These were non-agitating groups which rose spontaneously and, like the club in Boston, were basically reading circles and discussion groups.[10] Although it might be surprising that Haskell, a notorious San Francisco radical, would be drawn to the decidedly milder Nationalism, the transition was not merely a sudden opportunistic switch. As Haskell biographer Caroline Medan points out, "he had been evolving toward more moderate types of reform since [his] anarchist period in 1883." Medan also points out his economic motive. "Haskell already had a cooperative colony of his own," she reminds us, "and probably saw nationalism as a lucky coincidence which would popularize his project."[11]

Haskell entered the Nationalist movement via the Oakland Nationalist Club, which met bi-monthly at Hamilton Hall. He brought an appealing oratory style, along with other abilities, which he freely gave to the movement. As one observer noted:

> He could gather fifty seamen from the wharf at a half hour's notice in order to boost a lagging attendance and so keep up the appearance of success; he could frame a resolution or write a stinging letter of protest, circulate a petition, and if necessary sing a duet with his wife.[12]

Working untiringly, he organized the First Nationalist Club of San Francisco, creatively named to compete with the Pacific Nationalist Club, which was actually first and still operating. The club's objective, as stated in a meeting program, was "Nationalization of land and industry, thereby the promotion of Brotherhood of humanity."[13] Reformers of all kinds flocked to the meetings—suffragists, grangers, free silver and free tax men—and formed a more practical program of reform than had really been proposed in *Looking Backward*. At various times the organization advocated the eight-hour work day, abolition of poll taxes, the direct election of United States senators and presidents, initiative, referendum, recall, free vocational schools and women's rights.

In the summer of 1889, as Haskell was forming his own circuit of Nationalist clubs throughout California and the West, he was still busy promoting and administering the Kaweah Colony, which he maintained represented "Bellamy's plan in action." *The Common-wealth* was still, at this time, a monthly journal published from San Francisco, where he maintained his residence with his wife, Annie, and young son Astaroth. He was also still active in various trade unions and organizations, and this period of incredible energy and productivity is testimony to the obsessive nature of his personality.

Haskell brought not only this energy, but also showmanship and promotion to the movement. An account of the 3rd Public Reception of the Nationalist Club of San Francisco, held at the Palace Hotel, was printed in the *Commonwealth*. It was the beginning of the link between Kaweah and Nationalism.

B.G. Haskell spoke and after explaining the ideas of the club, declared they were so simple that even a child could understand them. Astaroth Haskell, age 3½, demonstrated the truth of this assertion by then delivering from the President's [Haskell] table the following address:

"Ladies and gentlemen, I'll tell 'oo why I'm are socialist. I'm ain'ta 'Publican, nor a Democrat nor an Anarchist. 'Lem are hood'ums. Socialists are gentlemen and Nationalists are Socialists."

Great applause greeted the pretty, earnest baby and when, in response to the repeated calls, he gave an encore in all earnestness, it arose to almost a storm. After this, Mr. Haskell resumed his talk leading up to the question of Millionaires and Tramps when an interruption occurred by the entrance of a perfectly revolting specimen of the later product of the competitive system. A natty millionaire rose up to put him out when the piano, Mrs. Haskell at the keys, struck a chord and "Tramp and Millionaire" began a duet set to the air of "The Gypsy Countess." This was the climax piece of the evening and was realistic, artistic, and fetching.[14]

Conservation Heats Up

Just as the change in administration and attendant shift in policy prompted the long delayed investigation of the Colony timber claims, it also served to accelerate the conservation movement (the more likely term at the time would be preservation) taking hold in the adjacent Central Valley. By 1889, rumors of withdrawn forest land, particularly in accessible sequoia groves such as the Grant Grove and Converse Basin, being returned to the market was causing great concern. This concern involved more than just Big Trees.

Irrigation had changed the Valley from grazing and bonanza wheat farms to an orchard and irrigated crop economy. Now Valley farmers feared that excessive logging in the adjacent Sierra would adversely effect their much-coveted watershed. Deforestation, they predicted, would accelerate spring thaws, leaving little, if any, runoff for the later summer months. The rate of snow-melt had great impact on water supply as there were no dams and reservoirs on the rivers to control runoff. What was bad for the crops was bad for the entire county, particularly for those with vested interests in land values.

In May of 1889, the worried farmers petitioned the Land Commissioner urging him not to reverse the withdrawal from entry of the Grant Grove area. Not only did many farmers sign the petition, but also, among others, George Stewart, F.J. Walker and business partners J.D. Hyde and Daniel K. Zumwalt.[15] Hyde and Zumwalt were engaged in various irrigation projects, and Zumwalt was a land agent and attorney for the Southern Pacific Railroad. He was said to have sold more land in the area during his career than anyone.[16] The reply they received was less than satisfactory. While assuring them that the withdrawal was still in force, Commissioner Stockslager added ominously that "it must be apparent, however, that a reservation by order of the Commissioner of the Land Office is only temporary."[17]

In October of 1889, a meeting of agriculturists and other interested parties motioned to appoint a Forest Committee to petition the government to create a permanent forest preserve in the area. A petition was prepared and sent to Congress in November, but there was no response. Stewart, a member of the Forest Committee, concluded that the petition had never reached Congress after learning that Representative General William Vandever had introduced a bill in March of 1890 to create a national park protecting Yosemite Valley and the nearby Mariposa Grove, a considerable distance to the north. Vandever's bill (H.R. 8350) did not even mention the groves of Big Trees Stewart's petition had outlined for preservation "which [made them] think he never received much information regarding the Southern Sierra."[18]

Also discouraging to Stewart were rumors that the Garfield Grove, one of the last groves of Big Trees with absolutely no claims against it, and other areas were soon to be put back on the market. As spring gave way to summer, Stewart's *Visalia Delta* was calling attention to the efforts of lumbermen to obtain the few remaining sequoia groves. According to Stewart, it was then that he and F.J. Walker decided that the only way to save the Big Trees was to create a "National Park" similar to Yellowstone, created in 1872. Walker, who also worked at the *Delta*, informed Stewart that "he had ample free time and asked how much space could be occupied in the *Delta* agitating the question." All the space necessary, for as long as necessary, Stewart replied.[19] Thus began the campaign to create Sequoia National Park.

Stewart's Sequoia: The Garfield Grove

"Save the Big Trees!" read the headline of an editorial in Stewart's *Visalia Delta* on July 10, 1890. Bringing attention to efforts to restore withdrawn timber land to the market which would "result in forever removing from public control the finest body of grand sequoias that exists in the world," the *Delta* pointed out that there remained a grove of giant trees "over which the government has an undisputed right of control." That grove, Stewart explained, lay in Township 18 South, Range 30 East, Mt. Diablo Meridian. Translated, he was describing the Garfield Grove area, located a considerable distance south of the timber claims of the Kaweah Colony.

Stewart and colleague Frank Walker's campaign to create a national park concentrated on reserving the Garfield Grove area because, as the *Delta* had stated on July 3, 1890, "nearly all the [other] groves have already passed into private ownership. Certain tracts, like the Giant Forest, that were once on the market and filed on by applicants in good faith, should be restored to the market." The applicants referred to were, of course, the Kaweah Colonists. As efforts to create a national park intensified, Burnette Haskell certainly took notice and was especially interested and undoubtedly relieved to note the location of the proposed preserve. In fact, the *Kaweah Commonwealth* reprinted portions of a *Delta* article that came out on August 21, 1890, addressing that issue.

> While it is not claimed that the unbroken area clothed with sequoias is as large on the south fork of the Kaweah as that found in certain other localities, it is nevertheless true that this is by far the finest sequoia forest still under the undisputed control of the government. If it be claimed that the so-called Giant Forest...is still in the hands of the government, the reply is that this vast tract is already claimed by a colony of Socialists who seem to be entitled to their land under existing laws.

In addition to editorializing in the *Delta*, Stewart and Walker wrote letters to anyone they thought could help. As a result, the Secretary of the Interior John Noble began receiving correspondence from influential people all over the country urging the reservation of sequoia forest land. Many of these, such as *New York Tribune* editor W.A. Stiles, were undoubtedly writing at the behest of Stewart and Walker. Stiles, in a letter to his former college classmate who had become Secretary of Interior, stated, "I have received in my capacity as editor...several communications from California relating to a grove of Big Trees in Tulare County."[20]

On July 28, 1890, as a result of a vigorous letter writing campaign, numerous newspaper editorials, and various petitions (some of which were once thought lost or ignored), General William Vandever, Member of Congress for the 6th District of California, introduced a bill in the House of Representatives to reserve a certain tract of land, encompassing two townships containing the Garfield Grove and backcountry to its immediate east. It was virtually just as George Stewart had suggested and outlined.

While an earlier bill introduced by Vandever to reserve the Yosemite Valley and its watershed was languishing, this later Sequoia bill fairly raced through Congress. It was passed by the House on August 23, 1890. The Senate approved the bill on September 8, 1890 and it was promptly sent on to the President for final enactment into law.[21]

The Nationalist Disorder

While the conservation movement was steadily building in California, urged on by men such as John Muir and George Stewart, Nationalism had taken the country by storm. Nationalist Clubs had sprung up all over the country, in large cities and small towns, and Kaweah was no exception. Of course, it was natural that Kaweah would support an active Nationalist Club. The philosophies behind both were similar. In fact, the Socialist endeavor was actually being referred to in the press as a "Bellamy Colony."[22]

The Colony's own newspaper quickly became one part Colony booming sheet and one part Nationalist organ. It ran advertisements for other Nationalist publications in Los Angeles, San Francisco and Boston and published reprints of Nationalist essays and articles. Throughout the spring of 1890, it printed accounts of the local Nationalist meetings. A typical example ran in the March 1, 1890, issue:

> The Kaweah Colony Nationalist Club meeting opened with singing—minutes of last meeting read and approved—Solo by Mrs. Ting—Reading from Bellamy—Singing "The Old Arm Chair" by Mrs. Martin—Remarks upon the matter read by Mr. Hubbard, Dr. Hunter, Mr. Braddock, Mr. Herschede and Mr. Nuckey.
>
> Debate then followed upon the following question: "Resolved that it would be for the general benefit of the public for the United States Government to assume control of the [rail]roads." Mr. Hubbard and Mrs. Martin on the affirmative; Mr. Christie and Miss Kate Redstone on the negative. No vote was taken, the subject being left open for discussion.
>
> It was voted that Mr. Redstone and Mr. Plaisted represent the Club as delegates at the Nationalists Convention in San Francisco.
>
> Adjourned to meet next Saturday.

The growth of Nationalism and the network of clubs and newspapers across the country were an obvious source for publicizing the Kaweah Colony. Burnette Haskell took advantage of this, but in his zeal to control the movement he brought on disharmony that was reminiscent of early Kaweah Colony struggles. It showed a pattern Haskell seemed destined to repeat again and again.

A talented motivator and stump-speaker, Haskell organized Nationalist clubs in Ocean View, San Jose, Santa Rosa, Santa Cruz and Fresno.[23] He eventually saw the movement as a viable political party, announcing at one reception that the Nationalists would enter the municipal elections of 1890. That spring, the California Nationalist Convention was held. Its purpose was to unify the clubs by means of a central committee, broaden the clubs' influence and plan for upcoming elections.

At a meeting of his First Nationalist Club of San Francisco prior to the convention, Haskell failed to gain control of the delegation. Charges of fraud and mismanagement had begun to surface against Haskell, who desired decisive control of the delegation and thus, he hoped, control of the upcoming convention. He instead found the club divided, making a final fight for power inevitable.

When the convention convened in Metropolitan Hall in San Francisco on April 8, 1890, Haskell quickly met opposition on the issue of proxy votes. Several smaller clubs were unable to send delegates, and Haskell presented their proxy votes, backing them up with written permission for each proxy and strong arguments that to deny these proxies was to discriminate against the poor, who could not afford to vote in person.[24]

With Haskell proxies allowed, a subsequent battle ensued over election of a committee chairman, which became deadlocked between Haskell's choice, W.C. Owen, and a rival's, T.V. Cator. Again rose the issue of proxy votes. Caroline Medan described the scene in her 1950 biographical thesis on Haskell:

> Then, just before another vote was to be taken, Judge Wheeler, a Cator supporter, stepped out of the hall for a few moments, appointing a proxy to cast his vote. This proxy was not recognized, however, and Owen's victory resulted. Non-recognition of Wheeler's proxy in the balloting caused T.V. Cator and almost half of the delegates to walk out of the convention.
>
> That night, Annie [Haskell] wrote in her diary "We have met the enemy and they are ours." However, Annie was wrong. T.V. Cator

was not defeated. He had gone directly from the convention to the Palace Hotel and there had organized a "true" nationalist convention, adopting a set of principles and drawing up fifteen reasons why he and his followers had left the convention. The reasons were all Haskell in fifteen different forms.[25]

Pattern and Prophecy

This was one more example of Haskell's peculiar talent for influencing (read "fixing") elections. Charles Keller had seen that talent in action and, like Cator, was prompted to leave with his followers. Dr. Hunter had seen it, resulting in his tearful resignation as editor and ultimate sacrifice of his valuable printing press.

The convention's split and the subsequent press attack was devastating. The *San Francisco Star* noted that the San Francisco Nationalist movement had early been "seized upon" by Haskell and was from that moment on divided. It went on to call Haskell "one of the most thoroughly untrustworthy persons who ever fooled the unwary public, or made simple-hearted folks believe him a little tin god on wheels."[26]

Haskell's First Nationalists Club in San Francisco quickly faced failing attendance. Resignations and disagreement were increasing daily until an especially bitter May 21 meeting. The disintegration was nearly completed. Bellamy Nationalism was founded on the precept that human nature, being essentially good, would arrive at a rational and humane order devoted to the noblest ends of man, but Haskell's ego and incredible drive to dominate insisted on utter control of that process. His impatience served only to hasten the movement's decline.

Yet despite the decline of the movement in California, on a broader horizon Bellamy's brand of Nationalism continued to influence and incite enthusiasm worldwide and even helped recruit members to Kaweah from as far away as England. Philip Winser's memoir, which he penned in the 1930s, provides an excellent example of how Nationalism attracted members to Kaweah from so far away.

The eldest son of a dissenting Unitarian family, Philip Winser was struggling to keep the family farm solvent in Kent, England, when, with an ailing father, he came up with a plan to "wind things up, realize everything and pay off." He made "preparations for the sale [of the farm] and arrangements for migrating" were put into effect. After setting up his mother and remaining family in a house by the sea where they could take in boarders for income, Winser's personal plans "began to formulate."

> About this time [Winser wrote] Edward Bellamy's novel *Looking Backward* was being talked of a lot and I read it. The word, socialism, was not mentioned, but it sketched an idealized society on that order. I had been pondering the anomalies of society and how it was that the hardest workers seemed to get the worst of it, and couldn't solve the riddle. The answer seemed to come to me in this book, and I made up my mind if ever there should be a community who would try and work things out on those lines, I would endeavor to join them.[27]

Winser stumbled upon his utopia after a Boston cousin sent him literature on a Bellamy Nationalist club and movement. Included in that literature was an article describing the Kaweah Colony. It was "Bellamy's dream realized" in the mountains of the Sierra Nevada, Winser remembered thinking. Writing to the secretary of the Colony, Winser soon received notice of his acceptance. He promptly remitted the initial $100 and made plans to cross the Atlantic.

CHAPTER

10

THE ANNIE HASKELL DIARIES

I defy any man in this room to read Annie Fader Haskell's diary without falling in love with her.

—JOSEPH E. DOCTOR, Southern California
Historical Symposium, 1968

WHILE THE KAWEAH Colony and its primary settlement of Advance flourished during the summer of 1890, its founder and leading proponent had yet to establish a residence at the Colony. Burnette Haskell somehow managed to take active part in its administration and to even serve as editor of the weekly publication produced at the Colony from his San Francisco base, where he recruited membership, continued his labor agitation, and tried to coalesce the Nationalist movement for his own agenda. As the summer wore on, it became more and more apparent that the time was coming for Haskell to make a final and focused commitment to the Colony—a commitment that would involve relocating his family to the foothills of the Sierra Nevada.

Haskell's move to Kaweah marked a watershed event in his personal life. It was a defining moment in his marriage, and his commitment to that marriage stood trial in the pages of his wife's most remarkable diary. To understand their marriage and her feelings on the eve of their big move to Kaweah, it is necessary to double back in time once more, and in the process get to know one of Kaweah's most remarkable personalities—Annie Haskell.

A New Day Dawns

Anna Fader, like many young women of her time and ever since, had early on fallen in love with the romantic notion of love. As a teenager, she wrote the following poem:

> *It is hard in the Summer of Girlhood*
> *Ere the days begin to grow old*
> *To have one's heart once so joyous*
> *Grow hard and heartless and cold*
>
> *It is hard in the days when freedom*
> *Is ours, for a time, to keep*
> *To be chained with a nameless longing*
> *To a sorrow intense and deep.[1]*

The daughter of a sailor who had joined the Gold Rush, Anna was born in California's Trinity County in 1858. After completing school in Salinas, she continued to live with her family in Sonoma County.[2] In 1876, the 18-year-old Annie (as she was called) started what would prove to be a life-long discipline. A dedicated diarist, she filled exactly one page—no more and no less—of small, leather bound diaries every day for 65 years. In 1881, she wrote of a romance, an "Arthur, my Arthur, for whom my heart has called." And while Arthur evidently hinted at a future together ("He thinks by next fall he can get bread and butter enough for two. Oh! If it is not too late!"), by the spring of that year Annie was again lamenting a nameless longing:

> I get so weary trying to live without love. Perhaps some time my
> day shall dawn. I suppose it ought to be a consolation to me that if
> it don't dawn in this world, it will in the next. But it ain't. I want my
> happiness now. I have waited long and am tired.[3]

In the autumn of 1881, Annie moved out on her own and headed for the big city of San Francisco.[4] In the early 1880s, San Francisco was the largest, most cosmopolitan, most exciting city west of the Mississippi. She initially had a hard time finding room and board, becoming "more disgusted than discouraged" at the sorry condition of various boarding houses and homes for girls. She did manage to find work, however, at a workingmen's restaurant "slinging hash," and more importantly, accepted an invitation from a friend, Helen Haskell, to stay with her and her family for a while.[5]

The attraction between Annie Fader and Helen Haskell's brother was almost immediate. After only a couple days staying with the relatively well-to-do Haskells, Annie wrote:

> I have commenced [work at the restaurant]. I am tired. I rather Burnette might despise a girl who slings hash. But this evening he came down and insisted on my going there to sleep, as did Helen, and so though I had engaged a room I went. Oh, it will be so much nicer...Burnette was exceedingly enthusiastic on the subject of my conduct. He said I was a "queen among women." It is foolish for me to report it, but somehow it warms my heart how he honored me.[6]

Burnette Haskell was smitten with Annie. At a time in his life when he was finally discovering for himself his life's cause in the labor movement, he also found the time to stay up until the wee hours "discussing the theory of evolution until we were wild" with Annie, or to praise her "exquisite shoulders."·

"The idea!" Annie blushed onto the pages of her diary. "I have always disliked them so much, and I don't care, I hate such wide shoulders on a woman." Burnette, she was proud to report, insisted they were "classic."[7]

Married Life

Burnette Haskell proved to be less than the ideal husband to Annie. While she was probably guilty of idealizing love and marriage, she certainly hadn't bargained for the lifestyle into which she was thrust. The pattern of their married life was quickly set by the mid-1880s. Annie was either busy working for Burnette's various labor causes, or left alone at home while he was. Neither of these two basic situations made her very happy, although the 1886 birth of their son, Astaroth (Roth), seemed to alleviate some of her chronic loneliness.

By the late 1880s, Haskell was occupied with his labor organizations, the Kaweah Colony, and the Nationalist movement. While Annie actively participated in the Nationalist Clubs—helping to organize meetings and programs and often performing at them—a diary entry from that period was especially telling. In it, Annie summed up feelings countless wives (and indeed, any person married to an ambitious and inattentive spouse) have felt:

> I feel as if I were at a turning point in my life and I don't know what to do. I have no friends, not even in the world. If a man says to his wife "no woman, not even my wife, shall come between me and my ambition," what then? Dear me, I waited and waited this evening for Burnette to come to dinner. He did not come home till near 12 and then did not offer a word of explanation. I really don't know what to do. Nothing I can do pleases him.[8]

Haskell was not, in the words of one Kaweah historian, a very good husband. Annie complained he spent more time with "the Cause" than with her and she felt he was rather too attentive to a woman who later became his "traveling secretary." But, as Joe Doctor—a good storyteller fond of the human-interest side of history—once hinted, Annie too may have been guilty of extra-marital involvements.[9] She was obviously quite fond of Andrew Larsen, whom she referred to in her diary as her "dear Larloo."

During the spring of 1890, an ill Larsen lived at the Haskell home in San Francisco where Annie spent a great deal of time trying to nurse him back to health. She described him once, sitting disconsolately by the fire, as a weary shadow of his former big, strong healthy self. Another day she noted:

> Larloo is in bed. Poor old fellow. I am doing everything I can for him. I hope and pray it will do some good.[10]

By June, he was feeling better and was sent to Kaweah, where it was hoped the drier climate might help his consumption. "Larsen went away this morning," Annie wrote. "He looked pretty well, but I kissed him good-bye, as I don't know what might happen."[11]

While Joe Doctor went so far as to call Annie and Larsen "lovers,"[12] there is also the possibility that it was strictly an innocent, warm relationship. An argument can be made either way. Annie worked at keeping her marriage sound. She made efforts to become involved with her husband's projects, but found it tiring. In addition to her work for the Nationalist movement, Annie tried to keep involved with Haskell's most consuming ambition at the time—the Kaweah Colony. The Kaweah Co-Operative Colony Co. maintained a large non-resident membership in San Francisco (as they did in other cities such as Los Angeles, Denver, and New York) which met regularly. Haskell continued to head Colony operations from San Francisco. Amazingly enough, in the days before instant communication, Haskell even managed to oversee publication of the *Kaweah Commonwealth* at Advance, acting as Corresponding Editor. Later, after Dr. Hunter resigned as Editor, the journal's masthead noted that it was published "under the supervision of Burnette G. Haskell, Superintendent of Education."[13] It is hard to imagine how much direct "supervision" he could offer from over 200 miles away; but nonetheless, as long as Haskell remained in San Francisco, much of the Colony business and promotion was also centered in the City by the Bay.

The young couple, meanwhile, were having financial difficulties. On July 29, 1890, Annie wrote in her diary:

> Burnette and I have been talking over our situation. It looks mighty bad—and you bet, if we ever get out of this hole we are in, we will never get into a similar one. Everything goes wrong and there seems to be no way to get money and we are so deeply in debt on every side.[14]

The very next day, via a telegram from James Martin at the Colony, they got the news that Andrew Larsen had died. A shock, Annie admitted, although it was hardly unexpected. "It's so sad," she wrote. "Poor dear Larloo. I'm so glad I kissed him good-bye."[15]

Back in San Francisco, life went on. In September of 1890, Annie shared with her diary her feelings about Colony activities there in San Francisco:

I went to the Colony meeting this evening. Took the trolley. I did not want to go and talk foolishness, which I don't feel like doing. I abominate it. I loath it. I feel that way about everything and I am getting worse and worse every day. I suppose I think too much of myself. Sat up until after 1:00 a.m. last evening, or rather this morning, waiting for Burnette to come home, but the cars had stopped so I went to bed. He came in at 4:00 a.m.[16]

Reading the diary pages, one gets the idea that there may have been more than Nationalist clubs, labor meetings, or Colony business keeping Haskell out so late and so often in a city so filled with temptation. The solution to their troubles, both personal and financial, they could put off no longer. The time had come for them to move to the Kaweah Colony. Their very survival would depend on the success of the Colony and Haskell's dream of a cooperative world.

Off for the Colony

In September of 1890, a turning point had truly come in Annie Haskell's life, as she readied for the move with her husband to the Kaweah Colony. It was a turning point she dreaded. "Off for Visalia, off for the Colony," Annie wrote. "I never hated to start for any place as badly as I did today."[17]

While Annie certainly lacked the eager optimism that most new resident-members brought with them to the Colony grounds, shortly after her arrival her attitude exhibited a change for the positive. It is hard to know if this was really inspired by finally seeing the Colony first-hand, or simply prompted by her husband's badgering and cajoling. After first seeing the area, however, she was duly impressed with its natural beauty, noting in her diary that "it is a beautiful place, and I am satisfied with it."[18] High praise from a woman who only days before loathed and abominated everything.

Just one week later, Annie's first impressions of Advance appeared in the *Kaweah Commonwealth*:

> Now I have come to stay; and I am very glad that I got here before
> this unique town, this wonderful tent town, has spread its white
> wings and settled down the canyon, for it is wonderful.[19]

The "white wings" referred to the canvas of the tent homes. The
Colony still consisted of these temporary structures, but by the fall
of 1890, when Annie had arrived, plans were already underway to
re-locate the primary Colony settlement down canyon four miles to
some land the Colony had leased.

The optimism Annie exhibited in the pages of the *Common-*
wealth may have been forced to some degree—anything appearing
in the promotionally obsessed "booming sheet" had to be somewhat rose-tinted—but there was also significant cause for such
optimism. The Colony had finished their road to the timber. A
sawmill had been set up and logging operations had begun. They
had found a site for their permanent settlement further down
canyon with plenty of level land and available water which was
being referred to as Kaweah Townsite.

The Haskell family also had cause to feel optimistic. Annie,
Burnette and Roth would soon move into their own house on
homesteaded land not far from Kaweah Townsite. Annie had to
expect that at Kaweah, Burnette would not be so subject to the
distractions of the big city. The small family would be able to
spend time together and be part of a true community. Annie
described in glowing terms some of the inhabitants of that community in an article entitled "My First Impressions":

> There are ladies here whom it is a misfortune not to know, sweet
> aunt Margery who is, I am sure, one of the sweetest ladies upon the
> face of the earth. Mrs. Martin, who fairly decorates a room, she is
> so handsome, and Daisy who has grown like some beautiful flower,
> Mrs. Christie with her brilliant face. Mrs. Elford who looks so
> motherly and kind, Mrs. Essner always smiling, Mrs. Purdy who
> has a face like that of Evangeline, Mrs. Theophilus whose smiles
> are like the sunshine in a room and illumined the mist that hung
> over the road-camp. Last but not least is Mrs. Carpenter, a nice
> little woman.[20]

Annie also had an opportunity, during her first few weeks at the Colony, to visit the Colony's mill and venture even further into the forest to see the awe-inspiring giant sequoias. She wrote about many of the sites visitors to Sequoia National Park visit today, although some were known to Annie by different names. She saw the Karl Marx Tree, the B.G. Haskell Tree, Moro Rock and Round Meadow. But the thing that moved her the most was visiting the grave of Andrew Larsen. In a circle of cedar trees not far from the mill and the end of the road, Annie searched and searched until she found just one little flower, which she put on "poor Larloo's grave."[21]

Annie's diary continued to plot the course of her new community and track the ebb and flow of personal and collective optimism. Her entries during her first year at the Colony, from October 1890 through the latter part of 1891, are perhaps the best eyewitness account of what would prove to be a pivotal year in the Colony's history. It was also an uncommonly frank account of a pivotal year in Burnette and Annie's marriage.

At the outset of that first year at Kaweah, having had a chance to visit the various camps and meet many of the other Colony families—her new friends and neighbors—Annie felt compelled to wax prophetic in her diary:

> Oh, we will make a success of this Colony yet—but it will take time and we must have patience everyone.[22]

11

THE MILLING BEGINS

Our First Lumber
Tis but a chip of pine
Picked from a rough sawn board,
Yet many a chip of pine
A story may afford

—*Kaweah Commonwealth,*
July 26, 1890

EARLY IN THE summer of 1890, the Colony road had reached the pines after nearly four years of grueling work. The heavily timbered land that had long been considered inaccessible was now reachable on an impressive wagon road nearly 20 miles in length that climbed over 5,000 vertical feet. It had been made possible not by huge expenditures of capital, but by the cooperative sweat and labor of Colony members who toiled not for mere wages, but for the common good of the community they had joined. Of course, many had paid dearly to join that community and continued to pay, if not with cold hard cash, then with the sweat off of their brow. Still, those who joined had nearly all done so believing their cooperative resources would pay dividends to them all.

With the road complete into the timber belt, their most valuable resource was finally accessible. However, there was still much work to be done. A workable mill had to be established, which required equipment and still more labor. Only then could the felling, milling and transporting of lumber begin, which called for more equipment and some fairly specialized and skilled labor. The Kaweah Colony was fortunate, however, that certain members happened along when they did. Irvin Barnard was one such member.

Barnard and his Ajax Tractor

Irvin Barnard had been a farmer in the coastal town of Ventura, California, before joining the Kaweah Colony.[1] With his arrival as a resident member in 1890, the Colony gained some very important assets. For one thing, Barnard had considerable capital at hand; it was he who acquired the lease on a sizable tract of land in the lower North Fork canyon, which would eventually become Kaweah Townsite.

He also brought to the Colony a valuable Ajax steam traction engine, which was just the thing needed to power the sawmill they were establishing at the end of the road. Ajax traction engines were sold by A.B. Farquahar of York, Pennsylvania, a manufacturer of farm and sawmill equipment. According to the 1887-88 catalogue, there were four sizes of Ajax engines—from 8 to 14 horsepower—costing in the range of $1,175 up to $1,625. The number two engine, for instance, was a 10 h.p. unit which would use about 400 pounds of coal and 10 to 12 barrels of water in a day's operation. It had a 6½-inch diameter cylinder with a 9-inch stroke and operated at 275 rpm. Although these traction engines were equipped with steering gear and could be driven under their own power, they were also supplied with a removable tongue so that when used on a road a team could be used for steering.[2] In this way these portable engines could be pulled by team from job to job.

Getting Barnard's Ajax to the job site at the end of the Colony's road to the pines proved to be a considerable and eventful task. It is unclear how Barnard transported the engine the 200 miles from Ventura to Visalia. Freightage via the railroads would have been costly and driving it or pulling by team all that distance an ambitious and time-consuming trip, but Barnard was apparently a man of both means and ambition. In any event, the journey was

*Getting an Ajax steam traction engine across the various forks of the
Kaweah River presented a stiff challenge to the colonists.*

without mishap until reaching the foothills and a bridge across the
South Fork of the Kaweah in the village of Three Rivers, a few
miles from the Colony grounds.

Crossing on an old and infirm wooden bridge, the eight-ton Ajax,
along with its driver, crashed through into the rushing stream
below. The South Fork is not a large tributary—it is the smallest of
all of the Kaweah's forks—so this bridge was low and the fall
neither great nor fatal. Barnard suffered only a few bruises, but his
vest and a gold watch were swept away in the current and never
recovered.[3] The Ajax, fortunately, was recovered. With a great deal
of labor and a bit of ingenuity, the huge tractor was pulled out of

the streambed and tangled rubble of the collapsed bridge. Soon, however, Barnard faced the even greater task of crossing the much larger Middle Fork.

Swollen from a heavy spring runoff, the main Middle Fork of the Kaweah had recently taken its toll on a ferry built by the Colony, destroying it against the rocks. When Barnard arrived at the crossing, there was no way to cross, and he suddenly found himself not only stuck on the wrong side of the river, but in the middle of a Colony debate over building either another ferry or a bridge. The ensuing dispute was a prime example of the frustration Colony leaders often faced.

Barnard returned to Visalia, where he brought news of the ferry's demise and the current situation to Colony Secretary James Martin. In addition to needing to get the Ajax across, the Colony faced a much more urgent need of getting supplies across to a suddenly isolated settlement. With the deep snows in the Sierra that year, the swift-running torrent would likely continue for some time. It would be several weeks before the main fork could safely be forded. A way across was of paramount importance. Martin later recalled that "a short talk with Mr. Barnard convinced me that he was the very man needed to meet the situation."

Barnard had experience with ferries; he told Martin it was the most practical, least expensive and quickest way of re-establishing connections to the cut-off Colony. He outlined exactly what materials were needed. It was obvious to Martin, a trustee of the Colony, that an immediate decision was needed and in less than two days the materials arrived at the spot on the river where the new ferry would be built. Martin's unpublished history of the Colony continues the story as he remembered it:

> In the meantime at the Colony there had been, naturally, much talk with regard to the situation and what was to be done. When the material for a new ferry arrived it appeared to be a shock to a few ardent democrats that a matter of such importance had not been discussed at a special meeting. One member, who assumed to be more or less of an engineer, had induced a few to believe that a suspension bridge could be built of the worn-out wire cables

discarded by the street cars in San Francisco, which he thought could be obtained for the proverbial song. It was rather a wild suggestion, but it took with a few because of the idea of economy. They failed to recognize that the hauling and freight on the amount to build a suspension bridge that would stand the strain of four horses and a loaded wagon would amount to much more than the cost of a new ferry. Nor did it occur to them that a bridge built of worn-out cable did not commend itself on the score of safety. And besides, a ferry would have to be built to bring aross the river the material necessary for the construction of the tower to carry the cable across, and for supplies to the Colony while the bridge was being built.

There were, perhaps, twenty advocates of the suspension bridge idea who would have liked to take a day or two off to thrash the matter out in a meeting, but when the material arrived on the opposite bank for the ferry the question was settled. Argument was then changed to criticism. It was contended that a ferry was unsafe, and besides, what did Barnard know about ferry construction anyway? Barnard's reply to this was that he had quite recently fallen through a county bridge with his tractor and that fact had not tended to increase his affection for bridges, especially suspension bridges of amateur construction. "But," he said, "if it will afford comfort and relief to the timid, my tractor and myself shall be the first to cross on the new ferry; I will drive onto the ferry with a full head of steam and toot the whistle vigorously while crossing." This was regarded as fool-hardiness by the bridge advocates. The time was set for the crossing, and a small crowd assembled, some of whom rather expected to witness a tragedy. Barnard, however, made the crossing in safety while the echoes rang with a multiplicity of toots.[4]

On June 21, 1890, the Colony newspaper, which had been following the progress of the Ajax, proclaimed, "All engine difficulties are past. The whistle of the engine has been heard at Advance." The report added that it would remain there "until the return of Comrade Barnard, who will take his son up to the mill site with him and probably leave him in charge of the mill."

Cauldwell's Return

When Special Land Agent Andrew Cauldwell filed his investigative report on the Colony in July 1890, his involvement with the case was seemingly over. While the report was generally favorable toward the colonists, he had questioned the legality of the individual claimant's quit claim deeds to the Colony. While satisfied that the original intent of the entrymen was to "place their claims in a common pool after they had proved up and paid for their claims, to be worked co-operatively for their joint benefit," the withdrawal of the land and suspension of the claims changed matters.

Cauldwell's report explained how Colony leaders nonetheless "instituted and partially carried out the plan of getting quit claim deeds from filers."

> I am satisfied [Cauldwell wrote] that nearly all of those timber entrymen who made these quit claims did so through a misinterpretation of the law, their attorney [Haskell] having advised them that having once tendered their final proof and money in payment they could subsequently deed their equity in the claims to the Colony Company, notwithstanding the fact that the Land Office had refused to receive their proof and money.[5]

His ultimate recommendation was to cancel all the timber claims in the suspended townships without prejudice to any individual claimant "to the end that such as honestly intended to enter said timber lands for their own use and benefit can have an opportunity to make new filings thereon whenever the suspension is removed." This would have thus opened the door for anyone, be they Colony member or otherwise, to make brand new claims.

This recommendation was never heeded, and a growing conservation movement undoubtedly influenced the decision. In fact, with bills already introduced in Congress to preserve California forest land, Secretary of Interior John Noble, who was in favor of the movement, ordered the commissioner of the Government Land Office to renew suspensions on the townships containing sequoia trees until a complete report could be rendered concerning the location of the Big Trees.[6] Cauldwell, a temporary employee of the

Interior Department, was already familiar with the area and drew the assignment. It probably helped that the congressman for the district and author of two bills to set aside forest reserves, William Vandever, had personally written the Secretary of the Interior asking that Cauldwell be given a permanent appointment, citing the character of his work as evidence of his efficiency and fidelity.[7] Cauldwell returned in August to make a comprehensive report on the location, number and size of giant sequoias in and around the Giant Forest. This new assignment also marked a dramatic shift in Cauldwell's attitude toward and relationship with the Kaweah Colony.

By August, Barnard's Ajax had made its way up the Colony road to the timber, and a sawmill had been erected. Production that first summer did not, however, live up to expectations. Burnette Haskell later vented his frustrations concerning the mill's output:

> A total of 20,000 feet (at $10 per thousand) was cut during a three month's run with a mill whose capacity was 3,000 feet a day; the actual cut average 193 feet per day; less than a tenth of what ought to be done, and this mill was not run short handed. It is true that most of the time it did not run; that loggers were inexpert; that the mill was small and old; that picnics had to be organized; that the men had to come down for "General Meetings," that this foreman was bad and that foreman was worse; that the timber was small; that the oxen were lame, and a hundred other reasons, but the fact remains that results were not attained.[8]

Haskell was obviously bitter when he wrote this, but even the ceaselessly optimistic *Commonwealth* hinted at problems at the mill that summer. "Work at the sawmill is progressing fairly this week, considering the lack of help," they reported, exhibiting a rare instance of qualified negativity. "Comrades Barnard and Shaw have worked like Trojans to prepare the new edger for service. A fine new belt has also been put up, and several other improvements made which will add materially to the capacity of the mill."[9]

The *Commonwealth* later tried to put a positive spin on another unforeseen setback. "The oxen recently purchased," the paper noted, "are recovering strength and flesh in the pines. The exception is one of the weakest, whose neck was broken while grazing too close to a rocky bank."[10] Nonetheless, logging had begun and the Colony was finally producing lumber—the valuable and vast resource that would sustain their cooperative dream.

Cauldwell was well aware that the land upon which the colonists logged had not been patented nor deeded to them. It was still technically public land, and he was compelled to warn them against cutting timber upon it, insisting they desist at once. He had personally caught them in the act of "timber trespass"—cutting trees on public land—and at once reported the infraction to the Department of Interior on August 15, 1890.[11] This, however, was one fact that had no detrimental effect on production at the mill, for the warning was patently ignored. One can easily imagine the negative effect this had on Cauldwell's relationship with the Colony. Tensions between them grew.

Conservation Successes

Meanwhile, it should be remembered that Vandever had introduced his bill calling for the reservation of the Garfield Grove area and that it was successfully speeding through Congress. On September 11, 1890, the *Visalia Delta*, in reporting the rapid progression of Vandever's Sequoia bill, commented that:

> In these days of tardy legislation, it seems wonderful that this bill should be introduced in Congress and passed without opposition, and then taken to the Senate where it is favorably reported by the committee on public lands, then presented to the assembly and passed without debate. The bill will be presented to President Harrison to sign and there is not the least doubt but that our chief magistrate will affix the seal of his approval to the measure. Those who have taken an interest in the successful passage of the bill can well congratulate themselves with their splendid work.

Even the *Kaweah Commonwealth* saw the rapid passage of the bill, which it must be remembered reserved the Garfield Grove area many miles south of all the Colony claims, as good news. With its passage imminent, they proclaimed that "never were the prospects of Kaweah more bright than today!" and went on to explain that "this news assures the retention of our rights to the Giant Forest, as one National Park is all that is likely to be created for some time to come in this vicinity."[12] In other words, the Colony cheered the creation of a park reserve as outlined in Vandever's bill because it didn't encompass their land. They had dodged the bullet of legislated conservation.

The Yosemite Bill Bombshell
Introduced months before the Sequoia bill, the proposed legislation to create a federal reserve around the state-controlled Yosemite had come about in great part due to the agitation of John Muir and Robert Underwood Johnson, editor of *Century* magazine. Envisioned by Muir to protect the vast watersheds surrounding the Yosemite Valley, which was already protected by the state of California, the bill was introduced in March of 1890 by Representative Vandever.[13]

Johnson had a great deal of influence in Washington, and even after the bill had been introduced he worked hard to convince the House Committee on Public Lands that it did not go far enough. Armed with a statement and a map from John Muir, who urged that the Yosemite Reservation ought to include the Tuolumne River watershed and the Ritter Range to the east, Johnson lobbied for extension of the boundaries of the proposed reservation. He appeared before the Committee on Public Lands on June 2, 1890, and finally by late September achieved positive results. A second Yosemite bill was substituted and passed through both houses of Congress on September 30, the last day of the session, without the customary bill printing. This new bill provided for a park that was almost township for township like the one Muir had sketched for Johnson.[14] The substitute bill, which became law on October 1, 1890, created a park more than five times the size of the one originally proposed by Vandever. Yosemite became the second national park created in California in less than one week.

The substitute Yosemite bill, introduced in the eleventh hour and rushed into law, created not only a vastly enlarged Yosemite National Park, but with its added sections of text created General Grant National Park and added four townships to the newly created Sequoia National Park.

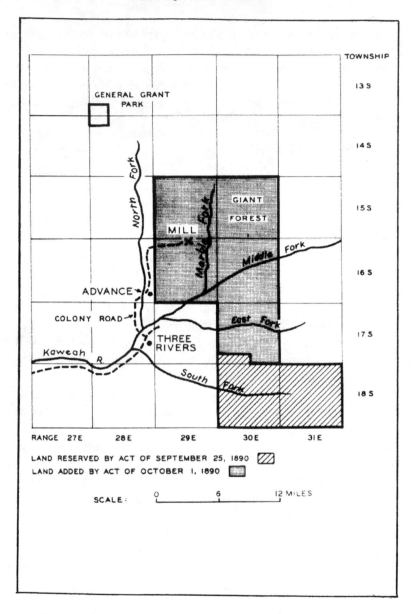

TOWNSHIP

13 S

GENERAL GRANT PARK

14 S

North Fork

GIANT

15 S

FOREST

MILL

Marble Fork

Middle Fork

16 S

ADVANCE

COLONY ROAD

East Fork

17 S

THREE RIVERS

Kaweah R.

South Fork

18 S

RANGE 27 E   28 E   29 E   30 E   31 E

LAND RESERVED BY ACT OF SEPTEMBER 25, 1890

LAND ADDED BY ACT OF OCTOBER 1, 1890

SCALE: 0   6   12 MILES

Map showing the boundaries of the original Sequoia National Park, created on September 25, 1890; and the enlarged boundaries after the park more than tripled in size through the bill passed to create Yosemite National Park on October 1, 1890.

116

Section Three of the Yosemite bill, which added to Sequoia National Park an area more than twice that which had so recently been reserved, described the addition only by township, section and range numbers; so it was unlikely that any of the politicians who passed this bill realized that the area added included the famed Giant Forest and all of the Kaweah Colony timber claims. Nowhere in the text was there any mention of the Sequoia bill passed only a week earlier, nor of the famed Giant Forest, Tulare County and the Kaweah Watershed.[15] With a road newly completed to the timber belt and claims filed on much of the land in question, it would have been hard to label this added land as worthless, which had historically been (and would continue to be) a key factor for consideration of reserving public lands.

Assured by the Committee that it was not "proposed in any manner to interfere with the rights of settlers or claimants," the bill was read and passed through the House without any debate. In the Senate, the bill was read and Senator George Edmunds of Vermont complained that it could not be understood and should be printed. Then someone spoke quietly to Edmunds, and he withdrew his objections. The bill passed the Senate without further debate.[16] The one thing these congressmen did understand was that forest preservation had become a very popular stance, so with the session nearly over, it is hardly surprising that they took the opportunity to cast their votes to save the Sierra forests.

The establishment of two national parks (and the mysterious enlargement of one) marked the end of the summer of 1890, a time of incredible activity and optimism for the Kaweah Colony. Several elements of Kaweah's story progressed at once during that exciting spring and summer: the road was finished and a sawmill erected; a community began to flourish at Advance; a Nationalist movement gained momentum and helped attract members to the utopian endeavor; a growing conservation movement took root and began to realize legislative success; a government Land Agent investigated, supported, and ultimately antagonized the Colony; and the driving force behind Kaweah—Burnette Haskell—finally focused his commitment solely on the Colony, moving his family to the Sierra settlement. As summer gave way to fall, all these divergent aspects converged at one place and time. In fact, Haskell and his wife, Annie, arrived at the Colony on the very day the Yosemite bill was signed into law.

It was several weeks before news of the bill's passage and the enlargement of Sequoia National Park reached California. It would be decades before the mystery surrounding this development finally came to light.

PART
III

A DREAM'S DEMISE
(1890 - 1891)

12

A CHALLENGE TO OPTIMISM

We hear today that our whole forest and Avalon are made by Congress into a park. Most of the colonists are sick.

—ANNIE HASKELL'S diary,
October 21, 1890

IT TOOK THREE full weeks before news of Sequoia's sudden enlargement reached those who had done so much towards realizing its establishment. George Stewart's *Visalia Delta* reported on October 23, 1890, that it was a "surprise to many to know that the park comprises seven townships instead of two townships and four sections as at first supposed," although the paper noted it had always been the intention of the originators of the bill, of whom Stewart was certainly one, to secure reservation of a greater area.

The Visalia newspaper undoubtedly spoke for Stewart personally when it explained:

> Those who have expressed dissatisfaction at the limited scope of the original Vandever park bill, in that it did not take in enough sequoia forests, cannot attribute it to narrowness in the conception of the originators of the movement. There was little sequoia timber remaining in the possession of the government, and there was no desire to interfere with vested rights or with those who had made application for timber land containing sequoias under the laws of the United States.[1]

Vandals of Capitalism

As news was so slow in making its way west from the nation's capital, one might surmise that Andrew Cauldwell's September 26 report recommending inclusion of Giant Forest and the surrounding townships into the park could hardly have made it all the way from Visalia to Washington in sufficient time to have had a causal effect on the park's enlargement. Obviously, there were others of influence in the capital who evidently shared Cauldwell's views, regardless of ever having read his report. But most people in Tulare County were little concerned with just who was responsible for the last-minute expansion of Sequoia—few people except those who were most dramatically effected by the news.

Burnette Haskell certainly had his theories. He claimed the purpose of the bill was "part of a plot to destroy Kaweah." In the November 1, 1890 issue of the *Commonwealth*, Haskell explained:

> The whole great San Joaquin Valley as a lumber market is in the hands of a gigantic lumber trust who have long watched us with a jealous eye. They well knew that as soon as we began producing lumber it would be sold at reasonable prices to the farmers of the valley and that their own prices would come down. Knowing also that our legal title to our lands was unassailable and seeing that we had at last got to the timber they did what monopoly always does under similar circumstances.

Haskell maintained that said monopolies had "flooded the colony with rumors that this bill takes away our lands." Of course, Haskell set the picture straight for *Commonwealth* readers. Aspects of his theory that he couldn't explain—such as how the hated lumber trust had been behind the legislation expanding the park—he ignored. And aspects of reality he disagreed with—such as his assertion that their legal title to the land was "unassailable"—he simply changed. (Title was only unassailable in that there was no title.)

Haskell was able to maintain his optimism and, in fact, presented a good argument for continued optimism. When, on October 25, 1890, the *Commonwealth* finally reported on the California parks bill and Sequoia's sudden enlargement, Haskell noted that while it "takes a portion of the Colony lands," it also "reserves the private rights and interests of the settler." Even the *Delta* agreed with this when it noted the provision in the bill honoring "any bona fide entry of land made within the limits."

"This is as it should be," the *Delta* editorialized, adding that the "rights of all applicants who made their filings in good faith should be respected and protected by the government."[2] It is obvious the *Delta* was specifically speaking of the colonists.

> Very well, then we propose to stay [Haskell wrote, steeling the resolve of the Colony]. Our colonists can rest easy. Our legal rights will be protected. Our homes preserved inviolate. The home of the American citizen is a sacred precinct, not to be invaded by the vandals of capitalism at their pleasure.[3]

Kaweah on the Move

The autumn of 1890 was a pivotal time for the Kaweah Colony. In addition to the creation and enlargement of Sequoia National Park and the arrival of the Haskells as permanent residents, the entire settlement was relocated down canyon to Kaweah Townsite.

Until that busy fall, the primary settlement of the Colony had been Advance, originally a road camp about four miles up-stream from where road construction began. Perched on a bluff with limited level land available, it was never really thought of as the site of a permanent Colony town. Indeed, most of the time the colonists lived there as mere squatters, although eventually some of the members actually filed homestead claims at and near Advance.

Before mid-1890, the Colony planned on eventually moving to a proposed town site at East Branch (as they called what is now known as Yucca Creek). This area, also known as Avalon by the Colony, was already the center of their agricultural endeavors. They dry-farmed and harvested hay there, had planted several small orchards and had begun work on a ditch and flumes for irrigation. After completing the road to the timber, they even built a spur road down to the confluence of East Branch and the North Fork of the Kaweah; but just as that road was being completed, a change in plans was prompted by the arrival of Comrade Irvin Barnard.

Barnard's financial assets have already been considered in telling of his Ajax steam engine, and further evidence of his means can be shown by a purchase he made of a 240-acre tract of land at the lower end of the North Fork canyon for $2,000.[4]

> *The canyon broadens here—with calm incline*
> *The hills up-billow from the oak clad plain;*
> *The river ripples blithely over stones*
> *Or rolls thru pools with soothing undertows.*[5]

This was how poetically inclined colonist Will Purdy described the area of the new settlement.

By late September, the big move had begun. The Colony newspaper noted that about 35 persons were already living at Kaweah Townsite. "As a place of residence," they proclaimed, "it seems to be a favorite."

In November, the *Commonwealth* gave some idea of the layout of the Kaweah Townsite:

> The post office will be located in one third of the annex to the printing office and residents will have to call for their mail. The store building will contain the store, the treasurer's office and reading room, with shelves for the colony library and files for papers. School will open in the school-tent on the hill south of the printing office. The blacksmith shop was moved to Kaweah where Vulcan Dudley will be nearer the river water that he loves so much.[6]

By late November, the move was mostly complete. The *Commonwealth* reported that "the new town is growing in rapidity and now looks on both sides of the river somewhat like a country city." Advance, by that time, had become almost entirely deserted and had "quite a desolate air."[7]

They Keep Cutting

After the Colony claims became a part of the new national park, Special Land Agent Cauldwell remained involved in the case and, in fact, matters heated up considerably between this agent of the government and the Kaweah Colony.

After completing their road and getting the Ajax traction engine to the pines, the colonists were able to start cutting trees and milling lumber.

On October 25, 1890, Cauldwell reported to the Department of the Interior that the colonists were continuing to cut timber on land now embraced in the forest reserve. In letters dated October 30 and November 10, the honorable William Vandever, according to Cauldwell's account, directed the Land Office to thoroughly investigate allegations that the Kaweah Co-Operative Colony Company was cutting within the reserve. Vandever allegedly instructed Cauldwell to "warn the trespassers to desist from further cutting and if they fail to do so lay the facts before the U.S. Attorney." By this time, Cauldwell had already gone to Los Angeles to consult with the U.S. Attorney, W. Cole, and "received from him the necessary instruction on how to proceed should I be ordered to stop the depredations."[8]

On November 12, Cauldwell received his official orders and paid a visit to James J. Martin. Martin maintained a Colony office in Visalia in the same building, ironically, as the local Land Office. It was there that Cauldwell paid the Colony secretary and trustee a visit, asking if his company intended to continue sawing timber in the park reserve. Martin, a man with an air of distinguished sophistication, didn't hesitate in answering in the affirmative.

> I then and there [Cauldwell wrote] officially notified said James J. Martin, a manager of the Kaweah Colony Company, to desist from cutting of timber on said forest reservation. In reply he said he didn't think they would, as they were cutting the timber under legal advice.

Martin, in his proper English accent, went on to inform Cauldwell that he could only give a definitive answer after calling a meeting of the trustees.

On November 24, Martin delivered that definitive answer. He informed Agent Cauldwell, in no uncertain terms, that the Colony was cutting timber on one of their own claims, and that they would continue to cut timber upon their claims in the forest reservation until restrained from doing so by force![9]

Arrested!

On December 4, 1890, the *Tulare County Times* reported that "B.G. Haskell, H.T. Taylor and William Christie were arrested in Kaweah for illegal lumber cutting." A fourth trustee, James J. Martin, was "picked up" in Visalia. Annie Haskell's diary provides this first-hand account:

> Well, there has been quite a sensation. There were two deputies— and they were very nice. They have all gone to Los Angeles and will have to find bail. Mrs. Taylor felt awfully badly—she was crying and so Lizzie and I tried to comfort [her.] Burnette sent word for me to teach the school in his absence.[10]

After Martin had informed Cauldwell that they would continue to cut until restrained by force, the government agent at once "proceeded to lay the facts before the U.S. Attorney." Cauldwell's report for November 26, 1890 shows the vehemence with which he now opposed the Colony:

In my judgment said trustees are the proper ones to proceed against, as the rank and file of the colonists simply obey their orders. It is a socialist organization, in my opinion, under semi-military rule. The majority of its members are un-naturalized foreigners.

These comments were quite in contrast to Cauldwell's first report filed in July, wherein he claimed the colonists appeared to be "a wonderfully 'happy family' of enthusiasts" and that so far as he could observe they were "above the average in intelligence." Cauldwell also earlier claimed he could not but help "testifying to their industry and perseverance in overcoming almost insurmountable difficulties in building their road." [11] There is no readily apparent explanation for his drastic change of heart.

In any event, Cauldwell's new opinion of the Colony and his recommendations to the U.S. Attorney resulted in the arrest of the Colony trustees. After posting bail, they still faced the expense of returning from Los Angeles, 200 miles away, as well as the cost of another future trip south to stand trial. While the other trustees were back in Kaweah well before Christmas, Haskell remained in Los Angeles and, as the holiday season approached, prepared for their impending trial.

In response to her suddenly-absent husband's request, Annie Haskell took charge of the school at Kaweah. The Colony had long been boastful of its school. Although Comrade Vest, who held a certificate in the California Department of Public Schools, failed to have Advance and its neighborhood declared a School District by the state early in 1890, he continued to maintain a school which was "conducted in accordance with the educational system of the state of California." [12] Vest had demanded legitimacy even if he couldn't obtain county funds.

When school resumed in September of 1890, Vest was pleased to announce that "he now had fifty-two pupils enrolled." [13] One of those pupils, Will Purdy, remembered fondly a supportive environment maintained at the school.

> *The wise preceptor, ardent as the rest*
> *Bore the unpoetic name of Vest*
> *His youthful charges openly exprest*
> *For buoyant spirits never were suppressed.*[14]

But that autumn Vest left Kaweah to take a job in Visalia as a school principal. Superintendent of Education Burnette Haskell had a difficult time keeping the post of Colony teacher filled, as he once explained:

> The teachers found it impossible to enforce discipline when a child, who deemed himself aggrieved, would in the class openly threaten that he would go home and get his father to call a meeting and remove the instructor. The boys and girls alike called the teachers by their first names, and came to school or not as they pleased. Complaints made to the parents were of no avail whatever, corporeal punishment of children being a "relic of barbarism."[15]

Annie, who later would become a career teacher, wasn't particularly thrilled with teaching at the Colony school that December. In fact, she hated it. She wrote in her diary that the children "behave most abominably and the accommodations are so bad and books so scarce that on the whole I am liable to have a very miserable two weeks of it." She described the school tent as "cold" although they finally "got a nice stove put in there." She herself sounded like a schoolgirl when she wrote, "oh how glad, glad, glad I was that it is Friday night." And just before the holiday vacation, her diary exclaimed "Thank Heaven! School is to end. I do hope I shant have to teach after the holidays."[16]

Christmas at Kaweah

> Christmas Eve. If Burnette were here I should be satisfied. I have just put some candy in the baby's stocking. I sent down one box for the tree tomorrow eve, and there will be a knife for him. He will fare slimly compared with other Christmases, but he will probably be just as happy.

So wrote Annie Haskell in her diary on December 24, 1890. It was her first Christmas at Kaweah. With her husband away, Annie

A group of Colony school kids.

lamented that for her it would "not be a very merry Christmas."
She had only been at Kaweah for a few months, and was finding it
difficult to adjust. Still, she admitted in her diary that next day,
"Mr. Martin did all in his power to make this a delightful day."

The *Kaweah Commonwealth* offered a description of the holiday
celebration shared by the community:

> Committees were appointed on arrangements and decorations, a
> fund was made up, someone was sent to Visalia to buy necessary
> presents, candies, nuts, etc. and a large fir tree was brought down
> from the Mill Camp for a Christmas tree. The hall was decorated
> with evergreens—pines and cedar brought down from the Mill
> Camp. A stage had been made for the event, upon which the

Christmas tree was placed and decorated. The piano was brought over from the restaurant, and Miss Abbie Purdy and Mr. Clark, our violinist, were the musicians of the evening.

The program consisted of recitation and songs by the children, a juggling exhibition by Al Redstone, and a dialogue between Frank and Harry Jackson representing an interesting conversation between father and son. After "Santa Claus" had made all the children happy with a bestowal of useful as well as ornamental presents, and after everybody in the room had been abundantly provided with cakes and candies, nuts and raisins, the room was cleared once more and those remaining tripped the "light fantastic" until the "wee small hours of the morning."[17]

Annie hardly felt like tripping the light fantastic, as the saying went, but she did note in her diary how "Roth enjoyed himself to say the least." Her entry for Christmas Day continued with an account of their first Kaweah Christmas and the wonderful time her five-year-old son enjoyed:

First, he had some candy in his stocking, and he kept exclaiming "ain't Santa Claus good!" Then Hambly brought up a great package from Uncle Benjie, which contained a box of three pies, a fine food basket, and a trumpet and candy cane.

Then this p.m. we went down to the restaurant where we enjoyed a nice turkey dinner, then we waited for the Christmas tree. Before the presents were distributed the children sang three songs and then this wonderful Santa Claus appeared. I watched Roth. He was awe-stricken and when presented with his presents said "Thank you, Santa Claus."

Annie closed her Christmas entry with a reminder of why the holiday season can be so sad for so many. "If Burnette had only been there," she wrote. "Poor old dear." For Annie, these feelings of loneliness were an increasingly common refrain. While life went on for her at Kaweah alone, her husband remained in Los Angeles preparing for a trial that could very well determine the fate of the Colony.

CHAPTER 13

DECISIONS, DECISIONS

I am not in a good mood. I feel like a powder magazine—awaiting the match.

—ANNIE HASKELL's diary,
January, 1891

ON APRIL 16, 1891, after deliberating for only 15 minutes, a jury delivered its verdict to the U.S. District Court in Los Angeles in the case against the trustees of the Kaweah Co-Operative Colony. Charged with illegally cutting timber on government land, the Colony leaders nervously awaited the jury's decision.

This was the second important decision for the Colony that month. A few days earlier the Secretary of the Interior ruled regarding their timber claims. Secretary Noble's decision addressed a provision to the bill, which enlarged Sequoia National Park to include the Colony claims. It was a provision on which Burnette Haskell and the colonists pinned their hopes. As they saw it, they were still entitled to their timber claims—existing rights, the provision stated, would be respected. Of course, the claims had been suspended back in 1885 and they never actually received patents on the land, but that was viewed as a mere technicality. The *Kaweah Commonwealth* assured members that they could rest easy. "Right and Justice will triumph in the end."[1] But as 1890 came to a close and the colonists could only await decisions out of their control, a sense of impending doom began to infiltrate the Colony. For some, it became a winter of discontent.

Annie's Winter Melancholy

Annie Haskell was prone to periods of depression, and this tendency was certainly heightened during her first turbulent months at Kaweah. Following her dread of moving there and a brief period of satisfaction at getting to know the community, Annie slipped into a rather deep melancholy that one can certainly sympathize with given her circumstances. First, she had to make the adjustment of living in the Spartan pioneer setting of Kaweah after years of life in cosmopolitan San Francisco. Next were the difficulties the Colony faced as a whole, and as always she faced the frustrations of being married to a husband who was, at best, inconsistent in his attentiveness.

Sometimes it seemed like nothing was going her way. She wrote of one day unpacking some boxes she hadn't realized were there, left out in the rain for some time "in which were some of my treasured possessions—ruined in a thousand pieces...I told baby [Roth, about five years old] I felt as if I could cry—he said 'well cry then. It don't annoy me.'"[2]

As winter approached, Annie was disgusted and resigned: "I guess there is no use my trying to care for anything. Nothing cares for me. I am like all women," she wrote, "always whining." For a while, when she and Burnette moved into their own house on land he homesteaded just a mile upstream from the new Kaweah Townsite, her depression lifted somewhat. Haskell called their homestead Arcady, and their little house of wood and canvas was complete with a piano, "tho I am sure it is awfully out of tune,"[3] Annie commented. Nonetheless, depression and general ill health quickly returned.

Haskell's extended absence exacerbated this depression. He spent a good deal of time in Los Angeles preparing for the impending trial. As legal counsel for the Kaweah Colony he also had to deal with other legal difficulties which took him to San Francisco to answer a charge of embezzlement by a disgruntled former colonist. Haskell managed to win acquittal of this charge in January, 1891.[4]

That same month, Annie's diary reflected her emotional state with a wonderful literary quality and attention to detail reminiscent of a great Victorian novel:

> I was very disappointed at not hearing from Burnette today—it seems as if everyone has forgotten me. To think that we creatures who have evolved from moisture & warmth like bugs under a stone should develop the capacity to endure such maddening misery as we do.
>
> Roth & I took a beautiful walk this morning on the side hill. Ah, the lovely grasses & ferns and the wonderful little plants & mosses growing on barren (but for them) rock. I wish I could grow such beautiful things on the barren rocks in my life.[5]

An Uninformed Congress

While the colonists pinned their hopes on Secretary Noble's upcoming decision regarding their claims, many had to wonder that winter how Congress even came to include that land as part of the new national park. While the bill enlarging Sequoia did provide that the permanent reservation of forest land would in no way affect any bona fide entry of land already made within its limits, it can be argued that Congress had no clear idea that there even were any existing claims. While the supplementary bill was neither debated nor printed, it should be noted that prior to passage of the bills creating national parks in California, Public Land Committee chairman Albert J. Payson had inquired of the Secretary of the Interior whether there were any adverse claims to the land. In an August 18, 1890 letter, Secretary Noble informed the senator that there were none.[6] Had Noble already struck a blow against the Colony?

Milton Greenbaum, in his 1942 thesis, maintained that Noble's answer was based on his belief that "an application to purchase under the Timber and Stone Act of 1878 does not effect a segregation of the land covered thereby." Greenbaum faults the Secretary for never having informed Congress of the existence of Kaweah, its status or accomplishments, basing this assertion on a careful perusal of the Secretary's outgoing correspondence. But, in defense of the Secretary, one has to ask why he would have informed Congress of the Colony claims when the land on which they had filed was not slated as part of the original Sequoia Park reserve, and the supplementary Yosemite bill which eventually set aside that land was not introduced until very late in the session. Therefore, when Noble responded in mid-August that there were no adverse claims on proposed park land, he was telling the truth as things then stood.[7]

This, however, is not to say that he wasn't keenly aware of the Kaweah colonists. Of course, in the months leading up to the passage of the park bills, Noble's knowledge of the colonists would have been based primarily on Cauldwell's first report, as well as that of the first land agent who investigated the Colony: B.F. Allen. Both Allen and Cauldwell had originally commented, in their official reports, that the colonists had made many improvements on the land. Farmland had been cultivated and a newspaper was being published and they both reported the existence of stores and shops and numerous other improvements, not the least of which was 18 miles of first-rate mountain road. But in the months immediately following the park's establishment, Noble's perception of the colonists via subsequent reports by Cauldwell would have been shaded considerably darker.

It is hard to pinpoint the exact cause of Cauldwell's sudden shift in attitude toward the Colony. Perhaps Martin's challenging response to Cauldwell's cease and desist order contributed to the strained relations. It could have been personal, for there certainly were some abrasive personalities involved. And maybe, as the colonists themselves believed, it was purely political. For whatever reason, by late November, Cauldwell had denounced the colonists bitterly. His contemptuous actions had already contributed to the arrest of the Colony trustees, and in the intervening months before the trial, Cauldwell's remarks would help to further influence public opinion as well as that of Secretary Noble.

Colony Bunco Game

Cauldwell's comments seemed designed to arouse prejudice against the Colony. He stated that the trustees were operating a "bunco game par excellence" which was netting them huge returns. They worked the resident Colony members hard and in return furnished the "poor fools" meager rations and promises. Outside sources contributed "between three thousand and five thousand dollars per month" whereas only two or three hundred was spent on beans, oatmeal, flour, coffee, and tea—the only food they fed their "victims and workers." The surplus "evidently went into the pockets of the trustees." Was it any wonder, Cauldwell rhetorically asked, that "they resort to every dishonest means in their power to keep up the delusion?"[8]

The trustees, Cauldwell claimed, also poisoned the minds of newspaper editors throughout the country by means of "bogus letters from imaginary individuals lauding the Colony and condemning the government for attempting to deprive the honest colonists of their timber lands upon which they have made valuable improvements." The land agent who owed his job to the current Republican administration railed at "all the local Democratic, as well as Farmers' Alliance, Labor Union and other kindred papers" that helped the Colony leaders "spread abuse and lies" about the government.

Ironically enough, Haskell was at the same time accusing the lumber trusts of using the press to "further influence the public against Kaweah." An editorial in Haskell's *Commonwealth* in December of 1890 noted:

> There have been published all over the land during the past month vicious attacks upon Kaweah Colony and its managers. These have been instigated by capitalistic Herods who seek the young child's (Kaweah's) life. These attacks, coming simultaneously from all sides, show a concerted and well laid plan to crush the cooperative movement inaugurated so successfully in our beautiful mountain home.[9]

Several of the large San Francisco dailies, including the *Daily Times*, the *Examiner*, and the *Chronicle,* printed accounts that were less than favorable toward the Colony, but no paper attacked the Kaweah Colony as vehemently as the *San Francisco Star*, which had once said of Burnette Haskell that he was a "systematic teacher of arson and assassination and that if there can be any excuse for his conduct, it must be that he is mad."[10] James Martin claimed that the *Star* was an open enemy of Mr. Haskell and that the editor was "well known in San Francisco as being reckless in his statements."[11] Whether this was true or not, it is readily apparent that the *Star* and its editor were certainly ready to do battle with Haskell via the press.

On December 27, 1890, the *Star* explained to its readers, under the headline "They Fooled The Papers," that the "almost unequaled capacities for lying, characteristic of one (perhaps more) of the trustees of the Kaweah Joint Stock Colony, continue unimpaired." The paper pointed out that a recent dispatch in the *Examiner* to the effect that the government didn't have a very strong case against the Colony in the Los Angeles trial was the result of lies and bribes. "The purpose evidently was to inspire confidence," the *Star* surmised, "so that the remittances would continue to come in, to be appropriated by the sharpers and liars who ran the concern." The *Star* proudly pointed out that they published the *Examiner*'s dispatch with "but one line of comment, as we want to be fair, even in dealing with scoundrels."

Contrary Views

There were, it should be pointed out, individuals in the government who did not favor the way the case against the colonists was being conducted. In December of 1890, then acting commissioner of the General Land Office, W.M. Stone, felt hearings should be held on the reasons for the original suspension of the Colony's filings.

His successor in office, Lewis A. Groff, felt even more strongly about it, viewing the current charges against the Colony as "mere allegations or ex-parte evidence." In looking at their original filings, Groff felt the colonists had fully complied with all the requirements of the law. The default in carrying the claims to patent, he declared, was due to the failure of the government to fulfill its obligations early enough, noting the suspensions had been in effect for over five years and no proof of fraud had ever been offered.[12]

In a letter dated February 25, 1891, to Secretary Noble, Groff advocated that the colonists be granted a hearing and if they could establish the legitimacy of their original filings, they should receive a patent to the land or be indemnified by Congress for labor and money expended. When news of Groff's recommendations reached the Colony, a tangible sense of hope returned. The *Kaweah Commonwealth* ran headlines proclaiming the "Important Document from Land Commissioner Goff [sic]." "The Commissioner believes," they reported, "that the Colonists have protected the giant trees, and that they should be allowed to retain the lands they now hold on the reservation [national park]."[13]

The arrival of this news made possible a legitimate recovery of optimism in the Colony just as spring was making its triumphant return to Kaweah. March is the most beautiful month in the Sierra foothills, as spring arrives in a flood of water, sunshine and wildflowers. And everywhere, green! This was just the thing that might bring many of the colonists out of an almost unbearable winter funk due to various community and personal difficulties that had nearly extinguished any glimmer of hopefulness.

Meanwhile, optimism itself was embodied in the person of one new arrival to the Colony. Phil Winser recalled in his memoirs, after becoming a Kaweah Colony member from England, booking passage on the Cunarder Cephalonia from Liverpool to Boston in early 1891:

> We had an average run, not so rough as was prophesied for the time of year, with only slight qualms from me after leaving the Irish coast. Boston at last and the long gang plank led down to the dock. It was no simple matter of walking down, however, for questions were in order and I had hardly opened my mouth before I put my foot in it.
>
> Where was I going? Kaweah, Tulare County, California. What to do? Ah! There was that rub, a cooperative colony was something out of the ken of an immigration officer; explanation and floundering called for more interrogation, until in my ignorance I demanded to know the reason at being held up, when the others were fast passing down.
>
> "Well, if you don't like it, we can send you back" had a cooling effect and we finally arrived at some sort of mutual understanding.

Winser's memoir tells how he was met in Boston by his cousin, Harry Talbot, who "was kindness itself." Talbot invited the newly arrived immigrant to stay and see the sights and they attended a Nationalist club meeting which led to an interview with Edward Bellamy himself. Winser noted that Bellamy was quite interested in his adventure, but "shook his head at such an experiment being made a success except on a national scale." This weakened Winser's faith not one whit. He took a train cross-country, traveling "tourist sleeper and fell easily into its ways, hearing odds and ends of information from fellow occupants." One fellow urged him to change his destination and get off to join the imminent Oklahoma land rushes.

> Finally [Winser wrote], at dusk on a spring day, we rolled into Goshen, the land of alkali plain and the only reason for whose existence would seem to be that it was a junction. A local branch line ran to Visalia, the county seat of Tulare County, some seven miles away. I took a room at the Palace Hotel. When I took my walk next morning, curiosity at my garb became apparent. The streets of the day were deep in mud even in the middle of town; winter rains had been plentiful apparently.
>
> I hied me to J.J. Martin's residence near the outskirts. I learned many details about the colony and found the biweekly stage, carrying mail, passengers and supplies left the next morning.
>
> This would be February 23, 1891, if one mistakes not.[14]

An Unfortunate Situation

During the spring, both Annie Haskell and her child fought severe illness. In March, she wrote that the "baby is sick...I have consulted my medical book until I am crazy." A few days later she reported he was "pretty sick again today" and that it "distresses me more than I can tell. Poor little darling, he takes medicine like a little man." When Roth finally got better, a relieved Annie wrote, "I think he has no more fever... he can walk some now...It is a great strain off my mind." A few weeks after that she herself became so ill that several entries in her diary read only "sick." Later on, she was able to elaborate: "I was attacked with that awful, horrible disease—dysentery." With atypical understatement, she simply called it "very unpleasant," but later the pages of her diary seemed to moan "oh, the misery of it. Some of these days in bed I thought I would never be able to get up again and I didn't care much."

Though Annie often complained of various ailments, it would be a mistake to assume that she overplayed her illness or depression, or that she was by nature weak and frail. Her resilient, tough and amazing strength of character, as well as the rudimentary state of health care in the Colony, is best illustrated in the following passage:

> I awoke this morning with a bad toothache. Harry [a family friend living at Haskell's Arcady homestead] tried to cut it out but the pain was too severe. Then I let him knock it out with a nail and hammer, so thank Heaven, this evening I have no toothache![15]

While Commissioner Groff's recommendation provided hope for the Colony, Secretary Noble's decision quickly deflated it. On April 9, 1891, the *Tulare County Times* reported the bad news. "Secretary of the Interior Noble rejected about forty-three entries of the Kaweah colonists, land embraced in the Sequoia National Park."

Noble apparently disagreed with the view of his commissioners. He declared that the General Land Office had the right to withdraw the land in question from entry. The Secretary maintained that applications to purchase are not entries of lands, and parties making the same acquire no vested right thereby. Congress still had the power to dispose of the land until the settler had made his final entry. In this case, Congress disposed of the land by establishing a forest reservation before the claimants made final entry. It was an unfortunate situation, Noble admitted, but the colonists had "no vestige of right to the land, and their entries are canceled."[16]

As Greenbaum pointed out in his "History of the Kaweah Colony," Noble preferred to take refuge in a technicality in canceling the entries of the colonists. By taking the stand he did, not only were the colonists denied an administrative hearing on the original question of whether their entries were bona-fide, but they were unable to take the case to court. They couldn't appeal Noble's decision because no hearing had been held. If the colonists sought redress, they would have to get it from Congress.

A few months later the *Kaweah Commonwealth* finally admitted the dismal situation into which Noble's ruling had thrust them:

> The adverse decision of Secretary Noble has had a disheartening effect on many of our members, so that just at a time when funds are most necessary, the Trustees are again crippled for lack of funds.[17]

The Jury's Verdict

A few days after Noble's ruling, the trustees stood trial in Los Angeles for illegally cutting timber on government land. The proceedings were widely reported, detailed accounts appearing in newspapers throughout the state, including the *Los Angeles Times* and the *Los Angeles Herald.*

A star witness for the prosecution was none other than Land Agent Andrew Cauldwell. According to the *Times*, Cauldwell testified "that he had seen trees cut and that defendant Martin had told him that they had a legal right to cut them. [Cauldwell] admitted that defendant Taylor told him they were cutting on the Zobrist claim."[18] The defense maintained that the trees cut were on Colony member Zobrist's homestead claim, and were used solely for improvements thereon.

The following day the defense called its first witness: John Zobrist. He testified that in 1888 he homesteaded his claim, laid the foundation for his cabin and in the following month went to the Land Office in Visalia and attempted to file on the land, but that the registrar refused to allow him to do so, claiming it had been suspended by the commissioner in 1882. The *Herald* noted that "this is the vital law point of the case; as to whether the commissioner had any legal power to abrogate an act of Congress [the Timber and Stone Act of 1878] and close the land to entry."[19]

On the final day of the trial, the attorney for the Colony, Henry Dillon, argued at length the points of the Colony's case, maintaining that the commissioner had no power to suspend; that they were entitled to their homes and had a right to ask the court to interfere in the protections; and finally that they were entitled to take the lumber to support their improvements. The courts refused to consider the issue of whether the colonists had any right to the land—and considering Noble's recent decision on these grounds, it was obvious the Colony had a slim case in that respect—but were instead trying them on the assumption that the land was government domain, indisputably a part of Sequoia National Park. According to the *Herald*, "Haskell then addressed the jury, asking them if they could acquit his four confreres, and convict him alone, as he had been their unfortunate legal adviser and they had innocently relied upon his advice." The court commented on his generous plea and the jury retired to deliberate.

The *Visalia Delta* was one of many papers that reported "a verdict of guilty was returned."[20] The four trustees were each fined $301—Haskell's plea was ignored, and probably seen by the jury as simply a ploy to save the Colony company money—and they all returned to Kaweah to figure out what to do next.

Damage Control and Support from Afar

Commenting on the Secretary of the Interior's devastating decision concerning the Colony land claims, the *Commonwealth* reported that "as foreshadowed and expected, Secretary Noble declined to interfere in our behalf and leave our titles to be settled by the courts." The paper was putting what modern commentators would call a "positive spin" on a truly dismal situation. "All of us understanding the situation," the paper continued, "feel still more determined than ever to fight to a finish and we have no doubt of final victory. We propose to stay by the ship! What do you say?"[21]

It was already evident, however, that many were choosing not to stay by the ship. Even before Colony timber claims were canceled, a negative population flow was taking place at Kaweah. The *Commonwealth* reported on the loss of one prominent Kaweah family:

> Monday last witnessed quite an exodus, the departure of Mrs. E.C. Miles and family and Mrs. Ting, with their effects. Two four-horse teams were loaded with goods and people, the latter comprising

Mrs. Miles, Clara, George, Waldo, Kate, Mable and Benny Miles, Mrs. Peter Ting and baby, and Eliza Williams. Comrade Miles has already been away some weeks, preparing for the reception of his family, who will join the new co-operative colony to be established near Santa Monica.[22]

Even though some comrades had apparently given up on Kaweah, they still held hope for the dream of cooperation.

The establishment of Sequoia Park and Secretary Noble's decision undoubtedly hastened this exodus. This was particularly frustrating to Colony leaders, as they now needed membership dues more than ever. With logging operations suspended, no income was generated and expenses, particularly legal fees, were piling up.

To encourage new members, their propaganda tool—the *Kaweah Commonwealth*—had to paint a positive, hopeful picture. They quit printing notices of members leaving. They were, however, quick to mention new members arriving:

Quite a contingent of the Eastern group arrived in our midst during the week, namely: The Hopping Brothers, F.E. Westervelt, his wife and two children, and Mr. Gowan, his wife and granddaughter. We were all pleased to see them and bid them welcome to their new home in the hills.[23]

When the *Commonwealth* did later mention some members who had left, they were not shy about pointing out the failure that consequently beset them.

Some members became dissatisfied and sloughed off to form the Port Angeles colony where interest and profit were allowed; that colony is now dead. Later on, others left Kaweah to start "Esperanza colony," our institution being too democratic. Esperanza is now no more. Still later, because Kaweah was too "despotic," others left to form the Santa Monica colony; that enterprise has also departed this life.[24]

After news of the convictions in Los Angeles, Haskell again urged a call to arms via the *Commonwealth*. After a telegraphic dispatch that proclaimed the verdict being "guilty as charged," the paper urged on readers with typically Haskell prose:

But be brave and stand by the ship! Let those who are loyal to our great purpose quietly but firmly resolve never to give up the fight. After we are convicted, we shall give bonds, appeal and come home. Then wait until the trial of the title in the Equity cases, which alone are the ones that affect our status as settlers.[25]

A Defense Fund had by that time been established to help defer the mounting legal costs. This call was answered in places far and wide, as evidence in the following letter, which appeared in the *Commonwealth* that spring.

J.J. Martin, Esq. Visalia Cal., Dear Sir:

Herewith I send you a note for $10, which please place to my credit on account of membership fee. A few days ago I went to hear a lecture on "Bellamy's Gospel" by a very popular minister. He gave a glowing description of Kaweah—showed how it had been formed a few years ago, before Bellamy's book was written. It seems as though the time is now ripe for the unfolding of that better condition of mankind, which so many thousands of weary ones have been longing for.

With regard to the troubles as to Kaweah Lands; If justice be the gauge of our expectations, then we know that Kaweah will stand firm; but at the best it is a hard battle. I send $5 to the Defense Fund which is, unfortunately, all I can spare at present.

There are now, including myself, two members of Kaweah in Liverpool, and several who are in sympathy with the movement.

Kindly acknowledge receipt of $15 ($10 and $5 respectively).

Yours Fraternally, F.S. Savage.[26]

Not more than a year later, Fred Savage began his long journey, "around the Horn," to Kaweah.[27] Like his countryman Phil Winser, Savage seemed to have little doubt that the great experiment would still be flourishing when he arrived.

14

INCIDENT AT ATWELL'S MILL

*The reign of the Cossack they thought was in Russia, not America; but
they had yet much to learn about our capitalist-owned land of the free and
the home of the brave.*

—JAMES J. MARTIN, *History of the Kaweah Colony*

EVEN WITH SECRETARY Noble's adverse decision and the
conviction of the trustees for illegally cutting timber, the leaders of
the Kaweah Colony refused to give up. By late spring they had,
however, decided not to continue cutting at the mill site at the end
of their road. As the *Commonwealth* noted on May 28, 1891, the
trustees had decided that "it was best not to cut any more lumber on
our claims until the civil cases are decided; and this decision
cannot be had until September." The paper went on to explain that
to continue cutting would surely provoke "more arrests and
persecutions from the Trust using the machinery of the Government." But that course of inaction left the Colony without any
source of income except membership payments from new members, which Haskell realized were being adversely affected by
what he called "the Associated Press slanders telegraphed throughout the country." [1]

With nearly 200 people living at the Colony that needed basic
supplies and an urgent need for lumber to build homes at the new
Kaweah Townsite, the Colony had a pressing need to investigate

all their options. They learned that there were 320 acres of fine timber land—also located within the boundaries of the newly created Sequoia National Park, but which had been patented years before to Judge A.J. Atwell—on which a fully equipped mill had been operated in the past. For two years it had not been run on account of the death of the owner and the estate was currently in probate. As the *Commonwealth* reported under the headline "Joyful News," Irvin Barnard managed to obtain a lease "on exceptionally favorable terms the land, mill machinery, etc., complete!"

> The inhabitants of this county [the reporter continued] will have their cheap lumber after all; we shall have work and food; and money to fight our cases in Court for our own lands and print and publish a million copies of the history of the outrages we have been subjected to.[2]

Atwell's Mill was located over 20 miles from Kaweah, on the already existing road to the high alpine valley of Mineral King, which had experienced a brief mining boom in the 1870s. By 1891, the area was beginning to flourish as a mountain resort destination. While Mineral King itself was not within the park boundaries, its proximity to national park lands and the already established road and resort status made it a natural choice as the site for the temporary headquarters for the first administrators of Sequoia National Park. When the Kaweah colonists made the decision and arrangements to relocate their lumbering operations to Atwell's Mill—privately owned land that was within the park boundaries—they were well aware of whose path they would inevitably cross.

Cavalry to Oversee Park

In January of 1891, newspapers reported that Secretary of Interior Noble had "requested the Secretary of War to station a company of cavalry in the Sequoia National Park and in Yosemite to prevent depredations on the mammoth tree groves." The *Visalia Delta*, in an editorial, admitted that "just what their duties will be is not yet known, but they will be required to prevent the destruction of the forest, killing of game, etc."[3]

Earlier reports had pinpointed one specific threat, "the so-called Bellamy colonists, who have in part perfected a title to the lands on which these trees stand, and have expressed their purpose to hold their claims in spite of all opposition." Another threat were the "hoofed locusts," as grazing sheep herds were sometimes called.[4] The newly created parks encompassed many summer grazing lands of valley ranchers, much of which were on patented and privately owned land.

The *Delta* noted that "the Secretary of the Interior has a knotty problem on his hands. He cannot prevent people from occupying their own lands, nor is it reasonable to suppose that they will be prevented from passing to and from the same. What is to be done with these isolated fragments remains to be determined."[5] One such isolated fragment was Atwell's Mill, which the Kaweah Colony had leased. This dilemma of dealing with privately owned land within the park boundaries has been a recurring and ever-present one, and is still being debated today.

The first person who had to deal with this knotty problem in Sequoia National Park was Captain J.H. Dorst. The *Visalia Delta* reported that Captain Dorst, "commanding Troop K of the 4th U.S. Cavalry, who has been selected to take charge of the Sequoia National Park, arrived in Visalia and the following day departed for the mountains to select a temporary camping place for his command." The April 16, 1891, issue of the *Delta* continued, "Different places were examined but the spot that appeared to be most suitable is on the Mineral King road," at a place known as Red Hill.

As pointed out in Lary Dilsaver and William Tweed's book, *Challenge of the Big Trees*, Dorst's first task was "to locate the new Sequoia National Park, and the tiny General Grant National Park as well, and develop plans for policing the tracts." As the very first military superintendent of the state's very first national park, Captain Dorst found himself blazing new procedural trails. "He soon discovered," Dilsaver and Tweed point out, "that two roads entered Sequoia—the 1879 wagon road to Mineral King and the recently built Colony Mill road...ending at the now closed mill." Dorst decided to base his operation in Mineral King, even though the new park did not include the Mineral King Valley, because most people entering the park would probably do so via that route. From their temporary camp at Red Hill on the lower stretches of the road, "Dorst sent troops to assist the county in repairing winter damage to the roadway. On June 7, he entered Mineral King Valley, although the melting snowpack prevented establishment of a permanent camp there until June 29th.[6]

As the *Commonwealth* reported on May 23, 1891, Dorst's troops "passed up the canyon on the other side of the main river Sunday. They did not stop at Kaweah." The paper also noted that even though the Cavalry "has not yet entered the canyon of the North Fork, nor made its appearance at the Colony pinery," the trustees had already made their decision not to cut any more lumber at the Colony Mill.

This did not mean, however, that the Cavalry and the Colony would not meet. "As the Cavalry did not come to us," the *Commonwealth* pointed out, "we have gone to them!"

Disconcerting Neighbors

As everyone knows, there is always more than one side to any story. Several sources can be used in trying to reconstruct what happened at Atwell's Mill when the Colony began lumbering operations and the United States Cavalry tried to stop them. These include "The Atwell Mill Outrage," from James J. Martin's unpublished "History of the Kaweah Colony;" personal letters of Burnette G. Haskell; "Memories," the unpublished memoirs of Phil Winser, who worked at Atwell's Mill; and "Cutting Timber at Atwell's Mill," a special report to the Secretary of the Interior by Captain J.H. Dorst.

Remembering back to the incident some 40 years later, James Martin's ire was easily raised. He recalled that he thought "the reign of the Cossack was in Russia, not America; but [we] had yet much to learn about our capitalist-owned land of the free." Explaining how Irvin Barnard had leased the land and that George Purdy was foreman, Martin pointed out:

> They were both veterans, and had fought to preserve the Union. Their patriotic blood boiled when the troops came and ordered them

to stop cutting where there was no shadow of doubt as to their rights. Foreman Purdy is reported as saying: "And so this is the Union I fought to preserve; troops are now used to harass law-abiding settlers. No, by the Eternal, I'll not stop! I am in my rights here and doing my duty. The country is not at war, and if I am to be stopped it shall be through civil process, not military."[7]

Irvin Barnard had acquired the lease on Atwell's Mill on May 20, 1891, which, unlike the Colony Mill, was in close proximity to giant sequoia trees. First owned by Isham Mullenix during the end of the Mineral King mining rush, it was sold to A.J. Atwell in 1885.[8] Because of its remote location, the mill was never profitable. When the Colony acquired it, the county road accessing it was in bad condition and the mill had long lain idle, "but the need for lumber was urgent, and this was the best the situation offered."[9]

Mineral King, which had become headquarters of Captain Dorst and his Cavalry Troop K, was only a few miles further up the road from Atwell's Mill. The Colony and the Cavalry were now neighbors, and Dorst was well aware of the Colony's presence at and plans for Atwell's Mill.

As early as May 25, Dorst had written to one official asking for specific instructions in connection with his duty in charge of the park. He well anticipated difficulties and mentioned the Atwell sawmill, saying that "arrangements are now being made to commence works at that mill. I shall warn the owners that I can not allow any timber, big or little, to be cut down, and that I have written for information about the matter."

Dorst then received further instruction from Special Land Agent Andrew Cauldwell, who had already become quite a thorn in the collective side of the colonists. He told Dorst there was no objection letting the old logs lying about the mill be sawed up, "as they had been cut down some time before the park was established, and were an eyesore anyhow, but pending definite instructions he thought that no timber should be cut."[10]

On June 19, 1891, Dorst was riding by the sawmill and noticed that two or three pine or fir trees had been felled. "I inquired for the man in charge," Dorst recounted, "and was referred to Mr. Purdy.

He declined to stop the timber cutting without being restrained by the order of a civil court, and [stated] that he was not under military government."[11]

Dorst's Dilemma

Captain Dorst's first difficulty concerning the cutting of lumber at Atwell's Mill was determining just what the official government policy was. Agent Cauldwell, it has been noted, had told Dorst that he should allow no lumber to be cut. A few days later Dorst learned that Cauldwell had received a telegram, dated June 16, from the acting Secretary of the Interior, directing him to suspend action in the case of Atwell's Mill until the Secretary, who was on summer vacation, could be contacted.

With this knowledge, obtained at Cauldwell's Visalia office while the Land Agent was away in Yosemite, Dorst headed back to his camp via the Visalia-to-Three Rivers stage. "Mr. Barnard was one of the passengers," Dorst recalled. "He spoke to me of my visit to the mill and asked me about it. I told him of the telegram to Mr. Cauldwell and that there would probably be no interference with his cutting timber."[12] Though both men were probably very hopeful that the issue would somehow blow over and resolve itself, they undoubtedly knew better.

Finally, in early July of 1891, Dorst received the long-delayed response to his initial request for clarification on the issue. From the Acting Secretary came this reply:

> I approve of your action in regard to the saw-mill, but you will communicate with [Land Agent] Cauldwell, now near you, and report if you have any difficulty in the premises. You will prevent, by all means, the destruction of any of these great trees within the lines of your reservation.[13]

As this mentioned only the Big Trees—giant sequoia redwoods—Dorst felt that "the claim might be made that it should be construed to mean them only." None had been cut as yet, and so on July 6, he sent the following telegram to the Secretary:

Letter received. On June 19 found several pines or firs cut down at Atwell's mill. Parties refused to stop without orders of civil court. Afterwards was telegram to Mr. Cauldwell, dated 16th, directing suspension of action, case of Atwell's mill, pending your decision, and have done nothing since. Pines and firs still being cut, but no redwoods. Is this permitted; letter mentions redwoods only?[14]

On July 13, Dorst received the following reply at his camp:

Washington, D.C. July 9, 1891—You will not permit the cutting of any timber within the park until further orders. Chandler, Acting Secretary.[15]

That very afternoon, Dorst sent a copy of this telegram to Irvin Barnard, along with a letter stating, "I have the honor to request, therefore, that you will cause the cutting of timber to be discontinued on the tract of land...which you have leased, or claim to control, for I am informed that all that land lies within the limits of the park."[16] The letter was directed back to Kaweah, and into the hands of the Colony legal counsel, Burnette Haskell.

Haskell promptly sent his directions to Barnard. "Do not stop cutting except upon the actual threatening of armed force and the presence of troops sufficient to carry out the threat. Be dignified, cool, respectful, but determined."[17]

A confrontation was inevitable. Phil Winser, remembering back some 40 years later, recalled the confrontation with "a troop commander with little judgment." As Winser remembered:

[Dorst's] instructions were to stop all timber cutting in the Park and he interpreted that to mean us. A small detachment was sent up our road and made camp two or three miles further on; soldiers would be sent out on foot to run down predatory sheep men and a cavalry man on foot in such unknown mountains with the light air of those elevations certainly had a tough time.

I remember coming in from work one evening and seeing two of them stagger into camp at the last limit of endurance. Of course, we fed and rested them and the boys at the bunk house, knowing we might be interfered with, would fill them up with wild stories of what a terrible lot we were and our local reputation as reds and a bunch of "anarchists" helped the effect.

So one morning as Jim and I were putting in an undercut, who should ride up but a lieutenant and three or four troopers. He halted and said, "You will stop cutting this timber." We said nothing and kept chopping; then he got off his horse, came up to me and repeated the order, laying his hand on me, with the same result, so he remounted, hesitated a bit and said, "Well, I'll go and get men enough so you will stop." [18]

The Winchester Bluff

Captain Dorst continued the story from his point of view. "A corporal reported that one or two more trees had been cut at the mill, and I ordered Lieutenant Nolan with ten or eleven men to go up and stop any further cutting."

By this time, Dorst well knew with whom he was dealing and had concluded that the leaders were looking for an opportunity to claim persecution "and to use the sympathy it would excite to make the public blind to any defects in their claim to the Giant Forest, as well as gain recruits." [19]

Dorst's keen assessment was confirmed by James Martin himself, who later wrote that "the attorney's for the colony were hoping the act of restraint by force would actually take place, so that a basis for bringing the case before the Court could be established." [20]

Lieutenant Nolan was dispatched to execute, if necessary, this restraint by force. He and Dorst had "talked a good deal about what should be done in case the people at the mill compelled us to act against them." Dorst advised against the exercise of absolute force "except in the last extremity." [21] When Nolan arrived at the mill, about 30 men appeared and he was told he would be resisted. Phil Winser's account details this encounter from the colonists' point of view:

> Pretty soon [the] lieutenant and about ten troopers jingled up and ordered the cutting to cease, the only result being the crash of a nearby tree or two; no reply being made at any time. He must have

been an amiable man, reluctant to push things to extremes; a hot-headed one could have made trouble. Ours was straight bluff and the reputed Winchesters hidden in the brush were sheer figments of imagination.[22]

Dorst's side of the story noted that one of the colonists, "a deputy sheriff by the name of Bellah, told [Lt. Nolan] that he would consider an interference with work as a breach of the peace, and would arrest any one who attempted it." Dorst also mentioned that "none of the mill force had arms, at least in sight, but most had axes."

After Nolan's encounter, Dorst made the trip up from Red Hill camp. Along the road he met Barnard, who was headed to Visalia to have warrants issued for Nolan's arrest. They discussed just what would constitute an act of restraint by force. Barnard replied that "laying hands on his men while cutting trees and taking them away would be his idea of force." Barnard was hopeful that any application of force would be done in a manner as to leave no doubt, in a legal sense, of being defined as such. Dorst was simply eager to resolve the situation.

I reached Nolan's camp [Dorst wrote], about a half mile from the mill, shortly before midnight. I had been ailing for several days, and had a fever then, and did not feel competent to engage in any business where tact, good judgment, and clearness of mind were necessary. I sent a note to Mr. Purdy, intending to go to the mill after the fever subsided. It kept up and, unwilling to delay any longer, sent Lieutenant Nolan to the mill with two men to find out just how much force they wanted me to use.

The Lieutenant agreed to carry out this plan without further delay. Deputy Sheriff Bellah, whose official sense of duty seems to have been whatever Mr. Barnard dictated, stated that he would not interfere. Accordingly, several men took axes and commenced cutting. By order of the lieutenant, one soldier advanced to one of the men who was cutting, placed his hand on him and ordered him to stop. The man replied "I won't" and kept on cutting.[23]

After a number of like responses, Nolan decided not to press the matter any further and returned to camp and reported to Dorst. Shortly afterward, Purdy came to Dorst's camp and stated that "all work had been stopped until Mr. Barnard's return." Perhaps the rather histrionic show of physical restraint had some effect after all, although the colonists would never admit as much. Purdy had explained that it was not because of the army's orders, but that the "events of the past two or three days had caused a good deal of excitement, so much so that [the men] would not work steadily but at every opportunity break up into groups and commence talking."[24] They were simply too agitated to get any work done.

The next day Dorst received a copy of a telegram recently sent to Cauldwell:

> Washington, July 24, 1891—It appears that Atwell's mill is on patented land. If this is correct instruct Captain Dorst to defer action on all patented land until I can communicate with Secretary. George Chandler, Acting Secretary.

Dorst sent a copy of this telegram to Barnard along with a note stating "In compliance with the foregoing, you are respectfully notified that you will not be interfered with by me in your work at the mill."[25]

CHAPTER

15

RESIGNATION, SUICIDE
AND DISPUTE

*I have my belly full of "co-operation" and the "labor movement" at
last, you bet.*

—BURNETTE G. HASKELL, November, 1891

THE SUMMER OF 1891 was vastly different for the Kaweah
Colony than the summer only one year before. The previous year,
with their road complete and real hope that their land claims would
be resolved favorably, it looked as if the Kaweah Colony would
join that short list of successful American cooperative communities. Even during a troubled winter, hope remained alive. Annie
Haskell opened 1891 with the following entry in her diary:

> Another year has dawned. How they do roll away—one after the
> other, and yet it seems a long time since last New Year. Last New
> Year I caroused, this one I did not. I returned in time from "the
> hall" to welcome it in my own house, under my own roof. There is
> something in that. If Burnette had only been here. When I woke I
> found a little bird fluttering about. How it got in I don't know, but
> it surely came to bring us a message of good luck and happiness.

But soon she was complaining about the increasing bickering and tensions within a community struggling to survive. "This whole colony is full of people who can't mind their own business," Annie wrote in her diary. She was tired of people sticking their noses into "something that doesn't concern them," and lamented that her husband, Burnette, got "nothing but kicks for his pains and it makes me crazy."[1]

After it became increasingly apparent that the Colony's efforts at Atwell's Mill were a dismal failure, Haskell had taken about as many kicks as he could stand.

Failure at Atwell's Mill

It should be pointed out that while Captain Dorst's interference certainly had a debilitating effect on Colony logging, their Atwell's Mill operation was probably doomed from the start. The equipment, some of which was included in the lease from Atwell's heirs, was in poor shape. And the leased land surrounding the mill was already nearly logged out. Most of the useable pines and firs were gone, and the colonists had to resort to cutting giant sequoias, a very labor intensive undertaking which produced much wasted lumber. And finally there was the condition of the road, which always has rendered any large-scale operation in the Mineral King area economically impractical.

Burnette Haskell summed up why he felt Atwell's Mill failed in his article, "How Kaweah Fell," written in November of 1891:

> The Trustees issued to the resident members an imploring circular, urging the workers to more active and persistent effort at the mill. But this appeal had no permanent effect except to arouse antagonism. Work still continued in the same desultory fashion until the last of July, when Taylor was sent up to the mill. While there he discovered that the force had, with the carelessness of children, cut over their line on to government land, thus again exposing the Trustees to arrest and prison.[2]

The strength of any organization lies in the people involved, and through cooperation, many hoped the whole (the Kaweah Colony) would exceed the sum total of the parts (the members). No one had preached this more fervently than Burnette Haskell, who had always possessed great talent to motivate. In the circular urging members to work harder, Haskell wrote, "Individual selfishness now means inevitably the ruin of Kaweah. Do you want to live or die?"[3]

Haskell claimed that after five months, the operation at Atwell's Mill cut only one-tenth of the 2.5 million feet they had expected, and "instead of being produced for $10 [per thousand feet] or less, it had cost from $18 to $20, and it was sold for $10." Haskell added that "comment is superfluous, and whatever excuses may be made, the business failure is flat."[4]

Haskell Resigns

The run of bad luck and the failure of the sum total to live up to expectations had, by the summer of 1891, left Haskell disillusioned. On July 25th, Haskell, along with trustees Horace T. Taylor and William Christie, tendered their resignations from the Board of Directors. Notice was published in the *Kaweah Commonwealth*. The departing trustees, with forced graciousness, proclaimed:

> In our time of trial and trouble, the new blood and brain and energy of Barnard and Purdy and others have sprung to the front, able to lead us out. We salute and retire to the ranks. There let us stand shoulder to shoulder in the fight and give them loyal support.[5]

As the year progressed, there was much fighting but it certainly wasn't "shoulder to shoulder." Early in August, Annie noted in her diary:

> Burnette has resigned….and I was very glad of it. I wish he had never seen, heard, nor dreamed of this colony—but then we would never know what a mistake cooperation is.[6]

The *Kaweah Commonwealth* naturally did its best to put as positive a slant as possible on the news of the resignations, stating that it should not be looked upon by anybody as "being an evidence of any dissatisfaction with Kaweah." The paper claimed that Haskell, along with Taylor and Christie, had given up their office "solely because they know they can do better work in the ranks."[7]

Burnette Haskell, seen here at a small cabin on his Arcady homestead, had his belly full of "co-operation" by the summer of 1891, when he resigned as attorney, trustee and editor of the Commonwealth.

But why did Burnette Haskell, who had worked so hard and tirelessly on behalf of his cooperative dream, finally resign his position? One clue can be found in Haskell's resignation letter to the Board as legal counsel for the Colony:

> I herewith tender my resignation as the Attorney of this company. This resignation is made because I am firmly and finally convinced that my services are not appreciated.

Of course, it was more than a lack of appreciation that prompted Haskell's actions. We have already seen that he felt operations at Atwell's Mill were grossly mismanaged; and that workers had carelessly exposed the trustees to possible arrest by cutting trees beyond the lease boundaries. By closer examination of his resignation letter we see another root of Haskell's anger, and perhaps the root of much of the growing Colony discord:

In June of 1886, the Colony was formed and I have transacted its legal business ever since without ever having received a single cent of cash or single credit on the books for such services. I have never charged you a fee although I have never volunteered my services gratuitously. But I esteem it equitable that you should pay me for my time at the same rate at least that you paid for pick and shovel work on the grounds; and that such payment should be in cash as I received no subsistence from Kaweah Colony. I enclosed you therefore my bill to date.[8]

It may seem ironic that money had become such a motivating factor for Haskell. But the socialist agitator had never preached against the evils of money per se, but against the "competitive system" and "Capitalist scheme where Justice and Fraternity are sacrificed to the spirit of selfish greed." Justice and Fraternity were now being pushed aside by self-preservation throughout the Kaweah Colony.

Haskell, the idealist, had also become frustrated by what he perceived as sloppy bookkeeping. He had become a realist, sensing that the light at the end of the tunnel was an oncoming train. In his resignation letter he offered the following warning:

In resigning, I desire to again call your attention to the absolute necessity of observing your by-laws exactly, and especially of entering every financial transaction of the Company on the books. As your Attorney, I know that half of your most important affairs are not upon your books and I again warn you that in case a suit for dissolution should be brought, and this is liable to happen at any time, your Secretary [James Martin] and indeed the whole Board, would be placed in a difficult and dangerous position. The folly of continually postponing and neglecting the accounts of the Company is an invitation to criminal process in the hands of any disgruntled member and an actual ever-present danger which has no excuse whatever for being.

It doesn't take a lawyer to see that this warning also contains a thinly veiled threat by Haskell, perhaps the most disgruntled of any member at the time.

One other factor, which undoubtedly raised Haskell's ire that summer, was once described by Tulare County historian Joe Doctor:

Old man [Elphick] came to the Colony at the age of 80 after years of selling newspapers at Lotta Fountain in San Francisco. He invested his little savings in the colony with the assurance that he would be well taken care of to his dying day. It wasn't long coming. He reached the colony after a long hot ride by train and stage from San Francisco. It was July, and the day after his arrival the temperature soared to plus 100 degrees. Eager to be of assistance, the old man went out to work in the field of string beans and about noon he fell dead between the rows. There was an inquest but no cause of death established. Haskell told in his journal that he had suffered the most ignominious insult of all—that of being accused of doing the old man in for his money.[9]

The *San Francisco Chronicle* reported, with headlines reading "Elphick's Death—Rumors of Foul Play Freely Circulated," that the frugal old man had gone to Kaweah to see about recovering $800 he had allegedly loaned the Colony and had died mysteriously. Members of the Colony, disturbed by the rumors, signed and sent a petition to Haskell requesting that he clear up several questions raised by the old man's untimely death, including what happened to Elphick's money. Even though charges were never formally made, and the *San Francisco Examiner* later reported that Elphick was clearly not the victim of foul play, the implications had to have been crystal clear to Haskell.[10]

Frustrated at the disorganization of the Colony, feeling unappreciated and uncompensated, and finally accused—even if only an implied accusation—of murder, Haskell resigned one other post that summer. From the *Kaweah Commonwealth*, August 8, 1891:

> Mr. Haskell, with this issue of the paper, resigns as Superintendent of Education, and, under the by-laws, places the paper in Mr. Martin's hands as Secretary. He thanks all friends and comrades for the kind support given in the past and entreats its continuance for the future.

Suicide at Kaweah

In October of 1891, exactly one year and a day after moving to Kaweah, Annie Haskell wrote the following account in her diary:

Such a horrible thing. Frank Wigginton was found this morning in bed, with a bullet hole through his brain and a pistol in his hand. The shot was heard at 6:00 a.m. Everyone is horrified. It seems impossible to believe that it is a case of suicide and yet he must have done it himself somehow. Poor boy, he was the best of all the young fellows down there [Kaweah]. Everyone liked him. The news has made me sick.[11]

The *Kaweah Commonwealth* reported that the deceased was a "native of Ohio, about 27 years of age, and a resident of Kaweah for about one year." The newspaper also noted his "cheerful, kindly disposition with not a trace of moroseness in his nature." The *Commonwealth* further explained:

The coroner of Tulare County was summoned and upon his arrival an inquest was held. Not the slightest part of the testimony showed that he had deliberately contemplated suicide, on the contrary, all the testimony went to show that he was happy and contented and satisfied with life, and that he had made arrangements to build himself a permanent home here.[12]

The Visalia papers offered slightly different accounts of the tragedy and even hinted at a possible motive for the young man's suicide. The *Tulare County Times* described the event in rather graphic detail, noting that Wigginton was found "still in bed, the pistol grasped firmly in his right hand lying on his breast, while immediately between and a little above the eyes a gasping bleeding wound showed where the leaden messenger had sped on its deadly work."[13] The paper also noted that Wigginton was universally liked by associates and of a cheerful disposition "although of late he has complained of what he believed the unjust treatment of himself and his associates by the government." It is interesting to note that the *Tulare County Times* was still very supportive of the Colony at this time, while the *Visalia Delta*, which had become vituperative in its attacks on the Colony, offered a significantly different account of Wigginton's state of mind:

A few days ago [Wigginton] was hauling some wood, and he made the remark that that was the last load he would ever haul. Wigginton had spoken frequently of going away from the colony to earn enough money to build a house for the winter.[14]

It is perhaps reading too much between the lines to claim that the *Delta* inferred Wigginton's suicide was motivated by financial duress brought upon by a failing Colony, but when reporting an earlier suicide connected with Kaweah, blame is very clearly assigned to the Colony. On July 30, 1891, the *Visalia Delta* printed the following:

Last Saturday's [San Francisco] *Chronicle* contained a lengthy article relating how Gus Hodeck, a member of the Kaweah Colony, committed suicide owing to the persecution he had endured while at Kaweah. He joined the colony about two years ago, and because he had an opinion of his own regarding the management of the colony, and dared express it, he incurred the enmity of the so-called board of trustees. A mock trial was held and Hodeck was expelled from the colony, losing all the money he had paid in as membership fees. Thoroughly disheartened with his treatment, Hodeck returned to San Francisco, hoping to find work as a machinist in the Union iron works. Not meeting with success, he hired a room last Thursday, turned on a gas jet and suffered the death of asphyxiation. The *Chronicle*, in its opening paragraph, said "Driven to death by the Kaweah Colony" ought to have been the verdict of the Coroner's jury upon the remains of Gus Hodeck.

While the *Delta* could rationalize the obvious slanted bias of this report by labeling it the *Chronicle*'s account, it does mark a turning point in their reporting of the Colony, and foreshadows George Stewart's devastating series of exposés that appeared later that year.

Ting's Biting Letter

The *Delta* had, since the inception of the Kaweah Colony, reported with a remarkable restraint of judgment. It was particularly noteworthy that during its agitation to create a national park reserve, Stewart and the *Delta* were supportive of the Colony's claim to land in and around Giant Forest. But as 1891 progressed, the paper became decidedly less positive in its comments concerning the Colony, and in November published a four-part history and scathing exposé on the Kaweah Co-Operative Colony.

The vehemence with which Stewart now attacked the Colony might seem an abrupt about-face, but Stewart had been exposed to definite and mounting motivations. In October, he received a letter from former colonist Peter Ting, which may have prompted, or at least confirmed, Stewart's negative feelings for the Colony. Having heard that the *Delta* was willing to publish "true statements regarding the Kaweah Colony," Ting was pleased to offer a "few facts."

He prefaced his remarks by stating that he thought the best thing a local county newspaper could do would be to "expose such fraud and save families from being ruined by such vile creatures as the old Trustees of the Kaweah Colony." Ting called the last two years of Colony existence "nothing more than a confidence game" and criticized Haskell's despotic control of the so-called democratic process.

Ting put the question of the land claims into perspective when he wrote:

> In order to shield themselves from being blamed for deceiving the people at first in regard to the title of the land, they now make the plea that the Government is persecuting them and trying to take the Colony's land away, when in fact the Colony has never had any land and would have had but very few claims even if the individuals had got their land, for who would want to turn their claims over to the Colony when it is run by such men as Haskell, Redstone and Martin?[15]

One major theme of Stewart's series was that bickering and in-fighting had crippled the utopian enterprise. It had become a very prevalent and apt criticism. By the time of Wigginton's death in October 1891, members of the Colony were arguing and fighting over just about everything. Annie Haskell offered one particularly disturbing example in her diary the day after Wigginton's death:

> We all went down to attend the funeral. It is very sad. After Burnette made all the arrangements and appointed the time for the

funeral, then the Redstone outfit came over and took charge of things and hurried the funeral away two hours before the time.[16]

The Sweet Potato War

One episode that illustrates the depths to which the Colony had sunk—the bickering and fighting, the hardship and desperation—involved nothing more than a few sweet potatoes. Annie Haskell's diary offers a version of the incident:

> A gang of fourteen men came up to Green's place and began to dig, sack and haul away his sweet potatoes. They knocked him down, choked and mistreated the old man very badly. Owen and Burnette were there and interfered somewhat. They said they were coming here this p.m. to get the cow—but they did not. Burnette has been guarding the place all p.m. with a rifle.[17]

In an affidavit he prepared with Haskell's help, Albert W. Green, age 58 years, explained that in the event of his death, the affidavit could be used posthumously. Even though his injuries were, he stated, severe, he thought however that he would survive. Annie Haskell, commenting on his injuries in her diary, noted that Green seemed "to be hurt internally and is considerably bruised and can't sit up in bed without being lifted."[18]

In his affidavit, Green explained his membership in the Colony and the agreement he had made with the trustees to exchange produce for lumber and help in improving his land. He claimed the land was "waste ground that he worked hard—10 to 18 hours a day—to produce corn, squash, pumpkins and potatoes that he turned over to the Colony. They ate it up but did no improvement on my place in return."[19]

The *Visalia Delta* reported on the incident:

> On November 5th a number of the colonists repaired to the potato field and commenced to dig the spuds. Old man Green was incensed with the proceeding and made a feeble resistance. He stood on the potato sacks and he testified that he was thrown to the ground, hit on the body, choked and generally ill-treated.[20]

An explanation as to why these sweet potatoes came into dispute was offered by the *Tulare County Times:*

> There are two factions now in Kaweah, the minority headed by Burnette G. Haskell; the majority adhering to J.J. Martin. Among other property of the colony is a garden, which has been under the care of Mr. Green, one of the Haskell faction. In this garden was a patch of sweet potatoes, claimed as colony property, but to which Green set up an individual claim.[21]

In Green's account, it was Haskell's intervention that kept the mob, led by John Redstone, J.C. Weybright, Phil Winser and Irvin Barnard, from beating him to death. He claims Haskell exchanged words, keeping his hand in a pocket in which "presumably he had a gun"[22]

If we are unclear at this point as to what really happened, this account by Phil Winser from the December 5, 1891 *Commonwealth* (which was now under James Martin's control) should only add to the confusion. After stating the reasons why the potatoes were actually Colony property, the issue of the physical assault was addressed:

> We found Mr. Green, Mr. Haskell and Mr. Owen standing there, and the former became very excited and tried to stop us from digging by standing over the tools. He did this to Mr. Redstone and was quietly and gently pushed away by him. This was the extent of "Uncle John's" assault on Mr. Green, although one or two others removed him with rather more force, though doing him no bodily injury.
>
> As also is another story that Mr. Green would have been murdered had it not been for Mr. Haskell and his revolver. It is true Mr. Haskell called us to witness that Mr. Green was being murdered, but the revolver did not appear, and every one was too well aware of the harmless nature of our intention on Mr. Green's person to witness anything of the kind.

History certainly teaches us that there is always more than one side to any story. The *Tulare County Times*, one of the few outside newspapers that still supported the failing Colony and the Martin faction, addressed what they called a "trumped up" assault charge:

> Behind this was an ulterior motive. Saturday a general meeting of the colony was held. The Haskell faction desired to control the meeting and run everything their own way; to do this it was necessary to get a large number of the other side out of the way and so reduce the majority. If enough of these could be arrested and removed upon some charge, however flimsy, then Haskell would have control. The potato episode seemed to furnish the means to this end.[23]

What really happened? We can only speculate. Except for Annie Haskell's testimony in her diary about Green's injuries, one could easily suspect Haskell of just such a ruse. A Visalia court, however, found Weybright guilty of assault and fined him $25.[24] It seems most likely this dispute was really symptomatic of a growing sense of panic in Kaweah. When things were running smoothly, cooperation had seemed to work. But as the end drew near and even food was scarce, cooperation disintegrated under the strain of tough times—when cooperation was needed the most.

Colony Death Rattle

By the end of 1891, Haskell had become desperate for money and sold an article to the *San Francisco Examiner* entitled "How Kaweah Failed." The brilliant propagandist, once so tireless in his efforts to promote the Colony, was now driving the final nails into the coffin. Haskell, of course, was not the only one disillusioned with the Colony, nor was he the only one writing critically of the endeavor.

George Stewart's series of articles in the *Visalia Delta* came out about the same time as Haskell's *Examiner* piece. Both focused on the internal squabbles as one source of the Colony's downfall, but whereas Stewart pointed the finger of blame at the founders and leaders of the Colony, Haskell blamed the weakness of human nature. Stewart harshly criticized the misleading nature of Colony propaganda while Haskell railed against a capitalist conspiracy. Stewart noted the comparative luxury in which Colony Secretary James Martin lived while other colonists were reportedly near starvation; Haskell bemoaned the existence of "too many average men."

Shortly after Stewart's scathing series appeared, Haskell, Martin and H.T. Taylor were arrested for "using the mails for fraudulent purposes in sending out literature to people stating that the Colony owned thousands of acres of timber land."[25] So dispersed was the Colony by this time that only three of the five trustees named in the indictment could be arrested, as the other two had already left the Colony. (The charges were eventually dropped, but not before Haskell, Martin and Taylor were forced to appear at yet another court trial in Los Angeles.)

Indeed, by this time—January of 1892—the Kaweah Co-Operative Colony Company, having failed to "weather the storms of internal disintegration," had been dissolved. In its place had sprung the short-lived Industrial Co-Operative Union of Kaweah, with James Martin as president. But it was too late for any phoenix to rise from the Colony's ashes; split into irreparable schism and denied their only resource (timber), the Colony's reformation was in fact nothing more than its final death rattle.

The March/April, 1892 issue of the *Kaweah Commonwealth* printed the official minutes of the Kaweah Colony for 1892, stating that, on April 9th, the 50th General Meeting of the K.C.C.Co was "adjourned *sine die*, there being no quorum present." This was the last issue of the *Kaweah Commonwealth* published by the Colony—a Colony which, in any form, had ceased operation. A bitter Haskell later wrote:

> A few more than half of the resident members at the November meeting, 1891, abolished the time checks, took possession of the machinery and land of the colony, repudiated the credits of the old workers, and decided to continue the struggle as a small enterprise under the absolute power of one man. It is needless to say now that this attempt was as well a failure. They hoped to make a living here as small farmers thus cooperating. Whether this plan would have succeeded cuts no figure whatever with this history. We can leave them quarreling over the little property left, as we leave coyotes quarreling over a carcass.[26]

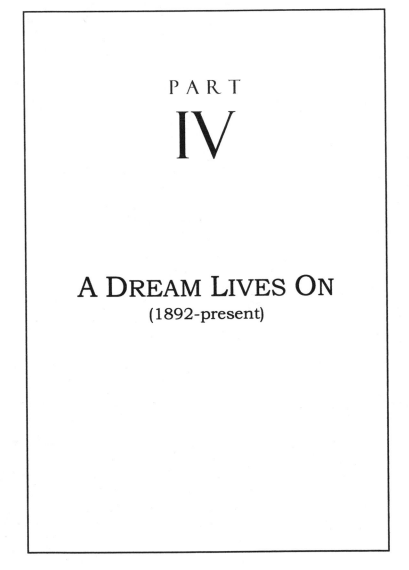

PART

IV

A DREAM LIVES ON
(1892-present)

16

THOSE WHO REMAINED

Kaweah Colony has failed. Those who had believed that they would be burglars of paradise, that they would reach upon this earth to the kingdom of heaven, have abandoned their purpose and are routed and disorganized, babbling many tongues.

—BURNETTE G. HASKELL, November, 1891

Recognizing in you a humanitarian of the highest order, I am submitting herewith a national matter for your personal consideration, which, while it remains unrequited remains also a discredit and disgrace to the honor and dignity of our great nation.

—JAMES J. MARTIN letter to Eleanor Roosevelt, 1935

VARIOUS FAMILIES AND individuals remained in and around Kaweah after the disintegration of the Colony. One account of those who stayed in the area comes from James Martin, who did not. His granddaughter, Olive Redstone Klaucke, well remembers her grandfather. Late in his life he lived with Olive and her parents, Al and Daisy Redstone, at the Daisy Dell ranch in See Canyon near San Luis Obispo, California. Olive described how "Grandpa Martin" would spend countless hours up in his loft apartment over the barn, busily writing memoirs and letters, many concerning the Kaweah Colony—a lifelong cause.[1]

In the mid-1930s, at nearly 90 years of age, James Martin wrote a history of the Kaweah Colony. The following is taken from a draft of that unpublished manuscript, now part of the J.J. Martin Papers at the Bancroft Library in Berkeley, California:

> The members who remained at Kaweah after the dissolution of the Colony were: H.T. Taylor, the Purdys, the Redstone and Brann families; the Winsers, the Hoppings and the Bellahs. The Haskells, with the Hildebrands and H.D. Cartwright, lived for a time at the nearby Haskell homestead at Arcady. Mr. C.F. Keller [founding member who left in anger in 1888] subsequently acquired the Halstead property, and for a few years was a Postmaster at Kaweah. Later he removed with his family to Santa Cruz.
>
> Philip Winser acquired some land at Kaweah, planted an apple orchard, worked at odd jobs between times, and did very well with his crops. Later he removed with his family to Bakersfield, and there engaged in the wholesale fruit business.
>
> Mr. Fred Savage, an absentee member, came from Liverpool, England, after the Colony was broken up, bought some land at Kaweah, planted an orchard, married, raised a family and made good. His two sturdy sons, born at Kaweah, both of whom are married, now run the farm. They each have families and comfortable homes.

A Square Deal from the New Deal

In addition to writing his history of Kaweah, James Martin carried out a campaign seeking recompense for perceived government wrongs against the Colony right up to his final days, including written communications with President Franklin D. Roosevelt and the politically influential First Lady Eleanor.

Shortly after the Colony folded in 1892, Martin's political agitation helped to get a bill introduced in Congress for financial compensation to the Colony for the road they had built to the newly established national park. But the bill was quickly killed in committee,[2] and what was left of the Kaweah Co-Operative Colony never received any money for the road they had labored four years to build. The road, which was extended to Giant Forest by the government in 1903, served as the only road into the heart of the national park until the mid-1920s.

To Martin, this was the final of many injustices by the United States government against the Kaweah Colony. The English-born

Martin left Kaweah not long after its demise and, despite his disheartening experience there, became involved in another cooperative colonization scheme in 1914, this time in Tasmania.[3] The Tasmania Colonizing Association hoped to attract settlers to their cooperative colony, but financial problems, land difficulties and a World War all conspired to dash these hopes. James Martin eventually ended up living with his daughter and son-in-law at their See Canyon apple ranch.

In his autumn years, Martin was a distinguished man with a head of snow-white hair and fine English manners. Even as an old man, working in the apple orchards, he insisted on wearing a necktie. His agitation regarding Kaweah and letter writing campaign never ceased, and in a letter to Eleanor Roosevelt he claimed:

> This is not an appeal to you for money but a request that you will use your womanly influence in securing justice to a number of loyal and worthy American citizens who were, and still are, the victims of a most unwarrantable outrage at the hands of a former capitalistic administration of our national government.[4]

His granddaughter, Olive, still recalls that Martin never had much money. He was more interested in bettering society as a whole than in personal gain, although certain embittered Kaweah colonists might argue the point. What he sought from the government 43 years after the Kaweah Colony disbanded is clearly set forth in his letter to President Roosevelt.

The letter, dated March 3, 1935, is quite lengthy at nearly 20 typed pages. Martin includes a history of the Kaweah Colony, and explains how in his view the Southern Pacific Railroad and the government conspired to ruin the Colony. Martin notes how shortly after he had an interview with Charles Crocker of the SPRR about a spur road to the Colony, their trouble commenced.

> The Colony had no idea at the time that freightage of lumber from points north to the valley was an exceedingly profitable feature of the SPRR and it was to its profiteering interest to stop the development of lumber in the mountains adjacent to the extensive lumber consuming area in the San Joaquin valley.

James J. Martin, Colony co-founder and secretary from its inception, never gave up seeking recompense from the United States government.

Martin did, however, note that the "rabid persecution" of the Colony did not commence until "after the Harrison (Republican—Capitalistic) Administration came into power." All had been fair and square, Martin pointed out, during the preceding Cleveland Administration. Martin then explained to FDR how, as Secretary of the Colony, he had:

[M]ade contact with an institution figuratively known as the "octopus." To this institution our government several years before had given an empire in territory—the best on Earth—for the construction of a railroad which, en pasant, was built practically upon the credit of the nation. This monster, as is well known, bled the struggling farmers and fruitgrowers of California with ex-orbitant transportation charges. The settlers of Mussel Slough district were also made to feel the blistering sting of its avaricious tentacles.

Martin finally got to the point in his letter. As recompense for past injustices, he asked for "sole right, in perpetuity, to cut and remove timber from what is now Sequoia National Park." He granted that such cutting should be "subject to supervision and direction of the Department of Forestry," but asked that the government appropriate "$250,000 to be expended in the complete rehabilitation of the Colony to its former state of earning capacity."

Martin closed by stating that he expected fair treatment from the "New Deal," which he believed to be a "Square Deal." An investigation was launched, which resulted in a Senate committee's recommendation to reimburse the Colony for the road, but the Senate refused to act.[5]

Of course, by that time, few Kaweah colonists were still even alive. James Martin was 90 years old. He died three years later at See Canyon, and one imagines him writing letters up in his loft over the barn right up until the very end.

The Hoppings of Kaweah

The Hoppings, even though they didn't arrive at the Colony until near the end, were nonetheless an important family in Kaweah's history. George W. Hopping was an active member of the New York group. A Civil War veteran, Hopping had a "brain for mathematics" and eventually became the chief accountant for the Seabury Johnson Co. of New York, wholesale druggists and chemical manufacturers (later to become Johnson & Johnson.) Hopping's grandson, Dr. Forest Grunigen, remembers that George was paid the handsome salary of $500 per month.[6]

One colonist remembers that as George Hopping had such a good position at the prominent firm, he "did not feel justified in throwing it up for the uncertainties of our endeavor. However, his heart was with us and he sent his sons and daughter in advance, by installments."[7]

Ralph and Burt arrived at the Colony sometime in 1891. Both worked at the Colony logging operation at Atwell's Mill, and Burt was a valuable mechanic. The Colony paper once reported that "the neat presswork of the *Commonwealth* latterly is owing to a good overhauling given the press by Burt Hopping."[8]

The Hopping brothers were popular, well-liked residents of what came to be known as the Redstone Park area of Kaweah, and it was not long before they made a committed alliance with the Redstone clan. Ralph Hopping married Kate Redstone and soon thereafter Burt married Kate's sister Dove.

Eventually other Hoppings arrived, including Guy, daughter Jesse, and finally the father, George. Colonist Phil Winser remembered the elder Hopping's arrival:

> By paying off Kaweah's mortgage, he acquired title to that 240 acres and thus insured greater permanency for the Redstone-Hopping section of Redstone Park and a choice of home sites for himself, Mrs. Hopping and two maiden sisters when they finally came West. Mrs. Hopping had French Louisiana blood, and carried a darkness of eye, good looks and vivacity of disposition. Ralph, the oldest son, was as dark as a Spaniard, while Burt was blonde, very good of profile and had an amiable disposition.[9]

The Hopping brothers left behind a considerable legacy in the local history of the Sequoia and Kaweah area. Guy Hopping served many years as a national park ranger, eventually becoming Superintendent of General Grant National Park in 1936. Ralph, in partnership with John Broder, operated the first pack touring business for visitors to Sequoia National Park. At Redstone Park, they established a hotel to serve as a way station, initiated a stage line from Visalia, opened a tent hotel in Giant Forest and began bringing tourists up to visit the famous Big Trees. Ralph was also an enthusiastic student of entomology, and later when serving as a ranger in General Grant Park, he discovered a species of theretofore unknown insect. This brought him great notice in the scientific world and launched his career as a entomologist.[10]

A Successful Partnership

Phil Winser had come to the Kaweah Colony during its last year of existence, but stuck around the area for quite some time. Horace Taylor, a colonist from its very inception, also stayed in the area long after the Colony ceased to exist. Shortly after the demise of the cooperative endeavor, Winser and Taylor labored together to build an irrigation ditch that to this day still supplies water to a number of properties in Kaweah.

Sometime in 1892, Taylor approached Winser, his nearest neighbor, and proposed they "take a ditch out of the North Fork above Arcady" down to his place, which would give them both all the water they'd need. They got Sam Halstead to pitch in $100 for supplies, as the ditch would pass through his land and thus be an improvement. After many months hard work, the ditch was complete and water flowed freely.

With the coming of irrigation water, the urge for owning land became strong for Winser. He wrote in his memoirs:

> We always wanted to become independent of working for others for wages and thought growing apples about as likely a way as any, for there were two or three rather good lots in the canyon. Mr. Purdy had just bought a little land from Halstead and we followed suit. Of course, we had to pay more now that it was irrigable, but the price was very moderate and I tried to forget the fact I had enhanced the price by my free work [building the ditch.]
>
> Having a start in land and water, we wrangled yearling apple trees from another neighbour I had worked for and set them out. Blanche's [Winser's wife] brother Bert came out about this time and would care for them in our absence.

Winser himself was absent because, although now a landowner and fledgling apple rancher in Kaweah, he needed to obtain work for wages. He was able to do so in Lemon Cove, a small citrus town about halfway between Kaweah and Visalia. Working long days during the particularly hot summer, Phil Winser "craved ice and hit on a plan." He and Blanche would have the stage bring ice from Visalia and they would make ice cream and lemonade and, "putting out a sale sign, supply the patrons traveling the hot, dusty road." [11]

Meanwhile, a fellow Englishman and former absentee-member of the defunct Kaweah Colony had made his way "around the Horn" to the Pacific coast. Fred Savage, son of a cabinet maker from Liverpool, took a great interest in social experiments and cooperative ventures. He was the same F.S. Savage who had sent money to Kaweah toward membership and the Defense Fund early in 1891. He had later spent a disastrous year at Topolobampo, Mexico, which was a "large scale attempt to clear, irrigate and cultivate a vast concession in Sinola cooperatively," on a similar line to the Kaweah Colony. As grandson Milton Savage recounts, Fred got "ashore there and about starved." He was able to find passage to San Diego and from there walked to Kaweah. [12]

Fred Savage was undoubtedly very hot and thirsty when his journey on foot to Kaweah, nearly complete, brought him to Lemon Cove, where he noticed Winser's sign advertising lemonade.

> It was this sign [Winser wrote in his memoirs] which lured in Fred Savage one hot day. A little conversation convinced Blanche that here was a man I must meet, so she induced him to stop that night and we talked.
>
> Then we sent him on up to Bert and when he returned, it was to get a job in Lemon Cove and we planned to pool our resources and extend our orchard enterprise together. And so it went, through the summer and autumn. Fred would come over some Sundays and we talked everything over; he sent to England for some savings and with my pay we were able to negotiate a further purchase of [some of Halstead's] land on which there was a clearing to be done by Bert.
>
> As soon as we returned to Kaweah we arranged a form of partnership to fit conditions; Blanche and I by virtue of holdings already established took two-fifths interest and Fred and Bert divided the remaining three-fifths equally; all outside earnings were

to be pooled and the common fund to supply housekeeping and ranch outlays.[13]

Thus began their profitable and successful partnership—a cooperative on a small scale that, unlike the Kaweah Colony, bore ample fruit for generations to come.

Haskell's Golden Dream

One colonist who did not stick around very long after the Colony's demise was the man who more than anyone had been responsible for its very existence. By 1892, with the Colony in a shambles, Burnette Haskell was barely eking out an existence at his Kaweah homestead. In April of 1892, he wrote in his journal:

> The motto on my mantlepiece reads "I owe much, I have nothing, I give the rest to the poor." That about states my case. Oh, if only I ever get a chance to get on top again, I'll not play the fool.[14]

Letters to both his parents, who were divorced, included pleas for a few dollars to buy supplies and proposals for them to come homestead at Kaweah, where valuable land was still available. Haskell had talked up the potential of the land as an orchard farm; even as Annie struggled just to keep a few scraggly plum trees alive by hand carrying water up from the river.

His once-successful father lived in San Francisco, selling a medicinal concoction called Gumptill's Sure Cure. The elder Haskell finally sold off his interest in Sure Cure and joined Burnette and Annie at Kaweah to try and make a go of the homestead.

The Kaweah Colony had been Haskell's dream of "a solution to the problem of poverty and wealth, the inequalities of destiny and fortune, and a road to human happiness."[15] But that dream had tragically failed. California, because of its peculiar history, had always been a state filled with dreamers. And unfortunately, like Haskell, many had failed to find their "mother lode."

Haskell was still a dreamer. In April 1892, he noted in his personal journals that he had discovered several what he called "specimens with free gold and silver" in and about the Kaweah canyon. Apparently his dream of bettering mankind through social reform still smoldered, for the idea of discovering mineral wealth prompted a plan:

> After careful consideration, I have solemnly determined if any mine is discovered and I make a fortune, I will use that fortune in order to make human beings better. This can be done by education, by assisting state control; by the establishment of prize funds for valor, perseverance, fidelity; by building up a labor farm and especially by checking corruption through making attorneys paid officers of the state. There are now 3,000 attorneys in San Francisco in a population of 300,000. This is one per cent. One-half of that ought to be enough. I will so use my fortune if I get it.[16]

But alas, again Haskell's dreams—noble though they were to better mankind by thinning the number of lawyers—were dashed. A few days later he wrote that he discovered "brass nails in shoes make gold stains on rock." He was "hugely disgusted" when he came home and re-examined all his ore-bearing specimens, being in doubt about every one of them.[17]

There was little left for Haskell to do. For the next couple of months he concentrated on trying to gain possession of as many Colony assets as possible. A considerable feud had ensued over who owned the printing press—private ownership had suddenly become a popular concept at Kaweah.

It quickly became obvious that Haskell simply wasn't cut out for the physical work of making his homestead profitable. While his wife and others labored to build ditches and plant orchards, Haskell decided he needed to return to the city. On June 20, 1892, his journal noted that "on Sunday I put an ad in the [San Francisco] papers saying I had returned to [legal] practice." Burnette Haskell, the famous labor agitator, newspaper editor and former attorney for the Kaweah Co-Operative Colony had returned to San Francisco and increased the number of lawyers in that city to 3,000 plus one.

A Marriage on the Rocks

In the summer of 1892, with Haskell now in San Francisco, letters between Burnette and Annie showed a very strained relationship. Annie struggled just to survive at Kaweah. Food and supplies were scarce. In one letter, Haskell claimed that he was "astonished, pained and surprised" at the situation. "I had no idea whatever but that you had ample supplies of everything you wished," he wrote. He shipped a box of supplies to nearby Exeter for Annie, and promised to send more "as soon as I get some money to spare." [18]

It was the beginning of the end for Burnette and Annie's marriage. Surviving letters and diaries allow them to tell us about the faltering relationship in their own words:

> June 23, 1892—My Dearest Wife: I am awful lonely here without you and Roth and if I could see any way in which I might be at Kaweah with you I would be there if I had to walk; but I don't. I am satisfied that if I stick to business and could only hold on for two months or so that I can make it go. I am neither drinking nor running around but am hard at work all the time. You ought to write. Good-bye dear.

By stating what he isn't doing, Haskell gives us a pretty clear indication of his past habits.

> Annie's diary, June 28, 1892—Had two letters from Burnette this evening. He was quite put out as he had not received letters from anyone here. Very strange, I should think.

> June 30, 1892—Dearest Annie: Your letter received. Also that of Roth and three from Dad. I was beginning to feel seriously alarmed and was glad to find everything OK. Don't you think your epistle was rather icy? Yours in the hope that your next letter will have imbibed some of the warmth you are probably having at Arcady.

Evidently Annie's next letter was not perceived by Burnette to be warm enough and certainly wasn't of a comparable length to his. On July 20, Burnette wrote to Annie:

> Your decidedly unsatisfactory letter of one page posted on Monday reached me this morning. I don't understand how you can have any complaint about my not writing. My letters have been long and frequent, yours have not. I wrote you on June 20th, 23rd, 26th, 27th, July 1st, 3rd, 7th, 8th, 10th, 13th, 18th—a total of 22 typewritten

pages, 500 words a page—for a total of nearly 11,000 words. It is best to be exact in this world. Perhaps it is not a question of letters that has aroused the emotion you feel? May not the propinquity of a person non gratia have influenced you to search for something wherefore to take the absent to task?

At this point, the modern reader has to be questioning the mental health of Burnette Haskell. Annie, however, seemed somehow used to it. By reading a letter Haskell wrote to Annie a few days later, we see how he was desperately trying to charm his way back into her good graces:

My Dearest Annie: The peculiar secret of my character is that I respond to things of like character…a chill or a rebuff seems to throw up an immediate barrier, despite my wishes. You know perfectly well that my love for you is sure, constant and steady. That outside of you and my child I don't care a rap for anything; you know too that for a long time I was, well, passionately in love with you, that around your every action clustered flowers of romance. I do not say those flowers are withered now; I do not believe they are; I feel them in my heart as much as I ever did; but they are closed up like buds that close at night time—it takes a warm sun to unclose them, not a chill wind. I have no doubt whatever but that your feelings are identical with mine; we both ought to make a continuous effort to show them and not the frosty ones. Let's get in a habit of having the sun shine. Perhaps then—when we get together again—it will always shine.[19]

They did indeed get together soon after that, for Annie returned to San Francisco before the year was over. There was little sunshine, however. A few years later, the marriage was all but over. Annie's diary tells the story:

January 1, 1897—I look forward to nothing but bitterness—as in the past year. So will it be in this—drunkenness, poverty, abuse, neglect. My child and myself crowded in a little closer, if possible, to the wall. Unless there is hope for me in me, myself, then there is nothing for me.

January 2, 1897—I have been accused of trying to poison the old man [Haskell's father] when he was down at Kaweah. Burnette was raving as usual this evening and said his father told him so—I did not believe his father told him any such thing—but called him up stairs and the old man said he did believe that I attempted to poison him shortly before I left Kaweah. I told the old man that I never heard of anything so abominable—two rotten men—with hearts of wolves to attack one helpless woman. Shame, shame. I asked Burnette if he believed such a thing—I begged him to have the decency to say he did not and he answered "I don't put it past you."

August, 1897—Burnette came over this evening in a raging fury. He had been drinking—said he would get a divorce from me and marry Mrs. O. and a lot more. Well, it was not a very pleasant thing. Burnette said he was glad I was going and hoped I would never come back.[20]

A Lonely Death

Annie eventually walked out on her husband and never did come back to him. The marriage was over. Ten years later, she learned that her ex-husband was seriously ill.

November, 1907—Roth says his father is very ill. Cannot walk nor hardly talk and he thinks it will be his last illness. It is very sad, I wish I knew that he is well taken care of and comfortable, but I do not see what I can do. Poor Burnette, his promise was so great, his gifts so brilliant. But that is all between himself and God.

There exists one rather interesting account of Haskell's final days, which comes to us via a letter scholar Rodney Ellsworth wrote to George Stewart in the 1920s. Ellsworth was doing historical research on Sequoia National Park and the Kaweah Colony. He wrote:

One evening while I was telling a friend of my mother's about my work, I mentioned the Kaweah Colony and to my utter amazement found that the woman I was talking to was an old friend of the Haskells. It seems that Mrs. Haskell accompanied her husband to Kaweah and lived there some time, but on her return to Oakland remained as silent as a sphinx. She left her husband and supported herself teaching. Burdette [sic] Haskell, broken and apparently unable to find comfort nor rest from the nemesis that pursued, sought solace in strong drink. For several years he lived in squalor in a mean hut of driftwood amid the lonely wastes of the San Francisco sand dunes. He died in poverty and wretchedness within the sound of the sea moaning on the tortured sands. Such is the sad destiny of those who would cure the disorder of society by ignoble methods.[21]

Perhaps Ellsworth, or the woman who provided him with the account of Haskell's final days, was guilty of some exaggeration and embellishment. But Haskell himself would easily have understood—indeed, the description of the "sea moaning on the tortured sands" sounds as if it could have come from Haskell's own pen.

On November 20, 1907, Burnette Gregor Haskell died. That night, Annie wept bitterly over "spoiled lives and unfulfilled hopes and unspeakable loneliness." She wrote in her diary:

> Burnette is gone. It seems when I write that, that there is no more to be said, but I think many thoughts. I feel so downhearted and dreary and think of a thousand things about Burnette, when he was young and full of enthusiasm.[22]

James Martin, who had worked so closely with Haskell to establish Kaweah and ultimately became his enemy when the Colony struggled and failed, wrote 40 years after their bitter falling out:

> It is hard to say a word in dispraise of Burnette G. Haskell, knowing how earnestly and unselfishly he worked in the interest of humanity. Haskell has since passed away, and though in the end we differed, I feel that no real animosity ever existed between us. I honor him for the good and noble work he did before he succumbed to the devilish obsession of the drug. Any of us might have fallen had we been by nature similarly constituted and situated. Peace be to him.[23]

CHAPTER

17

LET HISTORY JUDGE

Members of the colony, into whose hands this book may fall, will be amused at the following incident: Two old colony members, after an absence of nearly forty years, visited the Giant Forest, now known as the Sequoia National Park. Upon arriving at the Park they joined a bunch of sight-seers who were being escorted around by an official whose duty, apparently, was to show visitors the various places of interest. In their peregrinations they came upon the old Colony saw-mill, a feature, naturally, of considerable interest to these two old colonists. The mill is, or was at that time—it has since burned down—properly designated on the map and guide book issued by the park authorities as the "Colony Mill," but it seems this erring guide had formed a concept of his own in regard to history. He told this bunch of sight-seers: "This, ladies and gentlemen, is a structure that was erected some forty or more years ago, by a man named Connelly, who used it as a saw-mill, hence it is called "The Connelly Mill."

There were two, at least, in that group who knew differently. They smiled, and let it pass as a sample of the stuff histories in general are made of.

—JAMES J. MARTIN, History of the Kaweah Colony

THE KAWEAH COLONY provided fodder for a great deal of copy, both during its existence and after, but until the latter half of this century very little of what was written about the Colony came close to maintaining objectivity. This is an understandable failing from writers directly involved, but less forgivable from those who simply sacrificed their objectivity in order to make a point. Because of the lack of objectivity in all that was written about

Kaweah during its existence and for many years following, it is—in the words of one Tulare County historian—"a perplexing subject."[1] In his 1968 article for the Tulare County Historical Society's quarterly bulletin, Joe Doctor pointed out that Kaweah's history "is almost too well documented for the historian to tackle objectively." It seems a ludicrous statement, until one considers the overwhelming quantity and extreme bias of that documentation.

History's First Drafts

Kaweah garnered a great amount of press coverage from its very beginnings, and most of it was very slanted. We have already seen how certain newspapers, such as the *San Francisco Star*, were especially nasty in their attacks on the Colony. But conversely there were also many positive reports, which were often the work of non-resident members, which appeared in papers from New York, Boston, Denver and as far away as England and Ireland. For instance, a glowing account of Kaweah's successful Colony was once printed in the *Belfast Weekly Star* by a writer who had visited Kaweah late in 1890.[2]

The press coverage literally exploded for a number of reasons. For one thing, there was the controversy surrounding the establishment of Sequoia National Park and the legal question of the Colony's timber claims. There was the arrest of the trustees, the subsequent trials, and much that was legitimately newsworthy. It should also be noted that the leaders of the Colony were no strangers to the press. Burnette Haskell, a colorful labor agitator in San Francisco before founding the Colony, was able to fill scrapbooks with news clippings on himself before the Colony even existed.

For example, famed satirist Ambrose Bierce once wrote in his *San Francisco Wasp* column, "Prattle," that:

> B.G. Haskell is a gentleman who lives without work by preaching the dignity of labor. Under protection of the laws, he urges the abolition of law. He accumulates wealth by attacking the rights of property. He aspires to be, and to some extent is, a leader of industrial discontent, which is well enough; but as all who lead it must do, he leads it toward anarchy, which is not so well.[3]

As 1890 came to a close, the *Star* and Bierce were no longer in the minority in attacking Haskell and the Colony. By the end of 1891, when George Stewart published his hyper-critical series on the Colony in the *Delta*, even Haskell was contributing to the negative press on Kaweah. By reading his bitter and obviously subjective account of the Kaweah Colony in the November 29, 1891 issue of the *San Francisco Examiner* entitled "How Kaweah Fell," we see that history is always, by necessity, somewhat subjective simply because those who lived history were themselves subjective, being mere humans.

Newspapers, it has been said, are history's first drafts. Noting the bias with which so many reported on the Kaweah Colony, how can one ever get an accurate picture of what really happened via such first drafts. Even an account which was ostensibly an objective study by an outside observer invariably expressed a certain slant. In the summer of 1891, while the Colony still clung to a stubborn hope for success, William Carey Jones of the University of California visited the Colony and wrote a 30-page report which was eventually published in the *Quarterly Journal of Economics*. When the respected scholar, who eventually became dean of the School of Jurisprudence at the University of California, visited the Kaweah Colony, he undoubtedly relied on the colonists themselves for much of his information. It is also possible that his own political and social beliefs made him predisposed to forming a positive opinion of the Colony's ideals, a Colony which Jones concluded held "the brightest possible material prospects" which were obscured, if not destroyed, Jones maintained, by "the action of the government."

> In the matter of the controversy with the government, I can come to no other conclusion than that a great injustice has been done to those persons who in good faith made filings for timber claims in October, 1885. The law of the case is not so clear to my mind. It is difficult to find consistency in the decision of the Land Office...but even the law seems to me to incline in favor of the timberland claimants.[4]

Forty years after the demise of the Kaweah Colony—after the news coverage had long since died—other drafts of the Colony's history began to be written, but many of what were now historians rather than journalists blindly relied on biased reports or were themselves trying to make a point.

Academic Views

Carey McWilliams, in his well-known history of California farm labor, *Factories in the Field*, published in 1939, certainly set out to make a point. Using Kaweah as an example, he wrote:

> The Kaweah Colony forms an important chapter in the neglected history of early cooperative experiments in America. Into the story of cruel butchering of this genuinely progressive idea it is possible to read a phase of the social history, not only of California, but of the nation. If the Kaweah experiment had been permitted to succeed—the success of the colony was demonstrated at the time—the subsequent history of California might have been entirely different.[5]

McWilliams' brief account of Kaweah was far from in-depth and written from an obviously sympathetic point of view. He referred to Haskell as "one of the most idealistic and socially enlightened men of his generation in California." He noted that "the Kaweah experiment was not forgotten immediately; it was kept alive for demonstrative purposes. With fetid hypocrisy, the newspapers of California continued to use the Kaweah experiment as a stock illustration of the 'inevitable failure' of Socialism." It was the fault of the press, McWilliams maintained, that "the word Kaweah, if it has any meaning in the State today, has become associated with the notion of a cockeyed and irrational Socialism." McWilliams pointed out that the *Fresno Bee*, as late as 1928, ran a series of articles on the Kaweah Colony to illustrate "the follies of socialism."

McWilliams, on the other hand, used his version of the Kaweah story, with its slant leaning heavily to the left, for "demonstrative purposes," showing how an "unpardonably harsh and cruel" government squashed a potentially successful bid at workable socialism. This gave Kaweah, he maintained, "a tragic significance."

McWilliams was, in historian Kevin Starr's words, "a skilled writer possessed of style, rhetorical force, moral vision and socio-historical imagination,"[6] and caused considerable furor with *Factories in the Field*, which concluded with a ringing call for the collectivization of California agriculture. His portrayal of the Colony as victims of capitalistic greed and rampant land monopolization was, if not central to the argument set forth in his book, at least a colorful and rousing example that helped support his theory. Anytime history is purposely used as an example to support a point of view, objectivity and accuracy will take a back seat to the larger issues of supposed right and wrong. Burnette Haskell would have been proud to see historical objectivity concerning his Kaweah sacrificed just to be a part of McWilliams' landmark study on farm labor, and grateful that McWilliams kept the name Kaweah alive, motivating students for generations to come to investigate the story on their own.

Finally, 50 years after the Kaweah Colony's brief existence, scholarly histories began to be written. The story attracted numerous studies by historians from various walks of academic life. There is perhaps no knowing how many thesis papers and doctoral dissertations have been written on Kaweah and Sequoia National Park's establishment. Half a dozen, beginning with Ben Rothblat's 1936 master's thesis through Dan Kennedy's 1973 thesis were consulted in the writing of this book. Many more undoubtedly exist, as Kaweah was radical and offbeat enough to attract young students of history, eager to raise eyebrows with their efforts. Before long some of these scholarly works began to be published, such as Ruth Lewis's "Kaweah: An Experiment in Co-Operative Colonization" which appeared in the *Pacific Historical Review* in 1948. It was perhaps the first objective account of the Kaweah Colony to appear in print anywhere.

That same year an article on Kaweah entitled "A California Utopia: 1885-1890" appeared in the *Huntington Library Quarterly*. It was written by a young historian named Robert V. Hine, and became the basis for a chapter in his seminal work in utopian community studies, *California's Utopian Colonies*. The book, which was originally published in 1953 and reissued by Yale

University Press in 1966, quickly became the standard in its field. In 1983, University of California Press published a slightly expanded version of the book, which had already been in print 30 years, and it remains a part of their catalogue of titles. Not only does *California's Utopian Colonies* provide an objective, thorough study of Kaweah, but in it Hine was able to put the story in the larger context of a whole movement of utopian community endeavors which sprang up in California between 1850 and 1950, linked only by the eventual failure of them all.

Hine, the historian, writes with such a genuine concern for the people of Kaweah and other colonies that he deserves to be called a true humanitarian. And while writing about the many failures these characters suffer in the name of utopia, Robert Hine manages to maintain a genuine sense of hope. It is an optimism which, like many of the colonies discussed, is quintessentially Californian in nature.

> The psychological temper of the utopian [Hine wrote] constantly beckons to an unseen but nevertheless real goal; from one more experiment in community life may yet emerge—like a phoenix, momentarily dusted with the disappointments of the past—a resplendent, reformed mankind gathered in the ideal society.[7]

The Invisible Arm

In the early 1960s, one writer finally attempted to answer the central riddle behind the demise of the Kaweah Colony:

> That the Giant Forest is part of Sequoia National Park seems hardly a matter for discussion; it is its heart. Yet Sequoia Park was born without it. As established by Act of Congress on September 25, 1890, the park consisted of little more than the two townships that today form its rarely visited southern toe. Less than a week later, on the last day of the same session of Congress, the now famous forest and surrounding land [was] added.
>
> This somewhat erratic procedure has never been explained.[8]

With all that had been written about the Kaweah Colony in the first seven decades following its ill-fated existence, it is surprising that no one attempted to thoroughly investigate and explain the motivations for Sequoia's establishment and enlargement which drove the Colony into extinction. Certain writers, with a view from the left, accepted that the government acted unfairly toward the Colony without offering evidence of proof. Still others ignored the government's actions and simply pronounced the Colony doomed from the start because of its socialist politics or objectionable leadership—a flawed entity from the beginning that naturally would fall victim to internal dissolution and just plain bickering. But no outside observer ever really addressed the nagging questions surrounding the controversial actions of Congress toward the Colony and the mysterious circumstances involved in Sequoia's early history.

Oscar Berland, with his landmark article entitled "Giant Forest's Reservation: The Legend and the Mystery," finally set out to explain that erratic procedure and solve the mystery behind the sudden, last-minute enlargement of Sequoia National Park. The influence behind that sudden turn of events, which hastened the Colony's demise, is the great irony of Kaweah's history. Berland's work exposing that irony has greatly influenced students of Kaweah's history ever since.

Who was really responsible for the bill enlarging Sequoia, which was virtually railroaded through Congress? Those who felt its effect most had their theories. Both Burnette Haskell and James Martin, able to agree on little else during the last days of the Colony, felt they had been done in by the "invisible arm" of big business. Haskell went so far as to maintain that "at least one man had been acting as the paid agent" seeking to foster dissension within the Colony. Martin, a little less dramatic, indicted a very popular villain when, some 40 years later, he explained to a Sequoia National Park naturalist that the Southern Pacific Railroad was evidently "the one that started the machinery of Government against us." Martin pointed out, just as he had to President Roosevelt, that their trouble commenced immediately after he had interviewed Southern Pacific president Crocker in regards to the location of a proposed spur line to connect with the SP main line.

Martin also believed that *Visalia Delta* editor George Stewart was working with the railroad, whose interest was to "prevent the development of timber in the mountains adjacent to the big valley of lumber consumers." He concluded that Stewart had been a "snake in the grass" rather than the "innocent little lamb whose bleating saved the Big Trees from destruction."[9] But Martin and Haskell lacked hard evidence for their personal theories of conspiracy.

Finally, in the early 1960s, such evidence would be uncovered. When Oscar Berland, a young student of labor history from San Francisco, visited Sequoia he became intrigued with the park's history—a history involving a Socialist colony started by radical labor leaders. His interest piqued, Berland started researching the Kaweah Colony and found himself on a path which would eventually take him to the National Archives in Washington, D.C. Although his original interest had been California labor history, he became obsessed with the story of the Kaweah Colony and had every intention of writing a book on the subject.[10] Although that book has yet to be realized, his article for the *Sierra Club Bulletin*, which was published in 1962, remains a landmark study for both students of the Kaweah Colony and Sequoia National Park. It was an article both Haskell and Martin, with their invisible arm theories, would have loved.

In the article, Berland presented a clear and succinct history of the Colony as well as an overview of the concurrent agitation in Tulare County to save the Big Trees. He then focused on the two congressional bills that created, then enlarged, Sequoia National Park. The story then jumps ahead to a time when the Colony was long since dead:

> A beautiful park, belonging to the entire nation, stood as a strangely appropriate conclusion to Kaweah's unhappy story, with many ex-colonists among its most dedicated rangers and protectors. That was [when] George Stewart began to investigate the manner in which Sequoia Park had been enlarged. More than a quarter of a century had passed; it was time for histories to be written.[11]

Stewart's Search

As Berland explained, George Stewart went to his grave claiming he never understood exactly who was responsible for the mysterious bill that doomed the Colony. Berland followed a long trail of correspondence, and recounted Stewart's fascinating but unsuccessful attempt to discover the source of the legislation. "I did not learn at the time why or at whose suggestion the park was enlarged," Stewart confessed in a letter to *Century* magazine editor Robert Underwood Johnson in 1930. "I inquired later of John Muir and others...but no one could throw any light on the matter." [12]

While examining Stewart's search for suspects, Berland carefully recounted the steps that led to the reservation of the Giant Forest. He noted how the Sequoia bill (H.R. 11570) had passed through the House of Representatives less than a month after its introduction and that the land claimed by the Kaweah colonists was not included. Quoting Frank Walker, Berland's article points out that in his comments to the California Academy of Sciences, Walker said "It is generally thought [that the colonists] will substantiate their claims and acquire the land." Walker added the observation that "public sentiment seemed to favor" this acquisition of the land by the Kaweah Colony.

But as we have already seen, this bill, which was signed into law on September 25th, was not the only preservation legislation pending in Congress. It was another act—H.R. 12187, the substitute bill primarily concerned with reserving land around Yosemite—which enlarged Sequoia and so deeply impacted the Kaweah Colony. And it was there that the mystery began.

> [That] legislation [Berland concluded], unlike the measure that first established the park, was never discussed publicly, and hence its proponents could not be identified. The western press seemed unaware of its passage. Reference to the measure cannot be found even in the Minute Book of the House Committee on Public Lands, which ostensibly authored the bill. [13]

Who would have had the motive to introduce that bill in Congress? Who had the contacts to gather support? And who had the absolute power to push it through at the eleventh hour?

In attempting to discover who that might have been, Berland himself posed those questions and turned to the "Father of Sequoia Park" for some answers. George Stewart was never comfortable with the laudatory nickname his part in the establishment of Sequoia earned him. Perhaps this was because he knew there was much behind the course of events that even he himself did not understand. Berland's examination of Stewart's correspondence showed that the mystery of the second bill, adding Giant Forest to the Park he had supposedly "fathered," troubled Stewart late in his life, and when he died he still had not solved the disturbing puzzle concerning Sequoia's establishment. Yet Oscar Berland was able to glean several clues in Stewart's letters, and in his article offered a possible solution that Stewart never seemed to have imagined.

As earlier noted, the tacked-on section of the Yosemite bill which enlarged Sequoia was written in a language only understandable to land surveyors and agents, describing the land only in numbered townships, ranges, and sections. Where were recognizable descriptions such as "Kaweah watershed" or the "Giant Forest?" It is hard to imagine politicians back in Washington having any idea what this section of the bill encompassed, if indeed they actually read the entire bill. Someone, however, had to know exactly what this addition to the brand new national park entailed, and must have brought this suggestion to Congressman Vandever, who introduced both park bills. It is also worthy to note that Vandever, while representative for the large Sixth Congressional District, which included Tulare County and Sequoia, did not represent the Yosemite area to the north, nor was he a member of the Committee on Public Lands. Why then his concern with Yosemite?

Berland reminds us that Andrew Cauldwell had made recommendations to set aside Giant Forest and the surrounding land in a permanent reservation. This was, Berland pointed out, "The only proposal for the reservation of the Giant Forest of which any record appears."

Yet it is difficult to attribute the congressional action that followed to a temporary land agent's inexplicable change of mind. For one thing, the time interval between the report, written in Visalia and dated September 26, and the legislation introduced in Washington four days later seems too short for a causative relationship. For another, except on the one matter of the four townships around the Giant Forest, the legislation bears no resemblance to the proposals made in Cauldwell's Big Tree survey.

So if it wasn't Cauldwell, who was it? Berland discovered one very strong possibility. His article states:

> In his reply to Stewart's last communication on this problem, Robert Underwood Johnson had recalled "a Californian" who spoke off the record at a meeting of the House Committee on Public Lands which Johnson attended. This man, according to Johnson, "took up the matter of the text of the bill with General Vandever" and "may even have drawn the bill." But he couldn't remember his name.[14]

The Prime Suspect

During the period when this park legislation was being submitted, there was in fact a Californian, from Tulare County, in Washington, D.C. He was a guest of Representative Vandever and was well acquainted with land matters in the area. Ironically, his identity may have even been revealed in Stewart's *Visalia Delta*. An innocuous notice printed on September 18, 1890, amongst several other items of local news—comings and goings and social items—noted that "D.K. Zumwalt and wife returned last night from their eastern trip."

If Daniel K. Zumwalt is the suspect, what then was his motive? And why would it have been so well hidden—or at the very least unpublicized—that he was responsible for such heroic conservationist gains? (Zumwalt later took credit for being involved in General Grant Park's establishment, which was created in the very same congressional bill as Sequoia's enlargement.[15] This is further evidence of Zumwalt's involvement in the Sequoia mystery.)

As Oscar Berland pointed out, "It is reasonable to assume that in a matter of this magnitude, Zumwalt was not acting for himself." It is by no means a huge leap to a theory of conspiracy. Daniel Zumwalt was the local attorney and a land agent of the most "generously hated" railroad in the nation, the Southern Pacific. One biographer even credits him for having personally directed the railroad's activities during the Mussel Slough affair. For this very reason, Berland claimed it would have been "foolhardy for him to have associated his name with Giant Forest's reservation."[16]

This still does not address the question of motive, but the Southern Pacific Railroad had plenty. As pointed out before, even Colony leaders Haskell and Martin knew the railroad had motive to "prevent the development of timber...adjacent to the big valley of lumber consumers."[17] For one thing, the railroad made huge profits transporting Northern California lumber to the booming Central Valley. The railroad also had vast land holdings in the Valley, so would have been "as much concerned with the preservation of the surrounding watershed as any farmer," knowing that available water added much value to their land. (Conservationists, it should be reiterated, argued that logging the Sierra would drastically alter the snowmelt, adversely effecting their water supply in the summer months.) Berland even suggested that the railroad might have had an interest in the large logging operations in nearby Converse Basin, on the southern slopes of the Kings River canyon.

With Zumwalt and the railroad as suspects and a huge financial interest their motive, we turn to the matter of evidence. The railroad's name appears with impressive frequency among documents dealing with Sequoia National Park. The most striking example is one Oscar Berland found in the National Archives. It is a map of the full seven-township Sequoia (the original park established on September 25 comprised only the two southern-most townships) printed on Southern Pacific stationery and dated October 10, 1890. This map is the "smoking gun," for as Berland explained:

> On that date neither the colonists, the local conservationists, nor the California press were yet aware of the park's enlargement. Congressional documents *not* excepted, this is the earliest reference to Sequoia Park's boundaries extant.[18]

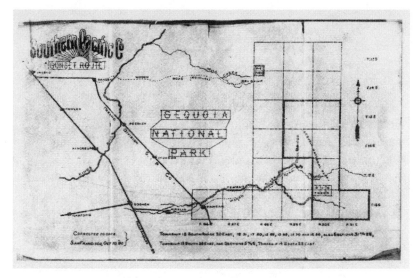

The now infamous SPRR map is the earliest reference to the enlarged Sequoia National Park boundary known to exist anywhere.

An Accepted Theory

No single work has had a greater impact on the subsequent study of the Kaweah Colony than Oscar Berland's 1962 *Sierra Club Bulletin* article. He blazed a trail, and armed with his theory of railroad involvement—supported by the now-famous Southern Pacific map—Berland and others since have been able to bring to light the mystery, drama and irony of the Kaweah/ Sequoia story.

In 1964, Douglas Hillman Strong wrote a dissertation for Syracuse University entitled "A History of Sequoia National Park." He relied heavily on Oscar Berland's work when discussing the Kaweah Colony and the park's establishment. Strong interviewed Berland a number of times and in his book, *Trees—or Timber?*, based on that dissertation, Strong reiterates Berland's central theory when he writes:

> The Southern Pacific could not come out in open support of the Park or its enlargement since to do so would have brought immedi-

ate suspicion and hostility. No corporation was more disliked or mistrusted in Tulare County. But a map of the enlarged Park on the Railroad's stationery, dated October 10, 1890, is evidence that the Southern Pacific initiated the park enlargement, for on that date no one else in California knew about it.[19]

How many visitors to today's Sequoia National Park, awed by the majestic beauty of a forest unequaled anywhere, appreciate that it was through the machinations of a powerful, self-serving monopoly that these trees were saved for posterity? Pondering this central irony brings up one last question. Did the establishment and enlargement of Sequoia, and the demise of the Kaweah Colony, really save the Big Trees of Giant Forest from destruction? Were they ever really in danger? In other words, what might have happened had Congress not set aside Giant Forest and its singular groves of giant sequoias?

Destruction of a Grand Forest

In Burnette Haskell's *Pen Picture of the Kaweah Co-Operative Colony*, written in 1889, the Colony's attitude toward the Big Trees was addressed:

> It would be nothing short of vandalism to indiscriminately destroy these sentinels of past centuries, as has been done in several parts of California, by ruthless ravagers of the Competitive system and care will be taken to preserve them in their primitive glory. It is gratifying to know that it is not the intention of this company to sweep from off the face of the earth these grand relics of past centuries. Portions of the forest will be cleared and cultivated, but the "Monarchs" will be left to reign supreme in their grandeur, to excite the awe and admiration of generations yet to come.[20]

Regardless of what Burnette Haskell may have written in 1889, if the Colony had survived—a survival made possible only by gaining title to their land claims and thus legal ownership of Giant Forest— the Big Trees of that famed forest would very likely have been felled sooner or later.

There are two possible scenarios that would have endangered the spectacular groves of Big Trees at Giant Forest. First, let us suppose Sequoia National Park had not been enlarged to include Giant Forest. It is easy to imagine big lumber interests such as Smith and Moore's Sanger Lumber Company acquiring title to that land and expanding their operations. In 1891, the company produced nearly 20 million board feet of lumber from the forests along the Kings River drainage just north of the Kaweah watershed. Still, this was not enough volume to make profitable their already enormous investments and the company eventually expanded its operations into a natural bowl known as Converse Basin, "where the really big trees are located." Converse Basin contained over 5,000 acres of some of the largest trees in the world.[21]

Even though the first year was a complete disaster, operations there continued for nearly ten years. Today, stump after giant stump dramatically litter the Converse Basin, and walking among the decimated giants, jutting up like gargantuan grave markers, one can't help but shudder at the possibility of a similar fate for Giant Forest only 20 miles away. With the Colony's road only a few miles shy of its groves, accessibility wouldn't have been a limiting factor for an aggressive outfit which, at nearby Converse Basin, demonstrated their willingness and ability to fell mammoth specimens despite the difficulty, danger and high percentage of waste.

And what if the Kaweah Colony had acquired title to Giant Forest along with their other timber claims? Even if we accept the theory that the Colony would never have logged the Big Trees, there remains a frightening scenario that would have spelled disaster for the grand forest.

Title to their timber claims would undoubtedly have contributed to a greater chance of success for the Kaweah Colony. There is no denying that when their claims were canceled and all hope of acquiring title extinguished, the Kaweah Colony lost any viable chance for success. But we have also seen that there were other factors contributing to the endeavor's demise, including mismanagement, internal disputes, and a tenuous capital base. Although gaining title to the timber land would have been beneficial, would it have guaranteed lasting prosperity and harmony?

One can easily imagine that even had the Kaweah Colony been granted title and established successful logging operations at Colony Mill, financial difficulties would have arisen (or simply continued.) With title to Giant Forest, and a lumber company 20 miles away possessed with the capital and propensity to expand, sale of land by the Colony would be one viable solution to many problems. Had the Colony owned Giant Forest, they may indeed never have cut down a single Big Tree, but they could very well have been forced into selling Giant Forest to someone who would. Fortunately, this is all pure speculation.

It is naïve to imagine the Big Trees of Giant Forest, left unprotected, *not* being destroyed. Giant sequoias by the thousands were destroyed at numerous locations: near Grant Grove, at Converse Basin, in the Tule River drainage to the south, and even at Atwell's Mill,[22] by the hand of the Kaweah Colony on patented private land within a newly created national park. Looking back, with our 100-year vantage point, for Giant Forest it ended up being a choice between survival of the Big Trees or the Kaweah Colony.

Granted, it did not have to be that way. Park boundaries could have been drawn to allow the Colony a chance at obtaining all the timber land they really needed—the pine and fir forests where they established their mill—but this wasn't the case. As we have seen, powerful forces had the motive and means to make sure the Kaweah Colony was denied any opportunity to produce lumber. As things turned out, the Big Trees of Giant Forest were the incidental beneficiary of a giant corporation's less than benevolent actions.

Does this, then, make the Kaweah colonists sacrificial lambs? Can we assume their motives were purely noble and their leaders innocent and uncorrupted? Of course not. Nothing is ever that simple. Human beings are not that simple, and history is lived and written by human beings.

The future, on the other hand, has also been and will always be imagined by the dreamer.

THE SPIRIT OF THE DREAMER

One duty only remains to those whose hearts were with Kaweah as a cooperative experiment; it is to let the truth be known. And is there no remedy, then, for the evils that oppress the poor? And is there no surety that the day is coming when justice and right shall reign on earth? I do not know; but I believe, and I hope, and I trust.

—BURNETTE HASKELL,
November, 1891

THIS NARRATIVE GREW out of an interest in local history. It has grown far beyond that. It is a story that epitomizes California and even America. This is not simply because of the prominence of such issues as land, labor and conservation. Kaweah's story is California's in the utterance of a single word—dream. The California Dream. Co-Operative Dreams.

Historian Kevin Starr used the word in the titles of his several volumes of California history. The first volume, *Americans and the California Dream, 1850-1915*, ends with a variation on Wallace Stegner's observation that California is like the rest of the United States, only more so:

> In a very real sense, the California dream was the American dream undergoing one of its most significant variations. The hope raised by promotional writers…was the simple yet subtle hope for a better life animating America since its foundation. California provided a special context for the working-out of this aspiration, intensified it,

201

indeed, gave it a probing, prophetic edge in which the good and evil of the American dream was sorted out and dramatized. In 1915, after sixty-five years of statehood, as, north and south, great expositions opened their gates, California, like America itself, remained an intriguing, unanswered question.[1]

How apt this is to Kaweah where the California dream underwent significant variation. Where hope was raised by promotional writers. Where a special context was provided for the working-out of aspirations. Where intriguing, unanswered questions certainly remain. And isn't the story of California filled with individuals who failed to achieve their dream? They include the countless seekers who came up short in the diggings of the Gold Rush; the settlers seeking land enough to raise food and family who were unable to compete with the wealthy land barons; the immigrants and economic refugees who envisioned eating the plentiful grapes right off the vine, but instead became a rootless migrant work force; even the star-struck youths coming to Hollywood to achieve fame and fortune only to end up desperate souls on a boulevard of broken dreams.

Starr reminds us that a culture that fails to internalize some understanding of its past tragedies and past ideals has no focus upon the promise of the future nor the dangers of the present. In that way, he maintains, the elusiveness or failure of the California dream can prove a blessing. Only by remembering those who struggled but failed can we further today's struggle for value and corrective action. "Old in error," Starr wrote, "California remains an American hope."[2]

From the very beginning, the story of Kaweah was a human story of flesh and blood and passion and hope. And while it centered on the dream of cooperation, it was a story of individuals.

There has long been a popular perception that the Kaweah Colony was destroyed by the bickering within. While we have seen that this was certainly a contributing factor to its demise, it is hoped that this book has shown there was much more at the heart of the problem. One reason for this perception, however, was the writings of Burnette Haskell. Even though he blamed governmental persecution and the long arm of capitalist monopolies for the demise of the Colony, in the end (and more than once in print,) he assigned blame to the failings of "too many average men." Disgusted with everyone's actions but his own, Haskell wrote that "men are not yet civilized enough to do right for right's sake alone and to labor for the love of production itself."[3] Never once did he concede that legal or management mistakes he, himself, may have made were a factor in the Colony's demise. With our knowledge of Haskell, this is hardly surprising.

Thus we can say that Haskell became disillusioned with cooperation because of the weakness of the individual. In his mind, the plan for cooperation did not fail; the individuals who took part did. Haskell once commented on the sheer variety of those individuals involved:

> The list of membership itself is a curious study. It is the United States in microcosm; among the members are old and young; rich and poor, wise and foolish, educated and ignorant, worker and professional man, united only by the common interest in Kaweah. There were temperance men and their opposites, churchmen and agnostics, free-thinkers, Darwinists and spiritualists, bad poets and good, musicians, artists, prophets and priests. There were dress-reform cranks and phonetic spelling fanatics, word-purists and vegetarians. It was a mad, mad world, and being so small its madness was the more visible.[4]

While Haskell noted that the cross section of individuals was reflective of America itself, he also felt that so varied a group was perhaps not the best of situations in such tight quarters, for while this "mad, mad world" may have been united in a common interest—Kaweah—they certainly were not united in how best to achieve its goal: cooperative utopia.

Little has been said in this book of other cooperative utopian experiments that preceded and followed Kaweah, or of Kaweah's place amongst them. The consideration of other colonies shall be left to other studies, for it is far too encompassing a subject to adequately deal with here. But a cursory look at some of the better known American community experiments—from Brook Farm to the Oneida Community, from the Mormons to the Shakers—reveals that those with the greatest longevity were those that relied on devotion to religious or spiritual doctrine. Those that were structured around political doctrine did not fare as well. Perhaps this is due to the almost impossible task of reconciling a society based on cooperation with a strong spirit of individualism. Strong-minded individuals are needed to achieve productivity, but that same spirit can be anathema to a system of enforced cooperation, which is what any political cooperative is by definition. Often times these systems of enforced cooperation become corrupted of their original intent—the good of the community—and the spirit of the individual becomes suppressed.

Such was the case some 25 years after the failure of the Kaweah experiment when, through a revolution Haskell probably would have at first cheered, a Bolshevik faction of Russian Marxists created Communist rule in Russia. Confronted with the formidable task of transforming the large, backward country into a leading industrial nation of the twentieth century, the great Soviet experiment eventually evolved and was controlled by Stalin's brand of totalitarianism.

Perhaps the ultimate example of enforced cooperation (and nationalist zeal) followed during a time of worldwide economic turmoil. The National Socialist German Worker's Party became the Nazi party, and its fuhrer will forever be considered the very embodiment of evil fascism.

John Humphrey Noyes, founder of the Oneida Community, once wrote that "a vast spiritual and intellectual excitement is one thing; and the institutions that rise out of it are another. We must not judge the excitement by the institutions."[5] We will not, then, judge the individuals of Kaweah and the excitement they felt for their ideals by the failure of Kaweah as an institution. Nor will we, as Haskell has done, blame these individuals for that failing, although it is tempting to assign some individual blame to Haskell himself. Instead, let us admire the effort—the spiritual and intellectual excitement they displayed, and learn from the shortcomings so visible from our vantage point of 100 years of hindsight.

Haskell called Kaweah a microcosm for the United States, and in so much that Kaweah's membership represented a sort of melting pot of individuals, that analogy holds true. America has always celebrated the spirit of the individual. America was founded on the liberties of the individual. The remarkable success of America, then, is that the spirit and liberty of the individual have somehow been integrated with the good of society. It is a precarious balance (where sometimes the good of society must be sacrificed to the rights of the individual), and one that was never achieved at Kaweah. This does not mean that we should not admire the effort these individuals who comprised Kaweah made toward that un-achieved goal. Society, as well as individuals, can learn from the mistakes of the past. As Robert Hine observed, "from one more experiment in community life may yet emerge—like a phoenix, momentarily dusted with the disappointments of the past—a re-splendent, reformed mankind gathered in the ideal society."[6]

Some never recovered from the disappointments of Kaweah. Haskell died a bitter, lonely and broken man at the relatively young age of 50, only 16 years after the failure of the Colony. With his "belly full of cooperation, you bet," he lost hope that any phoenix might rise from the ashes of his failed dreams.

Nearly 50 years after her days at Kaweah, Annie Haskell looked back. At 79 years of age, she wrote:

> No use thinking of that day so long past—when Burnette and I were married; my life, emotionally seemed to be like a troubled sea—the waves raged and the salt was bitter. I learned a little, I suffered much, and laughed a lot. If I had it all to relive—I wonder if I shouldn't do exactly the same, even with knowledge added. I wonder.[7]

Annie, following the end of her marriage and the death of Burnette Haskell, lived a long and full life. She found fulfillment in her son, Roth; her career as a school teacher; and ultimately in religion. Perhaps she learned, better than anyone, from the difficul-ties surrounding Kaweah and her tumultuous life with its founder. It was only a few years after Kaweah, as her marriage was disintegrating and the dawning of a new year brought with it only the promise of "drunkenness, poverty, abuse, and neglect," that Annie came to a realization:

> Unless there is hope for me in me, myself—then there is nothing for me.[8]

Only through the strength of individuals able to learn from failure and maintain hope in themselves can the dream of cooperation stay alive. And will that dream ever be fully realized? To echo Burnette Haskell's words, I do not know; but I believe, and I hope, and I trust.

NOTES

FOREWORD

1. *Tulare County Times*, August 20, 1891, under the headline "Kaweah, A Prosperous and Harmonious Colony," and *Tulare County Times*, December 3, 1891, "Kicking the Corpse," offer examples of that paper's continuing support. The Board of Supervisors' circular appeared in the March 3, 1892, issues of both the *Tulare County Times* and *Visalia Weekly Delta*.
2. Oscar Berland, personal journal, July 22, 1960.
3. This disclaimer ran in *The Kaweah Commonwealth* from October 4, 1890, through August 29, 1891.
4. Joseph E. Doctor, notes on his interview with surviving Kaweah colonists conducted in the 1940s. Shortly before his death in 1995, Joe Doctor donated all his notes and clippings on the Kaweah Colony to the author.
5. Doctor, op. cit., as well as interviews with the author, March/April, 1995.
6. Maren L. Carden, *Oneida: Utopian Community to Modern Corporation*, (Johns Hopkins Press, 1969), pp. 41-61.
7. Joseph E. Doctor, "Why Kaweah Failed," *Los Tulares*, No 78, September, 1968.

Part I: The Birth of a Dream (1885-1889)

CHAPTER 1—KELLER AND CALIFORNIA LAND

1. W.W. Robinson, *Land in California: The Story of Mission Lands, Ranchos, Squatters…*(University of California Press, Berkeley, 1948), p. 1.
2. Charles F. Keller papers, (Sequoia National Park historical archives). The Keller papers at Sequoia consist of an undated 5-page autobiographical manuscript and typed transcripts of two letters: Keller to his son, Carl, dated April 14, 1921; and another to Sequoia National Park superintendent Walter Fry dated March 7, 1913.

3. Stephen Whitney, *The Sierra Nevada, A Sierra Club Naturalists' Guide,* (Sierra Club Books, San Francisco, 1979), pp. 31-32; also see Lary M. Dilsaver and William C. Tweed, *Challenge of the Big Trees,* (Sequoia Natural History Association, Three Rivers, 1990), pp. 10-11.

4. Brooks D. Gist, *Empire Out of the Tules,* (Tulare, CA, 1976), pp. 57-60; also see *Visalia Weekly Delta,* June 25, 1959 (Golden Century Edition), an article entitled "Litigation in Water History."

5. *Visalia Weekly Delta,* June 25, 1959, "Bonanza Wheat Farms Came With Rails."

6. Carey McWilliams, *Factories in the Field,* 1939, (page number citations are from the 1971 edition published by Peregrine Publishers, Santa Barbara and Salt Lake City), pp. 20-21.

7. Ibid., pp. 12-14; also see Kevin Starr, *Americans and the California Dream, 1850-1915,* (Oxford University Press, 1973), p. 138. Both authors use the same particular Henry George quote to launch discussions of California land acquisition and its monopolistic nature.

8. Keller, op. cit.

9. Date of Keller's marriage from a newspaper obituary for Charles Keller, 1937, paper unidentified. Xeroxed clipping provided by Joann Tobin Bell, great granddaughter of Charles Keller.

10. As cited by McWilliams, *Factories in the Field,* p. 12-14.

11. William Deverell, *Railroad Crossing: Californians and the Railroad, 1850-1910,* (University of California Press, Berkeley, 1994), p. 32.

12. Deverell, op. cit.; Irving McKee, "Notable Memorials to Mussel Slough," *Pacific Historical Review* 17, (February, 1948,); Richard Orsi, "The Octopus Reconsidered: The Southern Pacific and Agricultural Modernization in California, 1865-1915," *California Historical Quarterly* 54, (Fall, 1975); and J.L. Brown, *The Mussel Slough Tragedy,* (1958), were all considered in synopsizing the story of Mussel Slough.

13. Frank Norris, *The Octopus, A Story of California,* originally published in 1901, (Signet Books, 1964), p. 42.

14. Keller, op. cit.

15. Douglas Hillman Strong, "History of Sequoia National Park," (an unpublished dissertation for Syracuse University, 1964), Sequoia National Park library, p. 74.

16. Keller, op. cit. It is interesting to note that in the three documents comprising the Keller papers, each has a different version of this very episode. In his 1913 letter to Fry, Keller implied merely overhearing the discussion; in the 1921 letter to his son, Carl, he claims he heard their conversation and introduced himself to join the discussion; and

in his autobiographical manuscript, presumably written quite late in life, Keller claims he had "read an advertisement of timber land being thrown upon the market." The version in the letter to his son seems the most likely.

CHAPTER 2—HASKELL AND THE LABOR MOVEMENT

1. Haskell Family Papers, Volume 6, *Genealogy*, Bancroft Library, Berkeley, CA. Burnette Haskell was obsessed with his genealogy and the beautifully hand-illustrated, brightly-colored book he composed attested to his interest. Upon re-discovering the book in 1902, 24 years after he began it, Haskell wrote, "The colors have not faded, paled nor changed. In the enthusiasm of 21 I began it; in the weariness of 45 I do feel a little happiness at its recovery. The colors have not changed but at 21 I believed in gold, and scarlet and vivid things— now, the book has not changed, but the skies look gray and somber."

2. Caroline Medan, "Burnette Gregor Haskell: California Radical," (M.A. Thesis, University of California, Berkeley, 1950), p. 2.

3. Haskell Family Papers, Volume 1, *Personal Reminisces and Memoranda of Burnette G. Haskell*, (hereafter referred to as B.G. Haskell journal), Bancroft Library, Berkeley, CA.

4. Oscar Berland, "Aborted Revolution: A Study in the Formative Years of the American Labor Movement, 1877-1886," (M.A. Thesis, San Francisco State College, 1966), pp. 52-53.

5. Frank Roney, *Irish Rebel and California Labor Leader: An Autobiography*, (edited by Ira B. Cross, University of California Press, Berkeley, CA, 1935), p. 338.

6. Ibid., p. 390.

7. Kevin Starr, *Endangered Dreams: The Great Depression in California*, (Oxford University Press, New York, 1996), p. 4.

8. Ibid., p. 6; Berland, op. cit., pp. 46-47.

9. Medan, op. cit., p. 7.

10. Ira Cross, *History of the Labor Movement in California*, (University of California Publications in Economics, Berkeley, CA 1935), p. 158.

11. John P. McKay, Bennett D. Hill and John Buckler, *A History of Western Society, 2nd Edition*, (Houghton Mifflin Co., Boston, 1983), pp. 788, 809-10; also see Mark Holloway, *Heavens on Earth, Utopian Communities in America, 1680-1880*, (Dover Publications, New York, 1966), pp. 104-07.

12. Berland, op. cit., pp. 54-55. Berland quotes and cites Annie Haskell's diary entry for September 23, 1882.

13. Ibid., p. 55; Medan, op. cit., pp. 11-18.

14. McKay et al, op. cit., pp. 904-05.

15. Cross, op. cit., p. 161.
16. *Truth*, November 3, 1883 and December 15, 1883. (A full collection of the labor newspaper *Truth* exists on microfilm at the Bancroft Library in Berkeley, CA).
17. Cross, op. cit., p. 164.
18. Medan, op. cit., pp. 53-55. Medan cites as her sources Paul S. Taylor, "History of the Pacific Coast Seamen," (M.A. Thesis, University of California, 1920), and William Martin Camp, *San Francisco Port of Gold*, (New York Doubleday, 1947).
19. Berland, op. cit., p. 58. In a footnote, Berland explains that John Hooper Redstone, according to family sources and an undated manuscript in his possession, had been associated with Giuseppe Mazzini in London in 1862, which was during the time Mazzini was involved in discussions which two years later led to the formation of the first International.
20. *Commonwealth*, Vol. 2, No. 15, May 24, 1889, (published by Burnette G. Haskell, San Francisco, CA), p. 71. This issue of the monthly journal of the Kaweah Colony included "A Brief History of Kaweah," which, judging from the style and content, was written by Haskell.
21. Annie Haskell diary, November 12, 1891, (via a transcription made by Oscar Berland).
22. Annie Haskell diary, October 13, 1882, (as cited by Caroline Medan).

CHAPTER 3—STEWART AND THE LAND OFFICE

1. Keller papers, letter to his son, Carl, April 14, 1921.
2. This is common knowledge for anyone, interested in history, who grew up in Three Rivers (the author's hometown.) This information could be verified in a number of places, from a Time-Line on file at the Three Rivers Historical Society, to Annie Mitchell's *Land of the Tules* (Valley Publishers, Fresno, CA, 1972), to discussions with current *Kaweah Commonwealth* publishers, John and Sarah Elliott.
3. Annie R. Mitchell, *The Way It Was*, (Tulare, CA, 1976), p. 104.
4. John Muir, *Our National Parks*, (Houghton Mifflin Co., Boston, 1901. Page citations are from *John Muir: The Eight Wilderness-Discovery Books*, published by Diadem Books, 1992), pp. 579-81.
5. Keller, op. cit.
6. James J. Martin letter to the editor of the *Fresno Bee*, (undated transcription, written circa 1929). Transcription contained in the Kaweah Collection of miscellaneous documents, Annie Mitchell History Room, Visalia Public Library.
7. Keller papers, op. cit.; also autobiographical manuscript and letter to Fry, March 3, 1913.

8. Keller papers, letter to Fry. It is unlikely Keller would have admitted, especially to Fry, not leading each and every claimant to the forest to see their quarter-section in person, as the law required.

9. George W. Stewart letter to Col. John R. White, Sequoia National Park superintendent, June 8, 1929. (George W. Stewart papers, Visalia Public Library). George W. Stewart, the prominent Visalia newspaper editor who later became known as the "father of Sequoia National Park," should not be confused with George R. Stewart, the author of such notable books as *The California Trail* and *Ordeal by Hunger.*

10. Mitchell, op. cit., p. 107.

11. Stewart letter to Enos Mills, Sequoia National Park historian, August 29, 1916.

12. Marc Reisner, *Cadillac Desert: The American West and Its Disappearing Water,* (Penguin Books, 1993, first published by Viking, 1986), pp. 43-44.

13. Stewart to E. Mills, August 29, 1916.

14. Keller papers, autobiographical manuscript.

15. Strong, "History of Sequoia National Park," p. 79-81.

16. Milton Greenbaum, "History of the Kaweah Colony," (M.A. Thesis, Brooklyn University, 1942), Sequoia National Park library. p. 8, citing *Report of Inspector G.C. Wharton to Commissioner of the General Land Office,* December 1, 1885.

17. Strong, op. cit., p. 82.

18. Keller, op. cit.

CHAPTER 4—ROAD WORK BEGINS

1. *Visalia Weekly Delta,* November 26, 1885.

2. Keller papers, letter to son, Carl, April 14, 1921.

3. Ibid.

4. Ibid.

5. Ibid.

6. *Commonwealth,* Vol. 2, No. 15, May 24, 1889. "A Brief History of Kaweah," p.72.

7. *Visalia Weekly Delta,* November 12, 1891. In November and December of 1891, the *Visalia Weekly Delta* ran a series on the history of the Kaweah Colony. It was very critical of the Colony and its leadership. The series was later bound into a book manuscript, with George Stewart listed as its author. A copy of that rare book is housed in the Annie Mitchell History Room of the Visalia Public Library. Citations for this series of articles will cite the *Delta* and date, rather than Stewart's bound manuscript history of the Colony.

8. *Commonwealth*, op. cit., pp. 71-72.
9. Keller papers, op. cit.
10. Ibid.
11. *Commonwealth*, op. cit., p. 72.
12. *San Francisco Examiner*, November 29, 1891, "How Kaweah Fell," by Burnette Haskell. A later version of this article appeared in *Out West* magazine in August, 1902, under the title "Kaweah: How and Why the Colony Died." (Hereafter cited as Haskell, *Out West*.)
13. James J. Martin letter to editor of *Fresno Bee*, circa 1929.
14. *Commonwealth*, Vol. 2, No. 15, May 24, 1889, p. 78.
15. Frank Roney, *Irish Rebel and California Labor Leader*, p. 475.
16. Oscar Berland, notes from an interview with Albert E. Redstone, December, 1960.
17. B.G. Haskell journal, entry dated December 17, 1885.
18. *Visalia Weekly Delta*, November 12, 1891.
19. *Commonwealth*, October, 1889, "A Visit to Kaweah...," p. 170.
20. *Visalia Weekly Delta*, November 12, 1891.
21. Philip Winser, "Memories," (original unpublished manuscript, 1931, Huntington Library, San Marino, CA), p. 109.
22. Ibid., p. 121.
23. *Visalia Weekly Delta*, November 12, 1891.

CHAPTER 5—CRISIS AND SETTLEMENT

1. Medan, "Burnette Gregor Haskell: A California Radical," pp. 74-75.
2. *Commonwealth*, Vol. 2, No. 15, May 24, 1889, p. 72.
3. "The Crisis," a circular issued by a committee headed by Burnette Haskell to the Kaweah Colony membership with the subtitle, "A Statement of the Legal and Moral Position of the Colony at the Present Time." November, 1887. (Sequoia National Park historical archives), p. 5.
4. Medan, op. cit., p. 75, citing Annie Haskell's diary, May 16, 1887.
5. "The Crisis," p. 5.
6. Ibid., p. 6.
7. *Visalia Weekly Delta*, November 12 and November 19, 1891; also, original copy of Articles of Incorporation filed in Tulare County, September 28, 1887, (Kaweah Colony collection, Visalia Public Library).
8. "The Crisis," p. 10.
9. Oscar Berland, research notes, citing a December 1, 1889 signed statement made by Andrew Larsen appearing in the *San Francisco Chronicle*, December, 8, 1889.
10. "The Crisis," pp. 17-18.

11. *San Francisco Chronicle*, December 1, 1889.
12. Ibid.; *Visalia Weekly Delta*, November 12, 1891.
13. *San Francisco Chronicle*, December 1, 1889.
14. *Visalia Weekly Delta*, November 12, 1891.
15. Robert V. Hine, *California's Utopian Colonies*, (University. of California Press, Berkeley, 1983), p. 92.
16. William Carey Jones, "The Kaweah Experiment in Co-Operation," (manuscript copy which later served as basis of an article in the *Quarterly Journal of Economics*, VI, October, 1891), Visalia Public Library, p. 9.
17. *Deed of Settlement and By-Laws of Kaweah Colony*, Article I, Sec. 20, adopted March 9, 1888. (Published as a supplement to the *Commonwealth*, March, 1889), p. 28.
18. Hine, op. cit., p. 87; *Visalia Weekly Delta*, December 3, 1891.

Part II: Living the Dream at Kaweah (1889-1890)

CHAPTER 6—PIONEERS OF KAWEAH

1. William Tweed, "The Kaweah Rivers—How Many Forks?" *Kaweah Quarterly*, (The Kaweah Land Trust Newsletter), Fall, 1995.
2. *Commonwealth*, October, 1889, "A Visit to Kaweah, Personal Observations and Reminiscences of Burnette G. Haskell Concerning the Kaweah Colony," p. 168.
3. Burnette Haskell, *A Pen Picture of the Kaweah Co-Operative Colony*, (San Francisco, 1889), p. 3.
4. *Kaweah Commonwealth*, Vol. III, No. 2, February, 1892. This, the penultimate issue of the Colony newspaper, included the "Secretary's Statement of Receipts in Cash and Time-Checks on Acct. of Membership fees from date of inception of Colony to January 1, 1892." The numbered list comprised 613 names, although several dozen had only $10 paid toward their membership.
5. Haskell, *Out West*, p. 315.
6. James J. Martin Family papers, from a 1936 unidentified newspaper clipping. Also miscellaneous papers and correspondence of James J. Martin, (Bancroft Library).
7. Winser, "Memories," pp. 114-15.
8. Phillip Redstone Hopping, "John Hooper Redstone: My Most Unforgettable Character," *Los Tulares*, No. 94, June, 1974, pp. 3-4.
9. Italia Crooks, *A Story of the Life of Bessie Humbolt Miles*, (published by Eleanor Esther Howell and David Weaver, 1979), Three Rivers Public Library, pp. 2-6; also, Peter Ting, "Reminiscences of my Early Life," (printed in *Tulare County Historical Society Newsletter*, date unknown/circa 1970, microfilm, Visalia Public Library), pp. 44-46.

10. *Kaweah Commonwealth*, Vol. 1, No. 15, April 26, 1890.

11. *Commonwealth*, Vol. 2, No. 15, May 24, 1889, p. 77.

12. Joseph E. Doctor, notes on interviews; also, Exeter *Sun*, "Memories of Kaweah Colony Revived," October 23, 1947; also see *The [new] Kaweah Commonwealth*, Vol. 4, No. 26, August 25, 1995, letter from Wilma Hengst Kauling in response to the author's "Colony Corner" article on the Hengst family. Wilma wrote: "Frank and Anna's first son, George Burnette, was born at the Colony in 1889. He spent his adult years in Visalia until his death in 1973. He would have to be the person referred to as 'Burnette Kaweah'."

13. Winser, op. cit., p. 125.

14. Tulare County Historical Society's foreword to "Kaweah: An Epic of the Old Colony." It should be noted they published Will Purdy's poem (written circa 1930) with the title "*An Epic* of the Old Colony," while I have elsewhere cited it as "*The Saga* of the Old Colony," as earlier copies of the manuscript at both the Bancroft Library and Visalia Public Library are so titled.

15. Winser, op. cit., p. 125.

16. Haskell, *Out West*, p. 315.

17. Ibid., p. 300.

CHAPTER 7—ON THE ROAD TO SUCCESS

1. *Commonwealth*, Vol. 1, No. 15, May 24, 1889, p. 74.

2. *Commonwealth*, Vol. 2, No. 16, June 24, 1889, p. 95.

3. Joseph E. Doctor, notes on interviews with Frank Hengst; also see "The Old Kaweah Colony Road," *Los Tulares*, No. 63, December, 1964, which describes a trip over the old road with Joe Doctor, James Corson, John Grunigen and other members of the historical society. It should be pointed out that the author has hiked the old Colony Mill Road several times.

4. Dilsaver and Tweed, *Challenge of the Big Trees*, p. 64.

5. Ibid., pp. 64-66

6. B.F. Allen, *Report to Commissioner, General Land Officer*, October 22, 1889, (Nat'l Archives, RG 49, microfilm, Bancroft Library), p. 1.

7. Ibid.

8. Ibid., pp. 20-21.

9. Ibid., pp. 22-23.

10. Ibid., pp. 27-29.

11. *Kaweah Commonwealth*, Vol. 1, No. 22, June 14, 1890.

12. *Kaweah Commonwealth*, Vol. 1, Nos. 29 and 30, August 2 and 9, 1890, from memorials written about Larsen by both Burnette and Annie Haskell.

13. *Kaweah Commonwealth*, Vol. 1, No. 27, July 19, 1890.
14. Oscar Berland, notes on his interview with Albert E. Redstone, December, 1960.
15. *Kaweah Commonwealth*, Vol. 1, No. 30, August 9, 1890.
16. Andrew Cauldwell, *Report to Commissioner, General Land Office*, July 16, 1890, (National Archives, RG 49, microfilm, Bancroft Library), p. 8.
17. Ibid., pp. 6-7.
18. Ibid., p. 7; Allen, op. cit., p. 27.

CHAPTER 8—FROM THE PAGES OF THE COMMONWEALTH

1. *Visalia Weekly Delta*, November 12, 1891; also Alfred Cridge, "Korrekt Kritique on the Kaweah Ko-Operative Kolony," a circular issued to the Non-resident members of the K.C.C. from the Democratic Element (The Kaweah Collection, Visalia Public Library); and the *Kaweah Commonwealth*, "The Coming Election," Vol. 1, No. 14, April 19, 1890.
2. *Visalia Weekly Delta*, November 12, 1891.
3. Ibid.
4. Cridge, op. cit.
5. *Kaweah Commonwealth*, "Some Words about our July General Meeting," Vol. 1, No. 26, July 12, 1890.
6. *Kaweah Commonwealth*, "May Day Festivities," Vol. 1, No. 17, May 10, 1890.
7. *Kaweah Commonwealth*, "Losing our Punt, Spring Wagon and Mail by the Rising River," Vol. 1, No. 19, May 24, 1890.
8. *Kaweah Commonwealth*, "Colony Notes," Vol. 1, No. 23, June 21, 1890.
9. Ibid.
10. *Kaweah Commonwealth*, "Colony Notes," Vol. 1, No. 25, July 5, 1890.
11. Ibid.
12. Winser, "Memories," p. 94
13. *Kaweah Commonwealth*, "Colony Notes," Vol. 1, No. 26, July 12, 1890.
14. Ibid.
15. Ibid.
16. Haskell, *A Pen Picture...*, p. 10.
17. *Kaweah Commonwealth*, "Official Directory of the Kaweah Co-Operative Colony," Vol. 2, No. 12, February 7, 1891.
18. *Kaweah Commonwealth*, "My First Impressions," by Annie Haskell, Vol. 1. No. 38, October 4, 1890.

19. Haskell, *Out West*, pp. 318-19.
20. *Kaweah Commonwealth*, Vol. 1, No. 43, November 8, 1890.
21. Haskell, *Out West*, p. 319.

CHAPTER 9—TWO RISING MOVEMENTS

1. Muir, *Our National Parks*, p. 566.
2. Dilsaver and Tweed, *Challenge of the Big Trees*, p. 53.
3. Ibid., p. 62.
4. Strong, "History of Sequoia National Park," p. 67, citing letter from Hyde and Lindsay to Hon. Surveyor General for California, May 31, 1880. (National Archives, RG 79.)
5. Ibid., p. 67; also George W. Stewart letter to Col. John R. White, June 8, 1929, (Stewart papers, Visalia Public Library).
6. Alfred Runte, *National Parks: The American Experience*, (University of Nebraska Press, 1997 3rd Edition), p. 48.
7. Strong, op. cit., p. 72.
8. Edward Bellamy, *Looking Backward 2000-1887*, Introduction to edition published by R.C. Elliott, 1966, (*Looking Backward* was originally published in 1888), p. *x*.
9. Ibid., p. *vii*.
10. Medan, "Burnette Gregor Haskell: A California Radical," p. 100.
11. Ibid., pp. 98-99.
12. Ibid., p. 102, citing Annie Haskell's diary for August 26, 1889.
13. Haskell Family Papers, Vol. 3, "Scraps collected by Anna Haskell in relation to the Nationalist Movement, S.F., 1889," which includes meeting programs, clippings, etc. (Bancroft Library).
14. Haskell Family Papers, op. cit., undated clipping from the *Commonwealth*.
15. Hyde/Stewart/Zumwalt et al. letter to Commissioner Stockslager, May 10, 1889, (Stewart papers, Visalia Public Library).
16. J.M. Quinn, *History of the State of California and Biographical Record of the San Joaquin Valley,* (Chicago, 1905), p. 631.
17. Stockslager letter to George Stewart, May 29, 1889, (Stewart papers, Visalia Public Library).
18. *Visalia Weekly Delta*, June 12, 1890.
19. George Stewart letter to Enos Mills, August 29, 1916 (Stewart papers, Visalia Public Library).
20. W.A. Stiles letter to John Noble, July 22, 1890, (National Archives RG 79, microfilm, Sequoia National Park).
21. Dilsaver and Tweed, *Challenge of the Big Trees*, pp. 67-68.
22. Ruth R. Lewis, "Kaweah: An Experiment in Co-Operative Coloniza-

tion," *Pacific Historical Review*, 1948, p. 436; also see the *Kaweah Commonwealth*, "A Bellamy Colony," (reprint of an article from the St. Louis *Globe Democrat*), Vol. 1, No. 30, August 9, 1890.

23. Medan, op. cit., p. 109.
24. Ibid., p. 115.
25. Ibid., pp. 117-118; also see Haskell Family Papers, Vol. 3, clippings from *San Francisco Examiner*, April 10, 1890 and the *Alta California*, April 9, 1890.
26. *San Francisco Star*, April 12, 1890.
27. Winser, "Memories," p. 70.

CHAPTER 10—THE ANNIE HASKELL DIARIES

1. Annie Haskell diary, June 14, 1877, (via a transcription from Oscar Berland papers).
2. Joseph E. Doctor, "Why Kaweah Failed," various drafts and research notes for a paper given at the *Southern Symposium of California Conference of Historical Societies*, February 23, 1968. (Later published in *Los Tulares*, No. 8, September, 1968).
3. Annie Haskell diary, March 21, 1881, (Oscar Berland papers).
4. Doctor, op. cit., much specific information on Annie Haskell is found in Doctor's early drafts and research notes, which are part of the materials he gave the author shortly before his death in 1995. Doctor's research included numerous transcriptions of Annie Haskell's diary, some he made himself and others provided him by Oscar Berland. Doctor also interviewed Burnette and Annie's son, Roth Haskell, in the 1940s; also see Annegret Ogden, "The 65 New Year's Eves of Anna Fader Haskell," *The Californians*, Nov/Dec., 1984, p. 7.
5. Doctor, op. cit.
6. Annie Haskell diary, November 14, 1881 (Oscar Berland papers).
7. Ibid., November 13, 1881.
8. Annie Haskell diary, August 20, 1889. (Haskell Family Papers, Bancroft Library, Berkeley, CA). Unless otherwise noted, citations are from Annie Haskell diary entries read and transcribed by the author. The Bancroft Library, in addition to housing all 65 years of the original diaries, has several years available on microfilm.
9. Doctor, op. cit.
10. Annie Haskell diaries, April 20 and 23, 1890.
11. Ibid., June 11, 1890.
12. Doctor, op. cit., Doctor wrote of a 1948 trip up the old Colony Mill road, accompanied by a former colonists, "Frank [Hengst], John [Grunigen] and I finally reached Colony Mill, after passing the

unmarked grave of Annie Haskell's lover, Andrew Larsen, the handsome young ship's captain."

13. *Kaweah Commonwealth*, Vol. 1, No. 15, April 26, 1890.
14. Annie Haskell diary, July 29, 1890.
15. Ibid., July 30, 1890.
16. Ibid., September 20, 1890.
17. Ibid., September 30, 1890.
18. Ibid., October 1, 1890.
19. *Kaweah Commonwealth*, "My First Impressions," Vol. 1, No. 38, October 4, 1890.
20. Ibid.
21. Annie Haskell diary, October 2, 1890.
22. Ibid., October 10, 1890.

CHAPTER 11—THE MILLING BEGINS

1. "Kaweah Colony Traction Engine," *Los Tulares*, No. 31, June, 1957.
2. Ibid.
3. James J. Martin, "History of the Kaweah Colony," (unpublished manuscript, drafts and notes, circa 1930, J.J. Martin Family papers, Bancroft Library), Sec. 5, p. 6.
4. Ibid., Sec. 5, pp. 6-7.
5. Andrew Cauldwell, *Report to Commissioner, General Land Office*, July 16, 1890, p. 10.
6. *Visalia Weekly Delta*, August 21, 1890.
7. William Vandever to John Noble, Secretary of the Interior, July 26 and August 5, 1890, (National Archives, RG 79, microfilm, Sequoia National Park).
8. Haskell, *Out West*, p. 321.
9. *Kaweah Commonwealth*, "Colony Notes," Vol. 1, No. 32, August 23, 1890.
10. Ibid., Vol. 1, No. 33, August 30, 1890.
11. Andrew Cauldwell, *Report to the Commissioner, General Land Office*, November 26, 1890, (National Archives, RG 49, microfilm, Bancroft Library), p. 1-2.
12. *Kaweah Commonwealth*, Vol. 1, No. 36, September 20, 1890.
13. Holway R. Jones, *John Muir and the Sierra Club Battle for Yosemite*, (Berkeley, CA, 1965), p. 43.
14. Ibid., p. 44.
15. Dilsaver and Tweed, *Challenge of the Big Trees*, p. 70.
16. Strong, "History of Sequoia National Park," pp. 120-21.

Part III: A Dream's Demise (1890-1891)

CHAPTER 12—A CHALLENGE TO OPTIMISM

1. *Visalia Weekly Delta*, October 23, 1890.
2. Ibid.
3. *Kaweah Commonwealth*, "The National Park Question," Vol. 1, No. 41, October 25, 1890.
4. Kaweah Colony documents, "To Whom It May Concern," circular issued by Board of Trustees, January 24, 1891, (Visalia Public Library, Kaweah Colony collection).
5. Will Purdy, "Kaweah: The Saga of the Old Colony," (manuscript copy of poem written circa 1930, Visalia Public Library, Kaweah Colony collection), p. 14.
6. *Kaweah Commonwealth*, Vol. 1, No. 44, November 15, 1890.
7. Ibid., Vol. 1, No 45, November 22, 1890.
8. Cauldwell, *Report to Commissioner, General Land Office*, November 26, 1890, p. 2.
9. Ibid., p. 3.
10. Annie Haskell diary, November 30, 1890.
11. Cauldwell, *Report to Commissioner, General Land Office*, July 16, 1890, pp. 8-10.
12. *Kaweah Commonwealth*, Vol. 1, No. 16, May 3, 1890.
13. Ibid., Vol. 1, No. 34, September 6, 1890.
14. Purdy, op cit., p. 8.
15. Haskell, *Out West*, p. 318.
16. Annie Haskell diaries, December 9, 15, 17, and 19, 1890.
17. *Kaweah Commonwealth*, Vol. 2, No. 6, December 1890.

CHAPTER 13—DECISIONS, DECISIONS

1. *Kaweah Commonwealth*, Vol. 1, No. 41, October 25, 1890.
2. Annie Haskell diary, January 18, 1891.
3. Ibid., November 5 and 13, 1890.
4. *Kaweah Commonwealth*, "Another Victory," Vol. 2, No. 7, January 3, 1891.
5. Annie Haskell diaries, January 19 and 20, 1891.
6. Milton Greenbaum, "History of the Kaweah Colony, (M.A. Thesis, Brooklyn College, 1942, Sequoia National Park library), p. 36.
7. Ibid.
8. Ibid., pp. 37-38, citing Cauldwell's *Report to Commissioner, General Land Office*, November 26, 1890.
9. *Kaweah Commonwealth*, "To the Comrades of Friends of Kaweah," Vol. 2, No. 5, December 20, 1890.

10. *San Francisco Star*, May 3, 1890.
11. *Kaweah Commonwealth*, Vol. 2, No. 4, December 13, 1890. In a reprint of a letter Martin wrote to the editor of the *Twentieth Century*, correcting statements they had copied from the *San Francisco Star*, Martin wrote: "While these statements were confined to the paper mentioned, they did comparatively little injury because of the obscurity and unreliability of their source, but when re-echoed in the *Twentieth Century*, they are at once brought to the notice of the world at large."
12. Greenbaum, op. cit., pp. 41-42, citing W.M. Stone's December 18, 1890 letter to Secretary Noble and Groff's February 25, 1891 letter to Noble.
13. *Kaweah Commonwealth*, Vol. 2, No. 15, February 28, 1891.
14. Winser, "Memories," pp. 72-92.
15. Annie Haskell diaries, January 19 and 20, 1891.
16. Ibid., June 7, 1891.
17. *Kaweah Commonwealth*, Vol. 2, No. 34, July 11, 1891.
18. *Los Angeles Times*, April 15, 1891.
19. *Los Angeles Herald*, April 15, 1891.
20. *Visalia Weekly Delta*, April 23, 1891.
21. *Kaweah Commonwealth*, Vol. 2, No. 27, May 23, 1891.
22. Ibid., Vol. 1, No. 32, August 26, 1890.
23. Ibid., Vol. 2, No. 23, April 25, 1891.
24. Ibid., Vol. 2, No. 26, May 16, 1891.
25. Ibid., Vol. 2, No. 23, April 25, 1891.
26. Ibid., Vol. 2, No. 22, April 18, 1891.
27. Interview with Kenneth "Milton" Savage, Jr., June, 1995, Three Rivers, CA.

CHAPTER 14—INCIDENT AT ATWELL'S MILL
1. *Kaweah Commonwealth*, Vol. 2, No. 32, June 27, 1891.
2. Ibid., Vol. 2. No. 27, May 23, 1891.
3. *Visalia Weekly Delta*, Jan. 1, 1891; *Tulare County Times*, Jan.1, 1891.
4. *Tulare County Times*, January 1, 1891; also see Muir, *Our National Parks*. Muir himself had once been a sheepherder and well knew the damage grazing herds could inflict. He often used, and probably coined, the term: "Hoofed locusts."
5. *Visalia Weekly Delta*, April 16, 1891.
6. Dilsaver and Tweed, *Challenge of the Big Trees*, pp. 76-77.
7. Martin, "History of the Kaweah Colony," Sec. 13, p. 1.
8. John F. Elliott, *Mineral King Historic District, Contextual History and Description*, (Mineral King Preservation Society, 1993), p. 47.

9. Martin, op. cit.
10. Capt. J.H. Dorst, *Special Report to the Secretary of the Interior Relative to Cutting Timber at Atwell's Mill*, September 8, 1891, (Sequoia National Park historical archives), p. 4.
11. Ibid.
12. Ibid., p. 5
13. Ibid., p. 6
14. Ibid.
15. Ibid.
16. Ibid., p. 7
17. Burnette Haskell letter to J.J. Martin, Irvin Barnard, H. Dillon, July 15, 1891 (Haskell Family Papers, Bancroft Library).
18. Winser, "Memories," p. 141.
19. Dorst, op. cit., p. 8.
20. Martin, op. cit., sec. 13, p. 3.
21. Dorst, op. cit., p.8.
22. Winser, op. cit., p. 142.
23. Dorst, op cit., pp. 10-11.
24. Ibid., p. 11.
25. Ibid., pp. 11-12.

CHAPTER 15—RESIGNATION, SUICIDE AND DISPUTE

1. Annie Haskell diary, January 7, 1891.
2. Haskell, *Out West*, p. 321.
3. Handwritten draft of a circular, "A Serious Word to the Members," signed by B. G. Haskell and H.T. Taylor, dated July 7, 1891, (Haskell Family Papers, Bancroft Library), p. 7.
4. Haskell, *Out West*, p. 322.
5. *Kaweah Commonwealth*, "A Word or So," Vol. 2, No. 38, August 8, 1891.
6. Annie Haskell diary, August 4, 1891.
7. *Kaweah Commonwealth*, "The Present Position," Vol. 2, No. 38, August 8, 1891
8. Burnette Haskell to the Board of Trustees and the Membership of the Kaweah Co-Operative Colony Company, July 25, 1891, (Haskell Family Papers, Bancroft Library).
9. Doctor, "Why Kaweah Failed," p. 3.
10. Kaweah Colony documents, undated petition to Burnette Haskell and A.W. Green to "furnish an explanation of the actions and conduct in relation to the late Father Elphick." Signed by, among others, James Martin, Irvin Barnard, Phil Winser, and George Purdy. (Bancroft

Library); also see Paul Kagan, *New World Utopias*, (Penguin Books, 1975), pp. 93-95, citing the *Chronicle* and *Examiner* stories.

11. Annie Haskell diary, October 2, 1891.
12. *Kaweah Commonwealth*, "A Sad Occurrence," Vol. 2, No. 46, October 3, 1891.
13. *Tulare County Times*, October 8, 1891.
14. *Visalia Weekly Delta*, October 8, 1891.
15. Peter Ting letter to the Editor, *Visalia Delta*, October 25, 1891, (from an original handwritten copy, Kaweah Colony collection, Visalia Public Library), p. 5.
16. Annie Haskell diary, October 3, 1891.
17. Ibid., November 5, 1891.
18. Ibid., November 6, 1891.
19. Albert W. Green to Tulare County District Attorney, November 11, 1891, (handwritten copy included as enclosure with Haskell letter to his father, Haskell Family Papers, Bancroft Library).
20. *Visalia Weekly Delta*, November 12, 1891.
21. *Tulare County Times*, November 12, 1891.
22. Green, op. cit.
23. *Tulare County Times*, November 12, 1891.
24. Ibid., November 26, 1891.
25. *Visalia Weekly Delta*, January 21, 1992.
26. Haskell, *Out West*, p. 322.

Part IV: A Dream Lives On (1882 - Present)

CHAPTER 16—THOSE WHO REMAINED

1. Author interview with Olive Redstone Klaucke, See Canyon, San Luis Obispo, CA, September, 1995.
2. Greenbaum, "History of the Kaweah Colony," pp. 56-58.
3. J.J. Martin papers, misc. clippings and letters, (Bancroft Library).
4. James J. Martin letter to Eleanor Roosevelt, undated handwritten draft, (Bancroft Library). Although the draft is undated, it was presumably written in 1935 when Martin also wrote to President Franklin D. Roosevelt.
5. Lewis, "Kaweah: An Experiment in Cooperative Colonization," p. 441.
6. Author's interview with Dr. Forest Grunigen, Three Rivers, CA, June, 1995.
7. Winser, "Memories," p. 116.
8. *Kaweah Commonwealth*, Vol. 2, No. 35, July 18, 1891.
9. Winser, op. cit., pp. 116-17.

10. Dilsaver and Tweed, *Challenge of the Big Trees*, pp. 89, 214.
11. Winser, op. cit., pp. 162-65.
12. Author's interview with Milton Savage, Three Rivers, CA, June, 1995.
13. Winser, op. cit., pp. 168-71.
14. B.G. Haskell journal, April 7, 1892.
15. Haskell, *Out West*, p. 300.
16. B.G. Haskell journal, April 12, 1892.
17. Ibid., April 15, 1892.
18. Haskell letter to Annie Haskell, July 22, 1892.
19. Haskell letter to Annie Haskell, July 28, 1892.
20. Annie Haskell diary entries from 1897, (via Oscar Berland papers).
21. Rodney Ellsworth letter to George W. Stewart, August 27, 1930, (Stewart papers, California State Library, Sacramento, CA).
22. Annie Haskell diary entries from 1907, (via Oscar Berland papers).
23. Martin, "History of the Kaweah Colony."

CHAPTER 17—LET HISTORY JUDGE
1. Doctor, "Why Kaweah Failed," p. 1.
2. *Kaweah Commonwealth*, "A Letter from Across the Ocean," reprint of an article from the Belfast Weekly *Star*, written by J. Bruce Wallace, "who was here about a month ago and made us a short visit." Vol. 2, No. 9, January 17, 1891.
3. *San Francisco Wasp*, June, 1886, from a Burnette Haskell scrapbook clipping, (Haskell Family Papers, Bancroft Library).
4. Jones, "The Kaweah Experiment in Co-Operation," p. 27-28.
5. McWilliams, *Factories in the Fields*, pp. 28-29.
6. Starr, *Endangered Dreams: The Great Depression in California*, pp. 262-264.
7. Hine, *California's Utopian Colonies*, p. 178.
8. Oscar Berland, "Giant Forest's Reservation: The Legend and the Mystery," *Sierra Club Bulletin*, Vol. 47, No. 9, December, 1962, p. 68.
9. James Martin letters to Frank Been, April 14 and 18, 1933, (Sequoia National Park archives.)
10. Author interview with Oscar Berland, El Cerrito, CA, May, 1995.
11. Berland, *Sierra Club Bulletin*, p. 74-75.
12. Ibid., p. 75, citing Stewart letter to Robert Underwood Johnson, December 6, 1930.
13. Ibid., p. 76.
14. Ibid., p. 76-77, citing Johnson letter to George Stewart, December 15, 1930.

15. George Stewart letter to Francis P. Farquhar, March 1, 1924; George Stewart letter to Col. John R. White, June 8, 1929, (Stewart papers, Visalia Public Library).
16. Berland, op. cit., p. 78.
17. Martin letter to Been, April 14, 1933.
18. Berland, op. cit., p. 78.
19. Douglas Hillman Strong, *Trees—or Timber? The Story of Sequoia and Kings Canyon National Parks*, (Sequoia Natural History Assoc., Three Rivers, 1968), p. 30.
20. Haskell, *A Pen Picture...*, p. 22.
21. Hank Johnston, *They Felled the Redwoods*, (Trans-Anglo Books, Los Angeles, 1966), pp. 32, 43-49.
22. Dilsaver and Tweed, *Challenge of the Big Trees*, p. 56; In addition to Johnston's account of giant sequoia logging in the Converse Basin, Floyd Otter's *Men of the Mammoth Forest*, (Edwards Bros., Ann Arbor, Michigan, 1963) offers an account of Big Tree logging in the Tule River country just to the south.

AFTERWORD—THE SPIRIT OF THE DREAMER

1. Starr, *Americans and the California Dream, 1850-1915*, pp. 443-44.
2. Ibid., p. 444.
3. Haskell, *Out West*, pp. 320, 322.
4. Ibid., p. 315.
5. John Humphrey Noyes, *History of American Socialisms*, (Hillary House Publisher, New York, 1961, originally published in 1870), p. 22.
6. Hine, *California's Utopian Colonies*, p. 178.
7. Annie Haskell diary, June 11, 1937 (via Oscar Berland papers).
8. Ibid., January 1, 1897.

BIBLIOGRAPHY

LETTERS, DIARIES, JOURNALS, MEMOIRS, GOVERNMENT REPORTS

Allen, B.F. *Report to Commissioner, General Land Office*, October 22, 1889, National Archives, RG49.

Cauldwell, Andrew. *Report to Commissioner, General Land Office*, July 16, 1890, National Archives, R49.

———. *Report to Commissioner, General Land Office*, November 26, 1890, National Archives, RG 49

———. *Supplemental Report to Commissioner, GLO*, April 6, 1891, National Archives, RG 49.

Corbett, Richard. Letter to Tom Waters, 1889-94, *Tom Waters Papers*, Bancroft Library, Berkeley, CA.

Cridge, Alfred. "Korrekt Kritique on the Kaweah Ko-Operative Kolony," circular published by *Democratic Element of Kaweah Colony*, 1890, Tulare County Public Library, Visalia, CA (hereafter Visalia Public Library).

Dorst, Capt. John. *Special Report to Secretary of Interior Relative to Cutting Timber at Atwell's Mill*, September 8, 1891, Sequoia National Park Library.

Haskell, Anna F. Diaries, 1887-92 (*Haskell Family Papers*), Bancroft Library.

Haskell, Burnette G. Letters, 1889-92; Personal Reminisces and Memoranda, 1885-86, 1892; Family Genealogy and Scrapbooks, (*Haskell Family Papers*), Bancroft Library.

Kaweah Colony. Collection of misc. documents, correspondence, time checks, circulars, pamphlets, etc., Bancroft Library.

———. Collection of misc. documents, correspondence, clippings, membership applications, Visalia Public Library.

———. Collection of misc. documents, including "The Crisis," Nov. 1887, Sequoia National Park Library.

Keller, Charles F. Manuscript collection, including undated autobiographical manuscript and letters to Walter Fry (March 7, 1913), and Carl Keller (April 14, 1921), Sequoia National Park Library

Martin, James J. Misc. correspondence, *J.J. Martin papers*, Bancroft Library.

———. "History of Kaweah Colony," unpublished manuscript, drafts and notes, (*J.J. Martin papers*), Bancroft Library.

National Archives. *Record Group 49*, "Conflict of Kaweah Colony Land Claims," misc. correspondence and reports pertaining to Kaweah Colony.

———. *Record Group 79; Entry 1,* "Sequoia and General Grant," misc. reports, correspondence pertaining to Sequoia National Park.

Stewart, George W. Papers/Misc. Correspondence, August, 1882-December, 1930, Visalia Public Library.

———. Papers/Misc. Correspondence, Manuscripts Collection, California State Historical Library, Sacramento, CA.

———. *History of Kaweah Colony*, bound manuscript, compiled from *Visalia Weekly Delta*, Nov./Dec. 1891, Visalia Public Library.

Winser, Philip. "Memories," original unpublished manuscript, 1931, Huntington Library, San Marino, CA/Sequoia National Park Library.

INTERVIEWS

Berland, Oscar. Interview with the author, El Cerrito, CA, May, 1995.

Doctor Joseph E. Interviews with the author, Exeter, CA, March/April, 1995.

Keller, Leland. Interview with the author, Three Rivers, CA, June, 1995 (Grandson of Charles Keller).

Klaucke, Olive. Interview with the author, See Canyon, CA, September, 1995 (Granddaughter of John Redstone and James Martin).

Grunigen, Forest. Interview with the author, Three Rivers, CA, June, 1995 (Grandson of George Hopping).

Redstone, Albert E. Interview with Oscar Berland, See Canyon, CA, 1960.

Savage, Kenneth Jr. Interview with the author, Three Rivers, CA, June, 1995 (Grandson of Fred Savage).

NEWSPAPERS

Commonwealth
Denver Labor Enquirer
Fresno Bee
Kaweah Commonwealth
The [new] *Kaweah Commonwealth*
Los Angeles Herald
Los Angeles Times
San Francisco Chronicle
San Francisco Examiner
San Francisco Star
Truth
Tulare County Times
Visalia Times-Delta
Visalia Weekly Delta

PUBLISHED BOOKS, MAGAZINE ARTICLES, HISTORICAL QUARTERLIES

Atwell, Walter G. and Albert W. *An Ancient Giant Speaks*, Erie Press, Three Rivers, CA, 1977.

Bellamy, Edward. *Looking Backward 2000-1887*, R.C. Elliott Publishing, 1966, (Originally published in 1888).

Berland, Oscar. "Giant Forest's Reservation: The Legend and the Mystery," *Sierra Club Bulletin*, Vol. 47, No. 9, December, 1962.

Brown, J.L. *The Mussel Slough Tragedy*, 1958.

Carden, Maren L. *Oneida: Utopian Community to Modern Corporation*, Johns Hopkins Press, 1969.

Crooks, Italia. *A Story of the Life of Bessie Humbolt Miles*, published by Eleanor Esther Howell/David Weaver, 1979, (Three Rivers Library).

Cross, Ira. *History of the Labor Movement in California*, Berkeley, CA, 1935.

Deverell, William. *Railroad Crossing: Californians and the Railroad, 1850-1910*, University of California Press, Berkeley, 1994.

Dilsaver, Lary M. and William C. Tweed. *Challenge of the Big Trees: A Resource History of Sequoia and Kings Canyon National Parks*, Sequoia Natural History Association, Three Rivers, 1989.

Doctor, Joseph E. "Why Kaweah Failed," *Los Tulares*, No. 78, September, 1968, (Tulare County Historical Society quarterly).

Bibliography

Farquhar, Francis P. *History of the Sierra Nevada*, Berkeley, CA, 1966.

——. "Legislative History of Sequoia and Kings Canyon National Parks," *Sierra Club Bulletin*, Vol. 26, No. 1, 1941.

Gist, Brooks D. *Empire Out of the Tules*, Tulare, CA, 1976.

Gronlund, Laurence. *The Co-Operative Commonwealth: An Exposition of Socialism*, Lee and Shepard, 1890, (originally published in 1884).

Haskell, Burnette G. *A Pen Picture of the Kaweah Co-Operative Colony*, San Francisco, CA, 1889, Bancroft Library/Visala Public Library.

——. "How Kaweah Failed," reprinted from *San Francisco Examiner*, November 29, 1891, Bancroft Library/Visalia Public Library.

——. "Kaweah: How and Why the Colony Died," *Out West Magazine*, August, 1902.

——. *The Haskell Journal, A Monthly Magazine*, Vol. 1, Nos. 1-4, 1898, (given to the author from the personal collection of Oscar Berland).

Hine, Robert V. *California's Utopian Colonies*, University of California Press, 1983 (Originally published in 1953).

Holloway, Mark. *Heavens on Earth: Utopian Communities in America, 1680-1880*, Dover Publications, New York, 1966.

Hopping, Philip R. "John Hooper Redstone: My Most Unforgettable Character," *Los Tulares*, No. 94, June, 1974.

Johnston, Hank. *They Felled the Redwoods*, Trans-Anglo Books, Los Angeles, 1966.

Jones, Holway. *John Muir and the Sierra Club Battle for Yosemite*, Berkeley, CA, 1965.

Kagan, Paul. *New World Utopias*, Penguin Books, New York, 1975.

Lewis, Oscar. *San Francisco: From Mission to Metropolis*, Howell-North Books, Berkeley, CA, 1966.

Lewis, Ruth R. "Kaweah: An Experiment in Co-Operative Colonization,"*Pacific Historical Review*, 1948.

McKay, John; Hill and Buckley. *A History of Western Society*, 2nd Edition, Houghton, Mifflen Company, Boston, 1983.

McKee, Irving. "Notable Memorials to Mussel Slough," *Pacific Historical Review*, No. 17, February, 1948.

McWilliams, Carey. *Factories in the Field*, Peregrine Publishers, 1971, (originally published in 1939).

——. *California: The Great Exception,* Greenwood Press, Westport, CT, 1971, (originally published by Current Books, New York, 1949).

Mitchell, Annie R. *The Way It Was*, Tulare, CA, 1976.

——. *Land of the Tules*, Valley Publishers, Fresno, CA, 1972.

——. *Visalia: Her First Fifty Years*, Exeter, CA, 1963.

Muir, John. *Our National Parks*, Houghton, Mifflen Company, Boston, 1901.

Bibliography

Norris, Frank. *The Octopus*, Signet Books, 1964, (originally published in 1901).

Noyes, John Humphrey. *History of American Socialisms*, Hillary House Publisher, New York, 1961, (originally published in 1870).

O'Connell, Jay. "Kaweah! A Dream's Demise," *The Californians: The Magazine of California History*, Vol. 12, No. 4.

———. "The Annie Haskell Diaries: Her First Turbulent Year at Kaweah," *The Californians*, Vol. 12, No. 4.

———. "Colony Corner," *The* [new] *Kaweah Commonwealth*, misc. issues, Three Rivers, CA, 1995-97.

Odgen, Annegret. "The 65 New Year's Eves of Anna Fader Haskell, 1876-1942," *The Californians*, November/December, 1984.

Orsi, Richard J. "The Octopus Reconsidered: The Southern Pacific and Agricultural Modernization in California," *California Historical Quarterly*, No. 54, Fall, 1975.

Quinn, J.M. *History of the State of California and Biographical Record of the San Joaquin Valley*, Chicago, 1905.

Reisner, Marc. *Cadillac Desert: The American West and Its Disappearing Water*, Penguin Books, New York, 1993 (revised and updated).

Robinson, W.W. *Land in California: The Story of Mission Lands, Ranchos, Squatters...*, University of California Press, Berkeley, 1948.

Roney, Frank. *Irish Rebel and California Labor Leader: An Autobiography*, edited by Ira Cross, Berkeley, CA, 1931.

Runte, Alfred. *National Parks: The American Experience*, 3rd Edition, University of Nebraska Press, 1997.

Starr, Kevin. *Americans and the California Dream, 1850-1915*, Oxford University Press, 1973.

———. *Endangered Dreams: The Great Depression in California*, Oxford University Press, 1996.

Strong, Douglas H. *Trees—or Timber? The Story of Sequoia and Kings Canyon National Parks*, Sequoia Natural History Assoc., Three Rivers, CA, 1986.

Terstegge, Mary Anne. "Creating a Park to Save the Big Trees," *Los Tulares*, No. 169, September, 1990.

Tweed, William. *Kaweah Remembered: The Story of the Kaweah Colony and The Founding of Sequoia National Park*, Sequoia Natural History Assoc., Three Rivers, CA, 1986.

———. "The Kaweah Rivers—How Many Forks?" *Kaweah Quarterly*, (The Kaweah Land Trust newsletter), Fall, 1995.

Ventura Historical Society. "Vandever: Ventura's First Congressman," *Ventura Historical Quarterly*, Vol. 20, No. 1, Fall, 1971.

Whitney, Stephen. *The Sierra Nevada: A Sierra Club Naturalists Guide*, Sierra Club Books, San Francisco, CA, 1979.

UNPUBLISHED MANUSCRIPTS, THESIS PAPERS, DISSERTATIONS, NOTES

Berland, Oscar. "Aborted Revolution: A Study in the Formative Years of the American Labor Movement, 1877-1886," M.A. Thesis, San Francisco State College, 1966.

——. Notes and drafts for "Giant Forest's Reservation," (article for *Sierra Club Bulletin*).

——. Book outline, research notes and correspondence pertaining to the Kaweah Colony.

Doctor, Joseph E. Misc. research notes and drafts of articles, (notes on interviews with Roth Haskell, Al Redstone, Frank Hengst, etc.)

Greenbaum, Milton. "History of the Kaweah Colony," M.A. Thesis, Brooklyn University, 1942, (Sequoia National Park Library).

Jones, William Carey. "The Kaweah Experiment in Co-Operation," original manuscript draft of article for *Quarterly Journal of Economics*, VI, October 1891, Bancroft Library/Visalia Public Library.

Junep, Herbert. "A Chronological History of Sequoia National Park," unpublished manuscript, 1937, Sequoia National Park Library.

Kennedy, Dane. "The Kaweah Colony," M.A. Thesis, University of California, Berkeley, 1973.

Medan, Caroline. "Burnette G. Haskell: California Radical," M.A. Thesis, University of California, Berkeley, 1950.

Rothblat, Ben. "The Kaweah Colony," M.A. Thesis, 1936, Sequoia National Park Library.

Strong, Douglas H. "History of Sequoia National Park," unpublished dissertation, Syracuse University, 1964, Sequoia National Park Library.

ACKNOWLEDGMENTS

WRITING A BOOK, I have discovered, is itself an experiment in cooperation. I was fortunate to have the help and cooperation of a number of people and organizations in the research, preparation and writing of this book, and I would like to thank them all. They included, in no particular order, Rick and Judy Dunn, David Geiser, Mike Herro, William Deverell, Jean and Michael Sherrell of *The Californians* magazine, Steve and Elizabeth LaMar (aka Burnette and Annie), George E. Hopping, C. Thomas Bell, Phil Noyes, Huell Howser, David Weaver, Eleanor K. Howell, Milton Savage, Dr. Forest Grunigen, Leland Keller, Robert Redstone and Olive Klaucke, Richard Challacomb, Jami Spittler, Mark Tilchen and the Sequoia Natural History Association, Terry Ommen and the Tulare County Historical Society, the Kaweah Land Trust and the Three Rivers Historical Society. I have undoubedtly left out many who helped, but thank them all nonetheless.

Through researching this book I learned the real worth of libraries and the rare talent of reference librarians. I owe a debt of gratitude to the staffs of the Bancroft Library in Berkeley; the California State Library in Sacramento; the Huntington Library in San Marino; the Tulare County Library in Visalia and Mary Anne Terstegge in that library's wonderful Annie Mitchell History Room; and the Sequoia National Park Library and Museum/Archives at the Ash Mountain park headquarters.

A number of people influenced my work by their own writings on the subject, and I was very fortunate to be able to enlist the further help of a select few—a triumvirate of experts, if you will—on this project. For their guidance, support and generosity in reading the various drafts of this book and offering their critiques and comments, I thank Oscar Berland, Robert Hine and William Tweed.

Joe Doctor deserves special thanks, and although he did not live to read even the early drafts of this book, he was a shaping influence nonetheless.

A writer is only as good as his editors. Over the years, Sarah Barton Elliott has taught me much and her eye for detail graces this book. Quinn Atherton made major contributions to the final version of this book and really helped to put me on track. I heartily thank them both.

For enthusiastic support and encouragement, I thank John and Sarah Elliott. As owners and publishers of *The Kaweah Commonwealth*, they have provided me with a rare opportunity and the community with a valued resource.

Special thanks to my parents, Pat and Shirley, for the good sense to move to the community of Three Rivers way back when and for fostering my creativity and curiosity. And finally, thanks to my wife, Susie, and son, J.P. (James Patrick), for making it all such a worthwhile journey.

INDEX

Index

Index

Illustrations

Cover photo (also frontispiece) courtesy J.R. Challacomb

Courtesy the Bancroft Library: pp. 17, 24, 43, 61, 70, 109, 125, 129, 158.
Courtesy the California State Library: p. 35.
Courtesy the Keller Family Collection: p. 11.
Courtesy *The Kaweah Commonwealth* collection: pp. 52, 77.
Courtesy Sequoia National Park: p. 174

Map on p. 116 courtesy the Sierra Club.
Map on p. 197 courtesy the National Archives

Maps on pp. *viii* and *ix* by the author.

ABOUT THE AUTHOR

Jay O'Connell grew up in Three Rivers, California, at the edge of Sequoia National Park. He has written articles for various magazine and writes a regular historical column for *The Kaweah Commonwealth*, the weekly newspaper serving Three Rivers and Sequoia & Kings Canyon National Parks.

O'Connell, who has worked as a television producer and production manager, is currently writing an historical novel about infamous nineteenth-century outlaws Evans and Sontag entitled *The Train Robber's Daughter*. He lives in the Los Angeles area with his wife and son.